SE 15 '20

WITHDRAWN

Legislating Gender and Sexuality in Africa

# Critical Human Rights

Scott Straus and Tyrell Haberkorn,
Series Editors; Steve J. Stern, Editor Emeritus

Books in the series Critical Human Rights emphasize research that opens new ways to think about and understand human rights. The series values in particular empirically grounded and intellectually open research that eschews simplified accounts of human rights events and processes.

Through an examination of laws on gender and sexuality in African states, this book highlights contemporary debates about morality, human rights, and the African subject. Decentering human rights as that which flows from the global to the domestic arena, the volume takes an African-centric, "local-local" view of how rights arguments take shape and emerge as forms of political practice. Drawing on case studies of seven countries, the book emphasizes the agency of African actors in human rights work and reveals contentious disagreements about gender, sexuality, ethics, and authenticity on the continent.

# Legislating Gender and Sexuality in Africa

*Human Rights, Society, and the State*

Edited by Lydia Boyd and
Emily Burrill

The University of Wisconsin Press

The University of Wisconsin Press
728 State Street, Suite 443
Madison, Wisconsin 53706
uwpress.wisc.edu

Gray's Inn House, 127 Clerkenwell Road
London ECIR 5DB, United Kingdom
eurospanbookstore.com

Copyright © 2020
The Board of Regents of the University of Wisconsin System
All rights reserved. Except in the case of brief quotations embedded in critical articles and reviews, no part of this publication may be reproduced, stored in a retrieval system, transmitted in any format or by any means—digital, electronic, mechanical, photocopying, recording, or otherwise—or conveyed via the internet or a website without written permission of the University of Wisconsin Press. Rights inquiries should be directed to rights@uwpress.wisc.edu.

Printed in the United States of America
This book may be available in a digital edition.

Library of Congress Cataloging-in-Publication Data

Names: Boyd, Lydia, editor. | Burrill, Emily, editor.
Title: Legislating gender and sexuality in Africa : human rights, society, and the state / edited by Lydia Boyd and Emily Burrill.
Other titles: Critical human rights.
Description: Madison, Wisconsin : The University of Wisconsin Press, [2020] | Series: Critical human rights | Includes bibliographical references and index.
Identifiers: LCCN 2019039028 | ISBN 9780299327408 (cloth)
Subjects: LCSH: Human rights—Africa. | Women's rights—Africa. | Gay rights—Africa. | Sexual minorities—Civil rights—Africa.
Classification: LCC JC599.A36 L44 2020 | DDC 323.3/4096—dc23
LC record available at https://lccn.loc.gov/2019039028

For Ivy, Charlie, and Rhys

# Contents

*List of Illustrations*     ix

*Acknowledgments*     xi

Introduction: Gender, Sexuality, and the State in Africa     3
**Lydia Boyd and Emily Burrill**

1  Legislating Marriage in Postcolonial Mali:
A History of the Present     25
**Emily Burrill**

2  Early Marriage and the Debates over Gender-Based
Rights in Niger     42
**Adeline Masquelier**

3  Where Are the Women? Gendered Experiences of
Land Resource Management in the Time of
Climate Change in Southern Burkina Faso     65
**Elisabeth Kago Ilboudo Nébié**

4  Sex, Schooling, and the Paradox of the
Readmission Policy in Malawi     84
**Rachel Silver**

5  The Debate over Comprehensive Sexuality Education
in Uganda: Barriers to Vernacularizing Reproductive
Rights     106
**Eunice Musiime and Leah Eryenyu**

6  Family Violence in the Refugee Claims of
Asylum Seekers from West Africa     125
**Charlotte Walker-Said**

7 Colonial Legacies, Electoral Politics, and the
  Production of (Anti)homosexuality in Senegal        150
  **Cheikh Ibrahima Niang, Ellen E. Foley, and
  Ndack Diop**

8 Making Rights Visible: The Embodied Nature of
  Debates over Sexual and Gender-Based Rights in
  Uganda                                              171
  **Lydia Boyd**

Epilogue: Entanglements of Law, Gender, and
Sexuality in Africa                                   193
**Dorothy L. Hodgson**

*Contributors*                                        199

*Index*                                               201

# Illustrations

I.1 African political map highlighting countries
featured in this volume     2

2.1 Poster advocating girls' education in
Dogondoutchi, Niger    49

3.1 Map of Sondré-Est    73

3.2 A typical household in Sondré-Est    73

3.3 The western border, delineated by a dirt road and
contested by the village of Sondré    75

Acknowledgments

This project began as an interdisciplinary conference held at the University of North Carolina, Chapel Hill, in April 2016. We want to thank the participants of that conference, especially Caroline Bledsoe, Ashley Currier, Harri Englund, Marc Epprecht, Lauren Jarvis, Alice Kang, Tom Kelley, Stacey Langwick, Benjamin Lawrance, Peter Redfield, Meredith Terretta, Matthew Thomann, and Robert Wyrod. The engaging discussions and presentations that unfolded over that two-day period laid the groundwork for this volume. That conference and subsequent support for this project were facilitated by an Interdisciplinary Initiatives grant from the College of Arts and Sciences at UNC. Other support has been provided by the UNC Provost's Committee on LGBTQ Life, UNC's Institute for the Arts and Humanities, and the Departments of African, African American, and Diaspora Studies, Women's and Gender Studies, History, and Anthropology, as well as the Program in Sexuality Studies, at UNC. UNC's African Studies Center provided additional support, including the funding for the map included at the beginning of this book. We also want to thank our colleagues at UNC who have contributed to and supported this project, especially our department chairs, Eunice Sahle and Silvia Tomášková.

A collaborative project such as this would not be possible without the hard work of all the authors. We are thankful for their engagement with this book's topic and for the insightful and wonderfully diverse chapters that have emerged from their scholarship. We are especially grateful for the contributions of Dorothy Hodgson, who agreed to write our epilogue during a year of professional transition and newly expanded administrative duties.

Our experience at the University of Wisconsin Press has been incredibly positive. We thank Gwen Walker and Scott Straus for their advice, feedback, and encouragement over the past year. We feel very fortunate to have had such experienced and knowledgeable editors guiding this book (and us) through the editing and publication processes.

Legislating Gender and
Sexuality in Africa

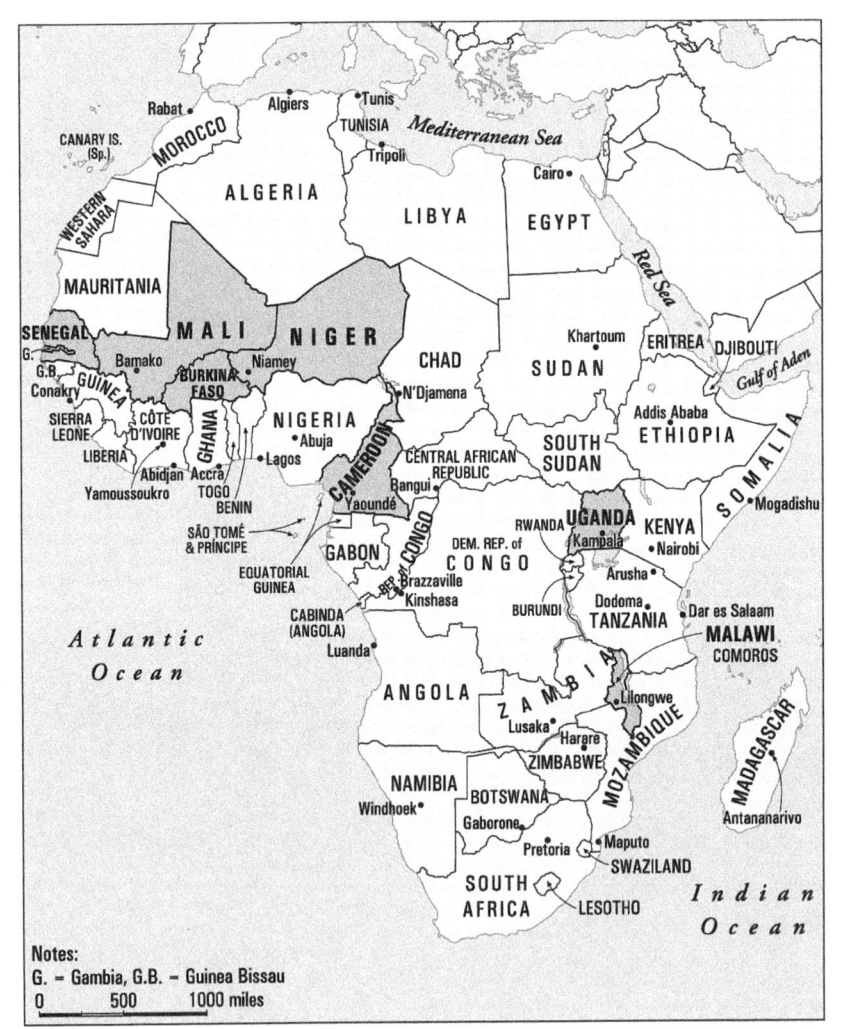

Figure I.1. African political map highlighting countries featured in this volume

Introduction

## Gender, Sexuality, and the State in Africa

LYDIA BOYD AND EMILY BURRILL

Over the past two decades, efforts to contest and redefine the frameworks that ascribe rights according to gendered and sexual status have provoked sustained legislative debate in several African countries. The focus of these debates has spanned a variety of issues, from marriage, divorce, and family law (Uganda, Mali, Niger) to legislation concerning homosexuality (Nigeria, Uganda), sexual violence and pornography (Uganda, South Africa, Kenya), and reproductive health rights (Malawi, Senegal). In one of the most widely followed of these cases, Uganda's national legislature drew international condemnation for its 2009 Anti-Homosexuality Bill, which heightened criminal penalties for same-sex sexual acts and sought to explicitly define and categorize illicit forms of sexual conduct.[1] In another case, in 2015, the Nigerian senate failed to pass what was known as the Gender Equality Law, which proposed sweeping reforms to property, inheritance, marriage, and divorce laws. Among other things, the law, which was overwhelmingly rejected by both Christian and Muslim legislators on religious grounds, sought to establish women's rights to shared marital property and child custody. These two failed laws are, on the face of it, quite different from one another: one sought to restrict rights and access under the constitution while the other sought to expand rights. Yet both, significantly, foregrounded moral language about interpersonal behavior and proper types of sexual intimacy in political projects of statecraft. These divergent legal efforts were moralizing enterprises, ones that explicitly aimed to define and reconstruct political subjecthood by mobilizing different arguments for and against gender and sexual rights.

This book explores such legislative turns that foreground issues of gender and sexuality in the articulation of human rights in African political contexts.[2] While there is a long history of the embeddedness of gender claims in human rights–driven work, since the 1990s a more formalized and forceful shift has emerged in the legislative realm when it comes to gender and sexuality. This is a shift shaped in part by broader political and economic changes linked to neoliberal policies that emphasize the autonomy of the individual and the freedom of the market and that have helped to redefine the transnational practice of human rights work. This book traces the rise and influence of this model for human rights with a focus on the variable ways Africans have responded to, engaged, and at times reframed the political tools associated with the global human rights apparatus. Above all, this book showcases how arguments are made for and against rights and how Africans craft and implement human rights on their own terms, engaging the state and the international realm in the process.

If one argument that runs through this volume is that African actors are not passive recipients of the beneficence of a transnational model for human rights that emerged in the second half of the twentieth century but key actors who transform, interpret, and apply human rights within their communities, a second argument is that in order to understand the struggles over human rights and their meanings, gender and sexuality must be foregrounded. Human rights are, at the core, arguments about not only governance and political obligation but also the kinds of subjects who are made visible to the state and the kinds of relationships between citizens that are deemed moral and worthy of protection. By examining unfolding debates over gender and sexual rights in African societies, we are able to trace and reveal the kinds of moral arguments over human rights that gain leverage and the ways competing interpretations for rights-based claims unfold. Gender-based and sexual rights have proved particularly contentious in recent years in Africa in part because debates over such rights highlight how experiences of gendered and sexual personhood are diverse, often contested, and sometimes in tension with global projects of sexual and gender identity making. This view of human rights privileges the multiple models for political agency and moral personhood that coexist within societies and that complicate the practice of human rights in Africa, as elsewhere. In this introduction, we trace some of the historical shifts that have helped define different eras in human rights work in Africa, with particular focus on the ways gender-based and sexual conflicts over rights claims have featured in such shifts.

Human rights, in their late twentieth-century iteration, are often described as an explicitly internationalist force that operates beyond the state and finds its modern origins in the legalistic frameworks crafted by post–World War II transnational organizations (Basu 2000; Asad 2003; Cornwall and Molyneux 2006). While there are instances of "vernacularization" of rights language and concepts, this transnational frame continues to characterize the emergence of rights as rooted in Western political and legalistic structures, positing non-Western culture as an impediment to rights (Merry 2006; Hunt 2007). "Culture" is often viewed as an obstacle to the universal claims of this global human rights framework; while some NGOs and rights organizations have made efforts to complicate frames for engaging culture, this perception of culture as a deterrent to the pursuit of rights remains markedly persistent when it comes to gender-based and sexual rights (Levitt and Merry 2011). In popular descriptions of struggles over such rights (such as activism against female circumcision and child marriage), African political actors are described in broad, monochromatic strokes, as tradition-bound and backward looking (Hodgson 2011). Yet in the examples engaged in this book, "rights" have emerged as something quite different in contemporary African publics: a critical part of the making and re-making of state power and political agency.

This volume showcases examples of African women and men grappling with rights across different national arenas in order to illustrate African innovations in modern human rights as the work of remaking legislation and political culture. Throughout the book, we see how demands for rights and critiques of rights frameworks are generated from the inside out, particularly when it comes to gender justice and sexual and reproductive rights. In 1995 Ugandan scholars Joe Oloka-Onyango and Sylvia Tamale argued that "women's human rights extend directly into the essential operations of the state, society, and the public (political) sphere," and such claims are not auxiliary to state legislative reforms, nor do they exist above them in the international sphere (1995, 711). The last twenty years have proven Oloka-Onyango and Tamale correct, and this volume is an effort to showcase in fine-grained detail some illustrations of just how this is so. Above all, we demonstrate that by taking up the vibrant contestation of rights-based claims by diverse political actors across Africa, the chapters in this volume complicate our understanding of modern human rights work. In building off the work of scholars who have argued persuasively for the global-local interconnection in human rights work (Stern and Straus 2014), we seek to emphasize how local processes and debates are engines for change with meaningful consequences.

This is an important claim to make in an era when many human rights theorists have emphasized the extrastate nature of modern rights work.[3] Samuel

Moyn (2010), in his influential revisionist history of human rights, argues that present-day human rights claims comprise a distinct movement that serves as a counterpoint to the rights of states. This dynamic is largely dependent upon a moral argument that prefigures the self-evidence of individual rights and that operates in the extrastate realm. In Moyn's work and the work of other notable human rights history scholars, human rights morph from a project that bolstered efforts at state building in the early and mid-twentieth century to a moral project focused instead on the rights of individuals, which are understood to stand above the rights granted by states and which draw their moral force from the evocation of physical suffering and social crisis (Moyn 2010; Williams 2010; Meister 2012; Hoffman 2016). Here, the rise of the nongovernmental realm in the post-1960s moment proved pivotal, with the founding of organizations like Amnesty International in 1961 marking a turning point where human rights work shifted from a project focused on political sovereignty and state building to a project that exists in a more diffuse, transnational realm, focused more on the individual and less on projects of collective self-determination. Yet as Bonny Ibhawoh (2018) has argued, this narrative relies on the supposition that African and other Global South anticolonialists dropped out of view after 1960 both as direct actors and as ideological influences. Ibhawoh warns us that this unidirectional "morphing" narrative—from human rights as a political tool associated with mid-twentieth-century independence movements to human rights as a diffuse moral authority associated with a powerful transnational realm—runs the risk of both erasing the anticolonial imprint on post-1960s human rights history and positing that the rise of authoritarian regimes in postcolonial Africa signaled an absolute turn away from rights-based claims within African political cultures and legislative projects (see also Jensen 2016).

In this volume, we advance a "both/and" argument: the rise of an international nongovernmental realm after 1960 advanced a global lexicon of moral personhood premised on individual rights beyond the state that has been deeply influential to human rights practice on the continent just as African statecraft, legislative reforms, and critiques of legislative action from within African states have engaged, pushed back against, and sometimes transformed these internationalist models. These are tensions that have only accelerated during the expansion of human rights work that has unfolded since the 1990s. We wish to pivot the focus away from questions about the apparent frictions existing between "global" human rights regimes and African states to consider the ways human rights practice unfolds on the ground in African countries. In this sense, we move beyond an emphasis on global-local dynamics toward what we consider the "local-local" dynamics of human rights debates and practices: the conflicts and entanglements that arise out of competing sets of moral arguments about human rights and what they should be. The reason we are compelled to make such a point is that there has been a historical formation of a perceived tension between the international realm and the African political realm outlined by scholars such as Ibhawoh, one that warrants some unraveling. In addressing such entanglements, we see how we might understand African interventions in the intimacy of rights: rights that are bound up in diverse experiences of sexuality, gender, subjectivity, and personhood and that populate landscapes of political economy.

## Histories of Global Human Rights in Africa, 1900–1970

Over the course of the twentieth century to the present, we see sustained but contested struggles to articulate a moral language of rights within political projects. The shape and scale have changed over time: gender and sexuality have shifted from the background to the foreground, as have issues of economic rights and state sovereignty. Here, we trace some of the contours of these historical transformations in an effort to show just a few of the ways the local, the national, and the international realms are theaters for working out the terms of these struggles. This leads us, in the second historical section, to the emphasis of this volume: a postcolonial, neoliberal African context in which struggles over gender-based and sexual rights are the terrain of the contemporary struggle over moral personhood and political sovereignty.

Early discursive and practical engagements with human rights within imperial contexts in Africa and the Global South were always already about gender and personhood, but not necessarily self-consciously so. Neither were they tied to the realm of formal rights. European imperialism introduced new elements of a hierarchical, (ostensibly) care-centered and humanitarian impulse rooted in an early human rights frame.[4] The nineteenth century gave rise to a European imperial maternalism that in turn gave rise to a form of empathy for distant others through religious formations (such as nineteenth-century missionary projects), the abolitionist movement in the United States and Britain, and European feminist arguments for colonialism as a force of protection for African women (Burton 1994; Scully 2011). The figure of the abject African or native woman was central to all of these projects, a figure in need of protection and liberation, something that colonial intervention could provide. As Gayatri Chakravorty Spivak famously argued about British reformers in South Asia, imperial intervention and reform in the name of humanitarian intervention were ultimately about "white men saving brown women from brown men" (1988, 297). This was also the case in African colonial contexts.

Early twentieth-century arguments that used humanitarian language to advocate for the expansion of empire coexisted with and later gave way to the proliferation of rights-based arguments that largely aligned with efforts to end colonialism in Africa and advocate for self-determination and social and economic equality. These were social and political movements that often, again, drew on arguments that emphasized the moral salvation of African women. This was a period when the language and ideals of human rights emerged as a force on the international political scene, intersecting with arguments about sovereignty, democratization, and socialism. Rights work here was explicitly about critiquing and reforming the colonial state and, later, advocating for African sovereignty, often on terms that hinged on the empathetic care for others. In the interwar period, a wave of "compassionate concern" emerged among journalists and writers who critiqued French colonialism in particular, noting that it was "hardly the humanitarian enterprise" that it was held up to be by those who made arguments for colonial uplift and the civilizing mission (Daughton 2011, 515). The focal point of many anticolonial writers in the 1920s was the brutal corvée labor system used throughout French West and Equatorial Africa, but "concern and care"–driven assessments of the colonial enterprise were about other things as well, such as European economic stability and political expediency. Thus, care-driven human rights claims about the state of the African male worker or the African woman were tied up with national and state-driven reform designs located in Europe. At the same time, Meredith Terretta (2017) demonstrates how lawyers associated with the French Communist Party and the League of the Rights of Man became ambivalently entangled with panblack anticolonialism across Madagascar, Martinique, and the Antilles, culminating in a unified legal battle for the rights of colonial subjects. Such international legalist movements both prefigure and inform later appeals for human rights on an international stage (Burke 2010; Jensen 2016; Thompson 2018); yet this period of human rights as a tool of anticolonial state building is often seen in contrast to the rise of the internationalist, extrastate rights regime that emerged after World War II.

Most modern histories of human rights point to the 1948 Universal Declaration of Human Rights as a watershed moment. A document crafted in the first years of the United Nations and in the wake of World War II, it heralded an emerging (though ultimately short-lived) faith in an international political authority that would help to articulate and forward a new moral order, one defined by the effort to protect the rights of individuals and groups from the unmitigated power of sovereign states (Terretta 2013, 393). However, if the

United Nations ultimately failed as an international organization with the jurisdiction to legislate and enforce "human rights," the advent of this international body marked a new era of extrastate governance. The United Nations' 1956 Supplementary Convention on the Abolition of Slavery, the Slave Trade, and Institutions and Practices Similar to Slavery, for example, included new language on the protection of human rights and provided a more substantial framework for defining and identifying slavery and slave-like practices. Forced marriage and child marriage figured prominently as a condition to prevent and abolish; in the 1956 supplement we see a direct critique of family and traditional practices as possible deterrents to the rights of the individual (Bunting, Lawrance, and Roberts 2016, 4–5). The UN Convention on Consent to Marriage, which was ratified in 1962 and entered into force in 1964, similarly included very specific language referencing the primacy of consent in human rights protections and signaled the family as a possible barrier to women's rights in marriage (Malitoris 2019). Thus, at the moment when we see formal international organizations and conventions emerging as gatekeepers in the realm of international human rights, we see the family and gendered relationships emerging as a "trouble spot" for rights, as a repository for cultural practices that held individuals back from achieving full rights. And here again, as in the humanitarian arguments that shaped political support for and against colonial rule, gender and sexuality figured prominently in debates over what constituted "rights."

Though the 1960s are often viewed as a turning point in human rights work, when an internationalist political realm in the form of the UN gave way to a new synergy between global capitalist markets and the expansion of a nongovernmental realm that defined, managed, and pursued transnational projects of "development" and humanitarian care (Moyn 2010; Williams 2010; Meister 2012), this was also the decade of African independence, and rights language featured prominently in new processes of African governance and state making. At the same time, those who fought for increased political rights for women at the height of African nationalist movements in the 1950s—rights to education, rights to hold office, rights to vote—witnessed a declension in the potential for gender-based arguments for rights in the 1960s as state makers and the political leaders of African independence turned toward platforms that emphasized the rights to political and economic sovereignty (Geiger 1987; Lazreg 1990; Allman 2009). Indeed, during the 1960s, "rights" were often invoked to describe broad processes of democratization in African states, as well as socialist projects in favor of economic liberation and equality. In President Milton Obote's Common Man's Charter of 1968 (a Uganda People's Congress Party document that was signed into law the following year), "rights" were used to describe political and personal freedoms such as speech and privacy.

The document also used the Swahili word for freedom, *uhuru*, a term that was invoked to describe not only political liberation but also economic freedom, or freedom from "feudalism," part of a larger political and economic "move to the left" spearheaded by Obote that year (and that would soon fail when Idi Amin took power in a military coup two years later). *Uhuru* was a term claimed by a number of independence-era African politicians, from Julius Nyerere, to Jomo Kenyatta, to Kwame Nkrumah, to discuss processes of political liberation. The use of the term was part of a broader intellectual effort to imagine the terms of both political independence and the scope of a new African internationalism and political solidarity, the ways that African political leaders might engage and imagine political "freedom" on terms parallel to and possibly divergent from those of the West (Englund 2006, 2). The scope of these debates over what constitutes a moral claim to "rights" is one that we return to in this volume, examining cases in which, like Obote's use of *uhuru*, African actors seek to refigure and redefine human rights in terms of diverse kinds of social obligations and orientations to justice and good governance. These cases, like those in the 1960s, demonstrate how local actors have long been central to the definition and deployment of human rights, seeking to define and root such claims in specific cultural orientations to notions of justice and civility.

### Transnational Frameworks, the State, and Local Actors from the 1990s to the Present

If there is some disagreement about the role of the state in managing and articulating rights-based projects in the mid-twentieth century, there is a widely held consensus that, at the present moment, human rights work is deeply shaped by broader changes in global governance and economic policy that have taken hold over the last few decades. Human rights emerge toward the end of the twentieth century as a new kind of transnational moralism, and the practice of human rights in this era is shaped by the dominance of transnational forms of governmentality (Hoffman 2016, 285). By the end of the twentieth century, the rising influence of an international rights regime framed key practical tensions, largely understood as occurring between the global and the state realms. Yet this attention to the dynamic between the international and the state levels—the global and a certain *kind* of local—often sidelines how rights work plays out domestically and how African actors pursue competing strategies and goals within their efforts to craft rights frameworks.

As the late capitalist political and economic order has taken shape, "rights" have become widely distilled into a focus on individual "freedoms"—or, as Gregory Mann (2015) writes of the 1990s in the Sahel region, "rights" become the freedom "to starve" (in the absence of state power to manage a famine that reshaped the region during that decade). Freedom, as the anthropologist Harri Englund, writing about Malawi, describes it, is experienced under these conditions as personal freedom; human rights as a discourse and practice are shaped by a rhetoric of personal empowerment and self-realization. Individuals are "freed" to realize their own potential, a perspective on rights and political agency that is narrow and that disallows, Englund (2006, 10; see also Chitonge 2015) has argued, the idea that empowerment and political change may be accessible as much through relationships with other people as it is through one's independence from others. As Pamela Scully has highlighted, one legacy of the rise of this model for human rights work is that other models for women's collective action and solidarity, especially those pursued through more "traditional" patterns of relationship building like kin groups, clientship, and ethnicity, are deemed "bastions of cultures hostile to women's rights" and antithetical to rights-based work (2011, 30; see also Merry 2006). These dynamics signal, in some ways, a new kind of "human rights paradox" (Stern and Straus 2014) in which we see the rise of a neoliberal regime that privileges the idea of the individual but within a singular framework that deemphasizes forms of African agency and innovation or the potential of alternative approaches.

This new language of human rights—of rights as individual "freedoms"—was at the center of a host of new constitutions in Africa in the 1990s, including in South Africa's first postapartheid constitution in 1996, Namibia's first constitution after gaining independence in 1990, and a new constitution in Uganda in 1995 following decades of political upheaval in that country. South Africa's constitution famously enshrined "gay rights" into the document by including a clause forbidding discrimination on the basis of sexual orientation, the first constitutional clause of its kind in the world. Human rights also featured prominently in Uganda's new constitution, with a clause that articulated the state's obligation to ensure the independence of nongovernmental institutions tasked with the responsibility of "protecting and promoting human rights." Yet again, it was not only a singular framework of neoliberal, individual rights that gained leverage during this period. The proliferation of rights-based language and constitutional protections that we see during this decade opened up new arenas for debate within African communities over how rights should be applied and for whom such protections should extend in practice.

Uganda's explicit constitutional reference to the interplay between civil society and the state when it came to human rights highlights how human rights during this period increasingly proved to be a point of interaction between the nongovernmental realm and the state and, by extension, between forms of global governance and state and community power. As Andrea Cornwall and Maxine Molyneux (2006) have noted in their own discussion of this period, the 1990s were marked by a strong overlap between projects of "development" and human rights, seen in the enshrining of rights talk in the broader realm of global aid and international governance, long considered separate fields of practice. Cornwall and Molyneux argue that from the 1990s onward rights talk has been "mainstreamed" (1177) into policy documents and political debates from the United Nations down to the local level. They note that many social activists in Africa and elsewhere welcomed this shift in part because "rights" provided a moral argument, drawing attention and resources toward issues like poverty and gender inequality, though on terms that heavily favored models of individual "empowerment" that were amenable to broader global economic strategies. But this shift is also notable, we argue, not only because it shaped the debate over rights as between the international realm and donor-dependent states (like those in Africa), which were "compelled" to take up rights frameworks advocated by global powers, but also because it introduced a domestic field of debate, one where local activists used international instruments to pressure their own states to engage with (and at times push back against) this emergent global rights regime.

The 1990s were notable as well for the increased attention paid to gender and sexual inequalities as rights-based concerns. Here, the interplay between the transnational realm and the local level has proved a critical point of concern, as international policy documents forged during this period continue to provide an (imperfect) legal framework to advocate for "rights" within the state. In 1990 Charlotte Bunch famously argued that women's rights are human rights, a rallying cry that permeated activism and policy in international legal circles and that implored states to act according to international conventions. A number of international conferences and instruments emerged over the course of the 1990s from this standpoint, ranging from the Platform for Action (a product of the UN's Fourth World Conference on Women in Beijing in 1995) to the UN General Assembly's Declaration on the Elimination of Violence against Women in 1993. While these were international tools and conferences that emerged to translate meaning and relevance between the global and the local, other efforts at creating more relevant and grounded African international tools followed quickly (Merry 2006). The Protocol to the African Charter on Human and Peoples' Rights on the Rights of Women in Africa, known as the Maputo Protocol, was adopted by the African Union in 2003 and entered into force in 2005. While this protocol builds on preexisting international human rights instruments, it locates universal concerns about women's rights as human rights in an expressly African context and pushes for a recognition that African conditions and concerns must be treated differently (Mukumu 2015). Thus, from the 1990s onward we see multiple arenas in which human rights have played out at the point where transnational and local connect. We also see an effort, in Maputo in particular, to create an African transnationalism that drives the "local-local" workings around human rights.

Despite the expansion of new tools to promote human rights practice during the late twentieth century, many scholars have pointed to the disingenuous nature of the promise of human rights in this era, particularly as structural adjustment has undermined the ability of states to provide social services such as health care and education and thus to ensure these rights for their citizens. The influence and attention that human rights issues garner in the West has also drawn criticism for the ways that the focus on rights-based issues may draw attention away from other kinds of unjust or nondemocratic actions on the part of African leaders. In Uganda, where Yoweri Museveni's increasingly autocratic regime has long been supported by Western powers, Sylvia Tamale (1998, 17) has noted that Museveni's efforts to promote gender-based rights may explain how he has been able to deflect Western attention away from broader problems with corruption and voter disenfranchisement in the country. And as we have noted, the dominance of a model of human rights that aligns with neoliberal models for economic empowerment often elides the possibility of other, non-Western models for gender-based solidarity and political action (Englund 2006; Scully 2011).

These criticisms of rights work point to the complexity and contentiousness of human rights in practice. Far from a singular and universal "good," human rights are aligned with a variety of political and economic formations at both the international and local levels, and rights-based practices have in turn taken a variety of forms within African communities. In the chapters that follow, we examine how rights-based legislative debates reveal not the dominance of a single framework for political action in African communities but rather the coexistence of multiple interpretations of what rights mean and do and the work of African activists and legislators to use rights frameworks to make arguments for the kinds of relationships between citizens and the state that should exist. In African states, the question of rights has increasingly been focused on issues of gender and sexuality, in large part because these issues highlight how and for whom "rights" should function.

### Legislating Gender and Sexuality: Morality, Personhood, and Political Agency

The proliferation of legislative debates over gender-based and sexual rights in Africa is not a new phenomenon, as the history we have outlined above has sought to demonstrate. Debates taken up in the present era have taken new forms and made use of new tools (especially international accords, like the Maputo Protocol), but the effort to define and extend rights in terms of age, gender, and sexuality has long been a central concern of African human rights work, whether on the part of Westerners or on the part of African activists. This is not only because human rights debates are about enshrining the privileges of citizenship but also because human rights make moral arguments about the kinds of persons states recognize and the kinds of obligations states and citizens believe ought to exist between people. The chapters in this book examine the complex dynamic between civil society, religious actors, and the state, and in so doing we reveal the multifaceted nature of rights-based projects in African communities in recent years. More than simply an effort to extend a global rights framework "from above" into African states, rights-based arguments in Africa take a variety of forms shaped by and in response to what are often competing moral arguments about what rights should mean and do. Human rights are in some instances applied to safeguard models of rights familiar in the West—those that enshrine the autonomy of the individual. In other instances we explore in this book, rights come to mean something different—they are ways of empowering collective notions of responsibility or of demarcating the differing kinds of political agency that may be granted to women versus men. In this sense, we are interested in the ways rights debates intersect with situated understandings of moral personhood, political obligation, and agency.

This volume takes up human rights work and the debates that surround it as what anthropologists understand as a social "practice" (Bourdieu 1990) shaped by broader global institutions and legal frameworks but brought into being through the situated actions and choices of people themselves. In taking up rights work as a social practice, we emphasize the ways such work can also be understood as an expression of political agency shaped by relationships of power, such as between the transnational realm and the state, between the state and the nongovernmental realm, and between state-level elites and the poor. In this way, we wish to emphasize how African actors, far from being simply subjects of rights-based advocacy, help form a lively, often contentious field of political debate and action, one whereby Africans themselves help reshape what rights mean and do within their communities. Often such political jockeying results in compromise, or processes of what Sally Engle Merry (2006) has termed "vernacularization," whereby Western human rights agendas are adapted in ways that incorporate local priorities and political goals. In some instances, this can be revolutionary, providing opportunity for the negotiation of new forms of political capital. In other instances, such as the case described by Rachel Silver in this volume, such compromise may complicate rights-based policy work. Malawi's Readmission Policy, which allows girls who have given birth to return to school, is possible in its current form only because it adheres to a politically neutral "middle ground" that values educational access for girls, Silver argues, while ignoring issues of gender inequality that contribute to high rates of adolescent pregnancy in the country. Rights workers who would seek to introduce sexual education and reproductive justice to the conversation in Malawi must navigate a precarious national and international terrain of contested morality-based arguments.

Examples such as this reveal not only how local debates over rights are framed in terms of African states' relationship to the global realm but also how such debates play out within African communities themselves, often on terms that seek to define expectations and experiences of moral personhood and social obligation. Debates over gender and sexual rights tend to exacerbate such conflicts, as older models for political authority that are based in social hierarchies of kinship and that presuppose the difference between and the different kinds of political power held by men and women conflict with newer ones that view men and women as equal and interchangeable actors. This dynamic is nowhere more obvious than in the numerous legislative efforts to limit the rights of sexual minorities over the past decade. In the early 2010s, Uganda's political arena was dominated by the debate over the failed Anti-Homosexuality Bill, which drew international condemnation but widespread local political support. In 2014 Nigeria passed a similar piece of legislation, the Same-Sex Marriage Prohibition Act, in spite of intense pressure and the threat of sanctions from European donors. The Democratic Republic of Congo proposed the Sexual Practices against Nature Bill in 2010, one of several legislative efforts in that country to heighten legal penalties for same-sex acts. And in 2013, when US president Barack Obama visited Senegal, President Macky Sall was cheered by his citizens for pushing back against the US demand to decriminalize homosexuality in that country (see Niang, Foley, and Diop, this volume). In these examples, sexual rights are often rejected because they are seen to challenge kin-based structures of political and social authority, bringing into question alternative models for collective belonging and agency. In some instances, local activists in favor of restrictions on homosexuality have forwarded the argument that successful human rights claims must recognize and acknowledge kin-based and gender-based hierarchies and that those that do not are immoral and even potentially socially or politically destabilizing (Boyd 2013). These arguments against sexual rights may be complicated as well by a changing political landscape, in particular the introduction of multiparty rule (a shift experienced in both Uganda and Senegal over the last two decades). Efforts at democratization may exacerbate and intensify competing claims to moral authority, amplifying religious or cultural arguments that are often couched in terms of their difference from a global, cosmopolitan sphere (see Niang, Foley, and Diop, this volume).

Such rejections of sexual rights underscore how human rights struggles are not only arguments over the definition and deployment of certain rights but also about how rights-based claims are rooted in categories of moral personhood, which may be demarcated and experienced differently in different places. Sexual personhood, shaped as it is by a constellation of relationships and moral norms governing reproduction, kinship, obligation, and desire, is perhaps especially fraught, contested, and often experienced in tension with globalizing projects for sexual identity making (Donham 1998; Boellstorff 2005, 2007). The chapters in this book are efforts to extend our understanding of how the rejection of concepts like sexual equality and sexual rights is not simply a rejection of "human rights" writ large but also a debate over how rights-based claims fit into a broader set of questions about moral agency and identity.

Even as efforts to advocate for sexual rights have struggled at the national level, women's rights activists have had legislative success in Africa, often by seeking to apply and modify international rights-based agreements for local contexts. Women's rights activists and lawmakers continue to push for increased legislation on marriage and family laws in African countries largely because these are opportunities to apply international tools, such as the Maputo Protocol, to advocate for an *African* rights-based approach to reform. But the investment in legal reform is not solely the purview of liberal or progressive actors: those who seek to bolster the authority of the paternal household head, limit external imprints on what they see as private or family matters, or protest neoliberal influence on social values also turn to legislative action as a strategy (Soares 2006). African activists and political actors use international human rights documents and other legal tools to engage "rights" at the level of the state and community, refashioning the state from the inside out (Kang 2015; Burrill, this volume). At the heart of most of these debates about gender, especially as they are manifested through marriage and family law projects, are conversations about consent, protection, and obligation. Thus, we see legal reform efforts as multivocal contests: fruitful arenas for different stakeholders who wish to define rights relative to social, family, and sexual or gender-based relationships. Often the terms of debate take up arguments about religion, culture, and moral behavior to make broader claims for ideal models of society. These are terms that highlight the different stakeholders in rights-based debates: How and for whom are "rights" being defined?

Because gender and sexual identity are in part shaped by social relationships, gender-based and sexual rights expose competing orientations to human rights themselves. Human rights claims, as they circulate at the global level, presume the value of individualism, equality, and autonomy, ideals that sometimes contrast with other models for personhood and collective political action that have historically existed in African and other cultural contexts. Human rights arguments are thus also moral arguments about the nature of personhood and social obligation, which can present contrasting models for social justice and political action. For instance, Africans' familiar criticisms of rights projects often point to the ways too much personal "freedom" (e.g., in terms of sexual identity or practice) may undermine other kinds of (often hierarchical and gender-based) models for collective political agency. These arguments seek to forward claims about the value not of autonomy and personal choice but of the agency derived from the maintenance of social bonds of interdependence between youth and elders, as well as women and men. The topics of gender and sexuality, situated as they are at the center of questions about humanity and human relations, are especially likely to lay bare these competing rights-based frameworks and the terms of debate over status, political obligation, and hierarchy within African societies. Because of this, we view legislative and political arguments surrounding gender and sexuality as a key front in the practice of human rights in Africa. The chapters in this book provide a window onto the complexity and diversity of rights-based advocacy and work in Africa and the often-competing perspectives used to define, reform, and sometimes reject rights-based models for political authority and action.

## The Chapters in This Volume

The chapters that follow draw on a range of topics relating to the contestation of gender and sexual rights in contemporary African societies. They have been selected in large part because they give a sense of the scope of what has been a broader trend to legislate gender and sexuality in African states in recent decades. That is, each case reveals something about the extent of explicit efforts to both extend new rights and limit the perceived expansion of rights relating to gender and sexuality on the continent. Some of these cases draw on efforts to revisit or revise decades-old laws that concern gender and sexuality—such as family and marriage laws in Mali (Burrill) and Niger (Masquelier). Others look at the ways more recent (1990s on) rights-based laws or social policies are being revised for the present era. These chapters, such as one focused on the debates following the revision of a sex education policy in

Uganda (Musiime and Eryenyu) and another examining a twenty-year-old policy that enshrined adolescent mothers' right to return to school (Silver), focus on the internal debates and competing sets of social actors who argue for and against different interpretations and versions of rights-based policies. Another set of chapters looks at the influence of the international realm on local experiences of political agency and rights and the ways efforts to codify "rights" from the global level down may be fraught in practice, reinterpreted in terms of local models of political power and influence (see Nébié's chapter on land tenure and Walker-Said's chapter on the tensions surrounding kinship that shape political asylum cases). A final set of chapters examines efforts to explicitly push back against an international realm that is perceived as advocating for "rights" that are considered in direct conflict with local norms and values (see Niang, Foley, and Diop on the rising antihomosexual sentiment in Senegal and Boyd on legislative efforts to restrict both homosexuality and pornography in Uganda). The authors in these cases seek to contextualize these political efforts in order to better understand the conflict over sexual and gender rights as something more complex and historically situated than simply a case of "culture versus rights." In these chapters and others, we seek to provide a sense of the kinds of activism surrounding gender-based and sexual legislation and policy on the continent, especially the ways such debates rarely simply play out as the adoption or rejection of a monolithic notion of human rights on a global scale. Rather, we wish to emphasize how rights debates reveal competing models for and moral investments in rights-based practice and agency in African communities.

Emily Burrill and Adeline Masquelier, for instance, both examine marriage and family law as platforms for working out different investments in rights and social values. Burrill discusses the ways Malian marriage laws have intersected with and diverged from rights-based arguments for marriage in that country since the 1990s. In particular, she examines the debates surrounding a 2009 effort to reform the Malian marriage code and religious leaders' assertions that efforts to raise the age of consent and to reform inheritance laws to favor women's rights to property would weaken marriage. Burrill argues that in the context of Mali since 2009, marriage law reform efforts are tied up in the disintegration and the restoration of the state itself and its membership in a larger international African community. Masquelier examines debates surrounding *mariage précoce*, or "early marriage," in Niger, where 75 percent of girls are married before the age of eighteen and where a narrative of children's rights and girls' rights to health have been mobilized in an effort to raise the age of consent in that country. In her discussion, she moves beyond debates about rights as a universal concept and delves into the way that gender ideologies are produced through activist discourse. Masquelier demonstrates that such ideologies reveal the different ideas of female vulnerability and moral womanhood that lie at the center of tensions over age of consent law.

Elisabeth Kago Ilboudo Nébié introduces the important issue of climate change to the volume's discussion of rights through her appraisal of women's involvement (or lack thereof) in land resource management in southern Burkina Faso. In her chapter, Nébié shows that reforms and concerns about climate change and land management are deeply gendered endeavors that weave together different expectations concerning property, mobility, and governance. Despite an increase in women's leadership in household decision-making as a result of men's labor migration, women's participation in formal community land management has not increased. This is in spite of top-down state policies that mandate gender quotas to achieve gender parity at local, regional, and state levels of government. Using ethnographic material and land resource management data, Nébié examines the exclusion of women from leadership positions in land resource management within their community in southern Burkina Faso, thereby revealing the limitations of state application of rights-based arguments for gender equality in the realm of land and resource management.

The chapters then move to themes of sexuality and reproduction. Rachel Silver in chapter 4 and Eunice Musiime and Leah Eryenyu in chapter 5 focus on the issue of youth sexuality: they take up the respective topics of school-age pregnancy in Malawi and the debates over a new comprehensive sexual education policy in Uganda. Sexual and reproductive health rights, or SRHR, as it is often abbreviated in Uganda, have become a major front in rights-based debates in that country as the media and political activists have honed in on health, especially maternal and reproductive health, as a political concern and tool of political critique leveled against President Museveni's thirty-year-old regime. But debates over sexuality have also mobilized religious activists who propose counterarguments in favor of "values" as a stabilizing force in the face of mounting political tension. These two competing arguments, for "rights" and for "values," have shaped discussion surrounding the Ministry of Education's new comprehensive sex education policy. Musiime and Eryenyu explore how these two sides of the debate reveal two dominant orientations to rights in Uganda today and their implications for efforts to address issues of social and gender-based inequality.

Silver examines a related issue in Malawi, the contested implementation of a twenty-year-old law that guarantees teenaged mothers the right to return to school after giving birth. Silver's chapter explores how this rights-based approach to girls' education is constrained in Malawi by broader social and political attitudes that have stigmatized youth sexuality. This chapter discusses how rights-based models for social and political change are situationally limited, especially when gender rights, such as the right to girls' education, depend upon and are shaped by a broader set of attitudes regarding sexuality and reproduction. She focuses in particular on the attitudes shaping policy within the government in Malawi and the tensions that inform relationships between the donor community, the NGO sector, and the state.

Charlotte Walker-Said examines the issues of gender-based violence and migration through the lens of human rights in her chapter. Through her focus on human trafficking cases involving women from Cameroon seeking asylum in the United States, Walker-Said investigates how rights are refracted through the lens of kinship and conflicting ideas about obligation and justice. This chapter examines kinship as a set of relationships that directly shape the kinds of claims to legal rights that migrants make, as well as the way the intimate relationships of family, gender, and kinship extend across and are transformed by state boundaries.

Cheikh Ibrahima Niang, Ellen Foley, and Ndack Diop turn to the increasingly fraught and politically volatile issue of the rights of sexual minorities in Senegal. They examine the recent backlash against homosexual rights as a "sexual panic" driven by increasing economic inequality and concerns about state failure. In this broader political-economic context, religious reformers have expanded their critique of what they characterize as a liberal sexuality that has contributed to a sense of moral and social chaos. The authors demonstrate that while the issue of antihomosexual violence has affected a number of African countries in the past decade, the historical acceptance of non-binary-gender expression in Senegal makes the recent public rejection of homosexuality by political leaders all the more surprising. This chapter provides the reader with a nuanced reading of the debates over homosexual rights in Africa and the reasons why campaigns for sexual rights, especially those that are led by global actors, have experienced limited success within many African communities.

Finally, Lydia Boyd examines rights through the lens of embodiment, specifically the ways debates over human rights often depend upon and engage the figure of the vulnerable victim. She draws upon examples of political protest related to two recent legislative efforts that have taken up the issue of gender and sexual equality in Uganda: the 2013 Anti-Pornography Bill, also known as the "anti–mini skirt bill," and the 2009 Anti-Homosexuality Bill. She analyzes how competing claims to "rights" in Uganda circulate and are oriented differently toward ideas of social obligation, hierarchy, and interdependence, highlighting both the possibilities for rights-based advocacy in Uganda and the limits on such projects.

Above all, the chapters in this volume tackle how arguments are made for and against rights and how Africans craft and implement human rights on their own terms, engaging the state and the international realm in the process. We believe this perspective is important in part because it reveals how African states and political actors are not now, nor have they ever been, passive agents in helping to define what human rights mean at either the national or the international level. Human rights, often understood as an imposition from outside, have long been and remain a means for making moral and legal claims within African communities, though on terms that are often fraught, contested, and open for debate.

## Notes

1. Uganda's Anti-Homosexuality Bill was briefly made law in 2014 before being nullified by the Constitutional Court on procedural grounds. Attorneys arguing against the law's passage successfully claimed that a parliamentary quorum had not been present when the bill was passed.

2. We focus here on the legislative arena because we are mainly interested in how people engage with law-making processes within states.

3. We use the term "extrastate" to refer to the arena above and outside the state. This highlights not simply an international or global realm but an arena defined by forces that differentiate themselves from state-based forms of authority, such as those associated with the nongovernmental and humanitarian sphere.

4. Philosophers and legal scholars point to an early history of human rights in Africa that predates European colonial rule—a prehistory of human rights in Africa, to use Bonny Ibhawoh's term—that outlines a concept of moral personhood and indigenous humanism (Wiredu and Gyekye 1992; Diagne 2009; Ibhawoh 2018). Indeed, rights have long been a point of debate and form of political agency in many African societies because a variety of models for rights and normative rules helped shape notions of freedom, belonging, and obligations between people and their communities prior to colonial rule . During the colonial period, African interpretations of moral personhood and indigenous humanism, as well as other rights formations, intersected with European expressions of rights through the paradoxical moral arguments that Europeans made to justify imperialism in the late eighteenth and early nineteenth centuries (Conklin 1998; Hunt 2007). These are the debates that provide the springboard for the contestations over rights that frame this book, yet it is important to recognize that "human rights" are not a purely modern concept in African societies.

## References

Allman, Jean. 2009. "The Disappearing of Hannah Kudjoe: Nationalism, Feminism, and the Tyrannies of History." *Journal of Women's History* 21 (3): 13–35.

Asad, Talal. 2003. *Formations of the Secular: Christianity, Islam, Modernity*. Stanford, CA: Stanford University Press.

Basu, Amrita. 2000. "Globalization of the Local / Localization of the Global: Mapping Transnational Women's Movements." *Meridians* 1 (1): 68–84.

Boellstorff, Tom. 2005. "Between Religion and Desire: Being Muslim and Gay in Indonesia." *American Anthropologist* 107 (4): 575–85.

———. 2007. "Queer Studies in the House of Anthropology." *Annual Review of Anthropology* 36:17–25.

Bourdieu, Pierre. 1990. *The Logic of Practice*. Translated by Richard Nice. Stanford, CA: Stanford University Press.

Boyd, Lydia. 2013. "The Problem with Freedom: Homosexuality and Human Rights in Uganda." *Anthropological Quarterly* 86 (3): 697–724.

Bunch, Charlotte. 1990. "Women's Rights as Human Rights: Toward a Re-vision of Human Rights." *Human Rights Quarterly* 12 (4): 486–98.

Bunting, Annie, Benjamin N. Lawrance, and Richard L. Roberts. 2016. "Introduction: Something Old, Something New? Conceptualizing Forced Marriage in Africa." In *Marriage by Force? Contestation over Consent and Coercion in Africa*, edited by Annie Bunting, Benjamin N. Lawrance, and Richard L. Roberts, 1–42. Athens: Ohio University Press.

Burke, Roland. 2010. *Decolonization and the Evolution of International Human Rights*. Philadelphia: University of Pennsylvania Press.

Burton, Antoinette. 1994. *Burdens of History: British Feminism, Indian Women, and Imperial Culture, 1865–1915*. Chapel Hill: University of North Carolina Press.

Chitonge, Horman. 2015. *Beyond Parliament: Human Rights and the Politics of Social Change in the Global South*. Leiden: Brill.

Conklin, Alice. 1998. "Colonialism and Human Rights, a Contradiction in Terms? The Case of France and West Africa, 1895–1914." *American Historical Review* 103 (2): 419–42.

Cornwall, Andrea, and Maxine Molyneux. 2006. "The Politics of Rights: Dilemmas for Feminist Praxis: An Introduction." *Third World Quarterly* 27 (7): 1175–91.

Daughton, J. P. 2011. "Behind the Imperial Curtain: International Humanitarian Efforts and the Critique of French Colonialism in the Interwar Years." *French Historical Studies* 34 (3): 503–28.

Diagne, Souleymane Bachir. 2009. "Individual, Community, and Human Rights." *Transition*, no. 101: 8–15.

Donham, Donald L. 1998. "Freeing South Africa: The 'Modernization' of Male-Male Sexuality in Soweto." *Cultural Anthropology* 13 (1): 3–21.

Englund, Harri. 2006. *Prisoners of Freedom: Human Rights and the African Poor*. Berkeley: University of California Press.

Geiger, Susan. 1987. "Women in Nationalist Struggle: TANU Activists in Dar es Salaam." *International Journal of African Historical Studies* 20 (1): 1–26.

Hodgson, Dorothy. 2011. "Introduction: Gender and Culture at the Limit of Rights." In *Gender and Culture at the Limit of Rights*, edited by Dorothy Hodgson, 1–16. Philadelphia: University of Pennsylvania Press.

Hoffman, Stefan-Ludwig. 2016. "Human Rights and History." *Past & Present* 232 (1): 279–310.
Hunt, Lynn. 2007. *Inventing Human Rights*. New York: W. W. Norton.
Ibhawoh, Bonny. 2018. *Human Rights in Africa*. Cambridge: Cambridge University Press.
Jensen, Steven L. B. 2016. *The Making of International Human Rights: The 1960s, Decolonization and the Reconstruction of Global Values*. Cambridge: Cambridge University Press.
Kang, Alice. 2015. *Bargaining for Women's Rights: Activism in an Aspiring Muslim Democracy*. Minneapolis: University of Minnesota Press.
Lazreg, Marnia. 1990. "Gender and Politics in Algeria: Unraveling the Religious Paradigm." *Signs: Journal of Women in Culture and Society* 15 (4): 755–80.
Levitt, Peggy, and Sally Engle Merry. 2011. "Making Women's Human Rights in the Vernacular: Navigating the Culture/Rights Divide." In *Gender and Culture at the Limit of Rights*, edited by Dorothy Hodgson, 81–100. Philadelphia: University of Pennsylvania Press.
Malitoris, Jessica. 2019. "The Promise of Marriage Consent: Family Politics, the United Nations, and Women's Rights in the United States, 1947–1967." PhD diss., Duke University.
Mann, Gregory. 2015. *From Empires to NGOs in the West African Sahel: The Road to Nongovernmentality*. Cambridge: Cambridge University Press.
Meister, Robert. 2012. *After Evil: A Politics of Human Rights*. New York: Columbia University Press.
Merry, Sally Engle. 2006. *Human Rights and Gender Violence: Translating International Law into Local Justice*. Chicago: University of Chicago Press.
Moyn, Samuel. 2010. *The Last Utopia: Human Rights in Histories*. Cambridge, MA: Harvard University Press.
Mukumu, Wairumu Irene. 2015. "The Maputo Protocol: Evaluating Women's Rights." *Pambazuka News*, June 11, 2015.
Oloka-Onyango, Joe, and Sylvia Tamale. 1995. "The Personal Is Political, or Why Women's Rights Are Indeed Human Rights: An African Perspective on International Feminism." *Human Rights Quarterly* 17 (4): 691–731.
Scully, Pamela. 2011. "Gender, History and Human Rights." In *Gender and Culture at the Limit of Rights*, edited by Dorothy Hodgson, 17–31. Philadelphia: University of Pennsylvania Press.
Soares, Benjamin F. 2006. "Islam in Mali in the Neoliberal Era." *African Affairs* 105 (418): 77–95.
Spivak, Gayatri Chakravorty. 1988. "Can the Subaltern Speak?" In *Marxism and the Interpretation of Culture*, edited by Cary Nelson and Lawrance Grossberg, 271–313. Urbana: University of Illinois Press.
Stern, Steve, and Scott Straus, eds. 2014. *The Human Rights Paradox: Universality and Its Discontents*. Madison: University of Wisconsin Press.
Tamale, Sylvia. 1998. *When Hens Begin to Crow: Gender and Parliamentary Politics in Uganda*. New York: Routledge.

Terretta, Meredith. 2013. "From Below and to the Left? Human Rights and Liberation Politics in Africa's Postcolonial Age." *Journal of World History* 24 (2): 389–416.

———. 2017. "Anti-colonial Lawyering, Postwar Human Rights, and Decolonization across Imperial Boundaries in Africa." *Canadian Journal of History* 52 (3): 448–78.

Thompson, Andrew. 2018. "Unravelling the Relationships between Humanitarianism, Human Rights, and Decolonization: Time for a Radical Rethink?" In *The Oxford Handbook on the Ends of Empire*, edited by Martin Thomas and Andrew Thompson, 453–76. Oxford: Oxford University Press.

Williams, Randall. 2010. *The Divided World: Human Rights and Its Violence*. Minneapolis: University of Minnesota Press.

Wiredu, Kwasi, and Kwame Gyekye. 1992. *Person and Community: Ghanaian Philosophical Studies I*. Washington, DC: Council for Research in Values and Philosophy.

# Legislating Marriage in Postcolonial Mali

## A History of the Present

EMILY BURRILL

Why does marriage matter to the modern state, and how? Organizationally, marriage makes households, organizes kin, and is the basis for multigenerational distribution of wealth. But marriage is also a site for the moral and values-based education that makes an informed citizenry or subjecthood and reinforces the nation; it is a site for different types of labor and knowledge production that can contribute to the reproduction of the state itself (Burrill 2015). Marriage reforms and marriage-related initiatives have long been projects of statecraft and nationcraft. While the topic of marriage as an element of statecraft that reveals debates over rights and gender in French Soudan (colonial Mali) has been taken up elsewhere, this chapter traces some of the elements of the relationship between marriagecraft and statecraft in the postcolonial context.[1] One strand of continuity between the colonial and the postcolonial periods is the following paradox: legislators' and state makers' efforts to render marriage legible through law and code often obscure the very reality of marriage for many. This is partially because of the realities of bifurcated legal pluralism: the secular state does not recognize certain pathways to marriage as binding, yet these non-state-approved pathways to marriage are the most culturally resonant and yield other, often more important types of assurances and social legibility outside the grasp of the state (Kamau 2009). As Rosa Da Jorio (2002) has noted, there are multiple "marriage scripts" in contemporary Mali, and these different avenues allow for a type of "venue shopping" that has been an enduring strategy for women and men who seek to make and break marital bonds according to their interests (see also Roberts 2005). Yet despite the popularity of non-state-regulated forms of marriage in Mali, different sets of actors invest significant energy in the work of marriagecraft as a state project. Marriage, then, is an important institution to the state with great potential to enhance the legitimacy or even the character of the state, apart from what we might think of as raw state power over a citizenry.

One of the broad political projects of marriagecraft is the locally situated engagement with human rights debates. While rights-infused debates were an essential part of marriage reform at different moments in the colonial period before 1960, talk of marriage has certainly become talk of human rights in a more deliberate and firm way since the 1990s. This is because of the groundswell in a human rights–conscious and human rights–invested global community since the Fourth World Conference on Women in Beijing in 1995; various treaties, trade relationships, aid packages, and diplomatic relations are tied to the stakes of human rights discourse. But beyond Beijing, this localized engagement with human rights derives much momentum from the 2003 Protocol to the African Charter on Human and Peoples' Rights on the Rights of Women in Africa, known as the Maputo Protocol.

Recently in Mali, rights talk—in particular, marriage rights talk—has emerged as a critical element in the formation of the state. As the introduction to this volume argues, human rights are not a "counterweight" to the state in Mali, but they are a way into reform: a local reinvestment in the state. In short, we see through our examination of the history of marriage reform in Mali that human rights are invoked not as something outside the state but as something that is part of state making itself and that is derived from a "local-local" articulation process. This is particularly important in a moment when Malian political actors find themselves rebuilding the state after collapse.

With these sets of arguments in mind, this chapter is an appraisal of marriage codes and their reform in postcolonial Mali. First, I offer a general overview of the Marriage and Guardianship Code of 1962, with a broad and syncretic discussion of marriage reform efforts in the 1990s and early 2000s. Other scholars have argued that what we see in debates about marriage reform in Mali—and elsewhere in the Global South—is symptomatic of the globalization of values, practices, and laws, as well as liberalization more broadly. This chapter is a contribution to that argument. Interest in reforming marriage in Mali has ebbed and flowed since the 1990s, with an acceleration of marriage reform activity in 2009. The chapter then moves to a closer examination of Mali's marriage and personal status code between 2009 and 2018, including first-person accounts that track elements of the press-based responses to changes in the code and the subsequent impact on a local feminist legal rights NGO. This discussion partially takes account of fast-moving political changes on the ground and puts them in conversation with earlier reform efforts, but it also reflects on the shape of marriage reform in the context of Malian state collapse and state regeneration. This chapter is a history of the present, and as such, it is an attempt to make some sense of change and continuities in the debates and stakes of marriage reform in Mali from 2009 to the present.

## Marriage Law in Mali from 1962 to 2009: A Brief History

When Mali became an independent nation, one of the first pieces of legislation ratified in the new state was the Marriage and Guardianship Code of 1962. The formation of the first piece of marriage legislation was marked by both disagreement and compromise. This marriage and family law code defined marriage as secular: civil marriage was the only marriage the state would recognize. The language of marital obligation dictated that a husband owed his wife protection, while she owed him obedience. The first postindependence code gave husbands unchecked authority over their wives, as husbands were legally empowered to restrict the movement and travel of their wives, just as they were able to restrict and control their wives' economic enterprises. Women's associations, which had fought so hard on the front lines in the struggle for independence, lobbied for the legal abolition of polygamy, a fight they did not win (Da Jorio 2002). Women's organizations did ensure that consent was the cornerstone of marriage, building on the ratification of the Mandel and Jacquinot Decrees in 1939 and 1952, respectively. Women organized to successfully abolish divorce through repudiation, just as they were able to ensure that there would be a stipulation that couples would have to consent to polygynous or monogamous marriage at the moment they signed the marriage contract. Women had the legal right to file for divorce if their husbands failed to provide for them in a material sense, and both women and men could seek legal divorce in cases of adultery, serious injury caused by the partner, alcoholism, or the spouse's inability to fulfill conjugal responsibilities. In cases of divorce, child custody and alimony were to be granted to the spouse in whose favor the court ruled. In cases of death of a parent, the surviving parent retained parental rights. According to the code, marrying couples were to sign for civil marriage first before engaging in religious or customary marriage celebrations. Mali's 1962 marriage code did not stand alone; it emerged from an international, immediate postcolonial moment in which organizations such as the United Nations were thinking very much about marriage as an element of statecraft. The UN Convention on Consent to Marriage of 1964, which established marriage consent standards as a human rights measure, illustrates this. It is therefore not a coincidence that a convention on consent to marriage emerged in 1964 in the context of widespread decolonization and global statecraft (Mazower 2013; Bunting, Lawrance, and Roberts 2016; Jensen 2016).

However, through the 1960s, there is little evidence that Malian women and men typically pursued civil marriages. Civil marriage laws meant very little to most people unless they worked for the state and therefore depended on the state for salary and pension benefits (Da Jorio 2002). For that matter, women's associations, which had been powerful and well organized through the late colonial period, retreated from the stage of formal political influence in the dawn of the new nation despite women politicians participating in the drafting of the constitution (Konare 1993; Da Jorio 1997). Indeed, this situation reflects political contours seen elsewhere in the immediate postindependence period in other African contexts, such as Algeria, Tunisia, Ghana, and Tanzania, where women contributed to the push for independence, crafting a language of the nation, organizing the population, and consequently finding themselves largely left out of the conversations on legal reform and statecraft in the 1960s and 1970s (Lazreg 1990; Geiger 1996; Allman 2009).

While there were no formal efforts to reform or address marriage and family law in the 1960s, leaders of the Union Soudanaise Rassemblement Démocratique Africain (US-RDA), which led Soudan Français to independence as the Republic of Mali, were concerned with a kind of crisis in the family: the perceived decline of youth morality throughout Mali in the postindependence 1960s (Mann 2015). In the 1960s, Mali saw an influx of cash and new resources from different parts of the world, the rise of dance halls, teahouses, and Western-style music and dress, and sexual liberation (Diawara et al. 2017). Schoolgirl pregnancies and pregnancy out of wedlock also increased in the 1960s, which the US-RDA saw as the ultimate sign of moral crisis (Mann 2015). Many social reformers believed that this crisis was tied to the weakening of the father and the rise of the individual self. The irony of this so-called moral decline is that it spread from urban contexts to villages via the very pathways that the US-RDA had forged in order to encourage a groundswell of African socialist political awakening and organizing: student and youth organizations (Mann 2015). Thus, challenges to the "model African household"—sexual promiscuity and pregnancy out of marriage—were the by-products of statecraft itself. Efforts to regulate youth behavior backfired for the leadership of the US-RDA, and political fissures often emerged along generational lines, with Malian student organizations rejecting the visions and policies of the government.

In 1968 General Moussa Traoré toppled the regime of Modibo Keita in a coup, an act that ushered in more than twenty years of authoritarian rule in Mali. Traoré's administration was known for its rigorous surveillance of suspected opponents, which often included teachers and the educated who were opposed to the military coup (Mann 2015). International human rights organizations, such as Amnesty International, took interest in Mali's deposed leaders and their detention in northern Malian prisons, as well as the suppression of democracy and the establishment of one-party rule. Over the course of Traoré's tenure, the Malian economy declined precipitously, and beginning in the early 1970s the region was plagued by the Sahel drought and subsequent famine. While Senegal, Mali's neighbor to the west, passed laws in the 1970s and 1980s concerning marriage and the family, this was an area of legal reform that went unaddressed in Mali under the Traoré regime. One way of understanding this lack is that the dominant political pressures and interests of the 1970s and 1980s were tied to economic development and structural adjustment; before the mid-1990s, it was not typical to consider human rights and development work as part of the same agenda (Cornwall and Molyneux 2006).

What is clear from a broad historical overview is that Mali's independence-era marriage and guardianship code did not garner much legislative or political attention until the 1990s. In many ways, the tide turned in the mid-1990s with the Fourth World Conference on Women in Beijing in 1995. For Mali in particular, the fall of the Traoré regime and the democratic election of Alpha Oumar Konaré made it possible for a surge of action in rights reform to take hold in civil society groups and nongovernmental organizations in the 1990s. And indeed, a lot of the energy of reform was directed toward the marriage code. However, despite the efforts of women's organizations, which rose to prominence during the Konaré administration, as well as other civil society and legal reform groups, efforts to revise Mali's Marriage and Guardianship Code were not fully realized in the 1990s and early 2000s. A major push for reform began in the late 1990s, with particular attention to the regulation of inheritance (making women and men equal in inheritance), raising the minimum marriage age for girls, and making women and men equal partners in marriage (Soares 2006). NGOs and international donors backed this internal effort at marriage reform, a dynamic that critics, particularly leaders of Islamic associations, decried. While President Konaré presented the texts to reform the code in 2002, in the dusk of his administration, the texts were withdrawn within a month due to massive backlash. At the time, the Malian and international press framed this failure to revise the code as a struggle between secularists and

Islamists, but others have looked more closely at the dynamics on the ground and suggest that this struggle was really about the complexities of an expanding and complex civil society in a neoliberal Global South context (Soares 2006). Rights discourse that emerged in full force in the mid-1990s from the Beijing platform was, in some ways, part of a larger wave of economic and social reforms attached to the growth of a donor aid community and the "NGOization" of Mali, a dynamic that many everyday Malians did not see improving their lives. Thus, the resistance to the marriage code reform at the end of Konaré's regime was a larger pushback against the perceived moral and economic failures of neoliberalism.

Meanwhile, change was afoot in the transnational human rights arena in Africa. In 2003 the African Union adopted the Maputo Protocol. The architects of Maputo squarely state in the instrument that their principal driver was the fact that, despite the ratification of the African Charter on Human and Peoples' Rights and other international human rights instruments by the majority of African states, women in Africa continued to be victims of discrimination and harmful practices. The origins of the effort leading to the Maputo Protocol are largely the product of Women in Law and Development in Africa (WiLDAF), a multinational African NGO dedicated to the advancement of women's rights as human rights. Part of what makes WiLDAF successful in its efforts to generate high-level change in the arena of international human rights law is the linkage that the organization forges between local concerns and broader human rights platforms (Hodgson 2002).

After 2002 the movement to reform the code withdrew from the main stage of legislative action in Mali. However, this is not to say that it went into complete hibernation; rather, civil society groups worked on the ground to develop localized, small-scale investment in internal processes of state reform. In fact, WiLDAF branches in Mali constituted a significant part of that effort. Malian reformers took up Maputo's international human rights instrument in order to engage the state and refashion legislation rather than work against it or outside it. This is a long-term political project of citizenship and rights literacy, one that requires investment from activists and buy-in from everyday Malians in order to be successful in the long run.

## Of Feminists and Dictators: Contestations over Marriage Reform

In the more recent political history of Mali, marriage continues to be an important but irreconcilable institution when it comes to state legitimacy. Through the 1990s and early 2000s, marriage was a no-win struggle because it pulled at forces that were often at cross-purposes in Mali, politically speaking. As a result, presidents have hesitated before taking it up, only turning to marriage reform in the lame-duck, end days of their administrations. This is because while marriage is critically important to the state, pressures from groups that legitimize the state differently also threaten to undermine the state when their stake in marriage is seemingly cast aside.

On August 3, 2009, the National Assembly of the Republic of Mali adopted the new Personal Status and Family Code, also commonly referred to as the Marriage Code. The new code was a long time in the making and was backed by President Amadou Toumani Touré, the minister of justice, and the attorney general. The National Assembly voted overwhelmingly to pass the code: 117 votes in support of the new code, 5 votes against the adoption of the code, and 4 abstentions. Different civil society organizations, Muslim organizations, elected state officials, and nongovernmental human rights organizations made contributions to the new code. Throughout the country in the lead-up to the vote, politicians and organizations backing the new code hosted information session–style debates and discussions on the existing code and the proposed provisions. The 2009 marriage and family code included reforms in the following areas: age of consent law (eighteen for both men and women, as opposed to age fifteen for girls), inheritance rights for men and women (men and women would be given equal inheritance rights from deceased parents, and children born out of wedlock would have rights to inherit), rights to adoption, and divorce. It explicitly outlawed repudiation, or *talaq*, as a divorce process. The new code also required that all marriages be registered with the government through a marriage certificate in order for the marriage to be recognized as legitimate; it removed language calling for a wife's obedience to her husband, instead stating that husbands and wives owe one another "loyalty and protection"; and it noted that the state recognizes marriage as a secular act.

While the proposed 2009 code introduced many reforms, some of the points that seemed to be the most contentious surrounded the issue of consent and the definition of marriage as secular, or *laïc*. The 2009 code, building off the 1962 definition of marriage as secular, required that a marriage be witnessed by an agent of the state in order for it to be considered valid. In practice, this was not different from the parameters in place.

The day after the National Assembly vote, my research collaborator and I visited the Bamako headquarters of L'Association pour le Progrès et la Défense des Femmes (APDF), a legal aid organization for Malian women and men seeking counseling or legal assistance in matters pertaining to family law. The organization was of particular interest to me not only because of its combined efforts in marital reconciliation and free or low-cost legal aid for women seeking divorce but also because of the contributions of its founder and former president, Fatoumata Siré Diakité, to the drafting of the new family and marriage code in Mali. On this particular morning, my research assistant and I walked into the small upper-floor office of the organization to find the staff members up in arms over headline articles in the weekly newspapers *26 Mars* and *Les Échos*. The newspaper articles accused the current president of the APDF of sending a letter to the head of the Mouvement Démocratique, the political party of the president of Mali, pledging the APDF's support of an unconstitutional third presidential bid for Touré. The *26 Mars* article was accompanied by a large photograph of Diakité and intimated that the letter had been sent to the Mouvement Démocratique on behalf of the APDF at her behest. Diakité had left her position as the president of the APDF a few years earlier to become the Malian ambassador to Germany, a powerful position, as Mali, one of the poorest countries in the world according to the UN, receives much of its foreign aid from Germany. The newspaper article in question suggested that Diakité, emboldened by her successful contributions to a new marriage and family code in Mali and her influential role as ambassador to Germany, was seeking a power grab and a political alliance with Touré. According to the newspaper article, Diakité was a power-hungry tyrant and supporter of a dictatorship; the democratically elected president of Mali, Touré, was set on a course to become the second dictator of Mali with the help of people such as Diakité; and the president's wife was modeling herself after the forceful and corrupt wife of the former dictator of Mali. In short, feminists and feminist sympathizers were akin to dictators. In this view, democratically elected officials who supported the marriage code reform were, in fact, tyrants who were operating not in the interests of the people but in their own self-serving attempt to be individually rewarded by an international community of foreign aid providers.

This accusation was a particularly powerful and aggressive framing of the Tourés and Diakité, because Mali had been ruled by Traoré's dictatorial regime from 1968 to 1991. Under Traoré, Diakité, who at the time was a professor at the University of Bamako, was punished for her critique of the dictatorial regime and her prodemocracy politics. The democratically elected Touré was in fact the military leader who led the overthrow of the dictator Traoré. One important root of this accusation was the National Assembly's passage of the reformed marriage code. Immediately following the code's passage and in the immediately following days, select Muslim organizations, namely, the Islamic High Council and the National Union of Muslim Women's Associations, protested the code, arguing that it privileged secularism and reflected the interests of an educated elite whose commitment resided with the international community and Western feminists rather than the people of Mali. The accusation that Diakité was a feminist dictator is a particularly sharp example of this opposition. Some suggested or even directly stated that Diakité, President Touré, and his wife, who are all Muslim, were, in fact, threatening the ability of Muslims to have good Muslim marriages and to abide by inheritance and child custody practices supported by the Koran and different interpretations of customary law in Mali.

The debates and discussions that circulate in the international media and human rights community often frame the failing of the marriage code reform as a sign of the oppositional relationship between and among democracy, women's rights, and Muslim societies. In the days immediately following President Touré's refusal to sign the 2009 marriage code, the BBC reported the "Mali Women's Rights Bill Blocked"; while the Voice of America proclaimed, "Mali Muslims Protest Increased Rights for Women." Malian news sources were similar in tone. The Malian newspaper *InfoMatin* stated on August 7, "The Family Code: Feminists Shout with Joy, While the Mosques Groan." Below this headline read another headline on the subject of the marriage and family code: "In the Name of a False Secularism." *Le Soir de Bamako* observed in an article titled "The Adoption of the New Family Code: Should We Expect the Worst?" that the adoption of the new family code seemed to be an effort "to catapult Mali onto the list of the most civilized nations in the world."

Indeed, members of this so-called civilized international human rights community had urged the Malian National Assembly to pass the new marriage code with no restrictions or amendments. Citing the fact that Mali is a signatory to the Convention on the Elimination of All Forms of Discrimination against Women (CEDAW), the United Nations Convention on the Rights of the Child, and the 2003 Maputo Protocol, the NGO Forum of the African Commission on Human and Peoples' Rights called for the code to be ratified as a sign of Mali's commitment to liberal human rights. However, Malian women's rights advocates and policy reformers were quick to point out that different civil society organizations, Muslim organizations, and state offices were heavily involved in the drafting of the language for the new code and that it was a multivocal affair. They hosted focus groups outside Bamako, with religious leaders, chiefs, and women's rights organizers meeting in rural village settings to hold "awareness-raising" workshops and legal literacy sessions on the old code and the proposals for the new one (Awid 2011). Despite these concerted efforts to engage the broader populace, the perception that many key provisions of the code were pressed upon Mali by the international human rights community persisted. The year 2009 felt quite a lot like 2002 all over again, in fact.

The reformed code, which was initially supported by President Touré, ultimately sat unsigned on the president's desk as he weighed the force of the public outcry against it, against him, and against his party. In the end, he sent the code back to the National Assembly unsigned, stating, "Societal change is not ordered by decree" (New Humanitarian 2009). The international press framed the failure of the code's passage as a mark against Mali's membership in a liberal international community, and some suggested that it is a further indication of the incompatibility of Muslim societies—particularly Muslim societies in poor African states—with democratic futures. This is, of course, an unnuanced read of Islam, feminism, and Malian history and society in general. In fact, the 2009 reform of Mali's marriage and family code arguably proposed a "Moroccan-style" approach to reform, dubbed as such because it mimicked the model of family and personal status code reform of the Moudawana, or Moroccan, family code of 2004. It relied heavily on the Koran to support proposed reforms but was still rejected and perceived as a direct threat by many in the Muslim community (Zoglin 2009; Wing 2011).

The code returned to the drawing board, and by April 2011 it was on the table of the law subcommittee of the Malian National Assembly. Although civil society organizations (CSOs) are not members of the law subcommittee, they can lobby the subcommittee with their interests. This was particularly important to the National Human Rights Commission and the Groupe Pivot Droit et Citoyenneté des Femmes, the latter of which is an umbrella group representing eight different women's associations. Lobbying and face-to-face contact with legislators were particularly important because of a shift in organizational responsibility for the drafting of the code under the Touré administration. Whereas the code reforms under President Konaré occurred under the purview of the Ministry for the Promotion of Women, Children, and the Family, the Ministry of Justice was the spearhead of reforms in 2011 (Wing 2011). Women's associations in Mali, which had consolidated some power to initiate change and lobby national politicians, as well as partner with international organizations, lost formal influence during Touré's administration, beginning in 2002. Political scientist Susanna Wing (2011) points out that under Konaré's administration, the Ministry of Justice was dissatisfied with the fact that the Ministry for the Promotion of Women, Children, and the Family stood on the leading edge of law reform when it came to marriage and child custody reform.

Despite animated debates over marriage and secularism in the 1990s and early 2000s, the secular Malian state had successfully shown that it was unwilling to yield to efforts to reform marriage and family law according to Islamic legal principles (Soares 2011). This seems to have shifted in late 2011:

on December 2 the National Assembly succeeded in adopting a revised version of the marriage and family code, one that reflected the interests and preferences of the Collectif des Associations Musulmanes. This 2011 code stated that "a woman must obey her husband" and that men are considered to be "head of the family." The legal age for marriage was established at eighteen years for males and sixteen for females. In certain cases, marriage could be authorized for individuals as young as fifteen years, and religious marriages would be legally recognized. According to international legal and human rights watchers, the 2011 code violated Mali's international obligations, set out in instruments such as CEDAW and the Maputo Protocol.

While many marriage and family law reforms under way in African contexts are designed to align constitutional law with international protocols on human rights, the 2011 constitutional reforms in Mali were a turn away from the international legal community. Some critics responded that the 2011 code made a mockery of human rights and consecrated discrimination and that the civil society groups in Mali that had been so instrumental in the first revision of 2009 were sidelined by the Islamic High Council (FIDH 2011).

## The 2012 Mali Crisis and Its Aftermath: The Intimacies of Marriagecraft and Statecraft

The family code was one of the last pieces of legislation signed into law by Touré before he was deposed in a coup d'état in late March 2012. Very shortly before what was to be the end of Touré's final term in office, young military officers led by an army captain overthrew the president, ultimately sending him into exile in Senegal. Within the capital, Bamako, Touré's approval ratings were quite low at the time of the putsch. While the international community broadly condemned the overthrow of the democratically elected president, many in Bamako supported his removal (Vogl and Callimachi 2012; Whitehouse 2012). One of the major reasons for dissatisfaction with the president was his mishandling of insurgencies in the northern part of the country. Subjected to the oscillations between abject neglect and overt suppression at the central state, the provinces of northern Mali have suffered tremendously throughout the colonial and postcolonial periods. Beginning in January 2012, a separatist struggle erupted between the state and northern secessionists with sustained complaints against the central government (Wing 2013). The conflict reached an apex when secessionists massacred eighty Malian soldiers at an outpost on the Niger border. Wives of soldiers organized demonstrations voicing their outrage at the president. On national television, military wives and mothers, who remained unnamed in media sources, grilled the president, demanding to know why the soldiers did not have enough ammunition and speculating that it must be Touré himself at the head of the rebellion (Vogl 2012). The women had been invited to the presidential palace as a publicity move that the president's advisors hoped would show that he was listening to Malian citizens, namely, the mothers and wives of the country. But rather than strengthen the president's ratings, the women's intense interrogation of the president galvanized popular disapproval of his leadership. This was, for many in Bamako at least, a culminating moment on a longer downward path of the weak and negligent state (Le Cocq et al. 2013).

Within ten days of the removal of the president, the three northern provinces of Mali fell to different secessionist and jihadi rebel groups, including Ansar Dine (a militant Islamist faction headed by a veteran of the early Tuareg rebellion in Mali), Al Qaeda in the Islamic Maghreb (AQIM), and the Nationalist Movement for the Liberation of Azawad (a secular and nationalist Tuareg separatist group known as MNLA). The takeover of the North, which comprises roughly two-thirds of the country, spawned a massive crisis of human displacement as hundreds of thousands of Malian civilians fled into the South and to neighboring countries (*Le Monde Afrique* 2012).

What happened in the following months has been documented and dissected by journalists, policy analysts, scholars, and human rights activists inside and outside Mali: the putschist army captain quickly fell out of favor in Bamako, ceding power to civilian politicians, but not before leading a bungled but violent attack on the interim civilian president; conflicts between Tuareg separatists and Islamist groups over ideology and purpose (as well as tactics and strategy) culminated in calamitous upheaval for Malian civilians, which spurred even more displacement; the French army, at the request of Mali's interim government, launched an attack on armed Islamist groups advancing southward in January 2013. The interim government of Mali realized its commitment to hold elections in the late summer of 2013 (despite vocal concerns that this was a rushed affair), resulting in the election of former prime minister Ibrahim Boubacar Keita to the office of the presidency.

In many ways, the election of the president was the first step down a path toward renewed statecraft, but for whom? The election of Keita unlocked billions of dollars in international aid funds that had been on hold since the coup (Hirsch 2013). In 2015 the central administration signed a peace accord with northern separatists, and military police now accompany Malian military operations as a monitoring safeguard against human rights abuses meted out by Malian soldiers (Human Rights Watch 2018). The 2015 peace accord, however, is weak and has been violated a number of times. Rebel groups and mujahideen continue targeted attacks on both civilians and military operations, making for a confusing and quickly changing landscape. It is hard to overstate the violence that Malians experienced in the north of Mali during the 2012–13 period and since. Civilians in northern Mali live in fear of physical attacks and violent, dismembering punishments in the name of a crude interpretation of Sharia law in the villages and towns occupied by Ansare Dine and AQIM. Gender-based violence and sexual violence have increased exponentially in connection with the violence in northern Mali, with single pregnant women and women with children born out of wedlock targeted in particular (Brown 2012).

But for many Malians, particularly rural Malians outside of Bamako, the coup, the subsequent crisis, and the current security uncertainties are part of a larger, ongoing trajectory of suffering and neglect (Bleck and Michelitch 2015). If this was the experience of Malian state infrastructure before the coup, why would civilians believe that things would change after the coup? And what does any of this have to do with personal status law and marriage and family codes?

Despite these doubts, lawyers and legal reformers in Mali continue to work for increased legibility in the arena of women's rights as human rights, and they continue to view personal status codes and marriage laws as the primary vehicles for those rights. Just as architects of the postcoup Malian state work to keep its load-bearing walls upright (Mali currently faces increasing insecurity in the North, and localized attacks against peacekeeping forces continue), marriage reform activists continue their work as well (FIDH 2017). They clearly view marriagecraft, in the legal sense, as an essential project of the fragile state as it seeks to maintain political stability.

On May 22, 2017, the African Court on Human and People's Rights (ACHPR) heard the case of the APDF and the Institute of Human Rights Development in Africa (IHRDA) versus the Republic of Mali. The APDF, which is of course a Malian association, and the IHRDA, which is a pan-African NGO based in Banjul, issued a statement outlining the August 2009 National Assembly majority passage of the revised personal status and family code. Their statement described the process taken up for the second reading of the code, the adoption of new provisions, and the elimination of ones introduced in 2009. The APDF and IHRDA alleged violation of women's rights under the Maputo Protocol, most notably, the violation of women's rights to inheritance, the failure to eliminate practices undermining the rights of women and children, and violation of the minimum age of marriage for girls. A year later, in May 2018, the ACHPR ruled that Mali was in violation of the Maputo Protocol because those provisions were inconsistent with the protocol. This was a landmark decision for at least two reasons. First, this was the first time that the court had ruled on a case that was solely about the violation of women's rights.

Before this ruling, cases heard before the ACHPR were primarily about violations of the Maputo Protocol, in addition to violations of another human rights instrument (*ACtHPR Monitor* 2017). Second, the court was liberal in its interpretation of the admissibility condition that applications must be filed "within a reasonable time." The complaint filed by the APDF and the IHRDA came more than four years after the complainants acknowledged understanding that the law violated Maputo. They argued that they needed time to study the Malian law in comparison with international law, but they also claimed that the climate of fear, intimidation, and threats delayed the process for submission (Banens 2018).

IHRDA executive director Gaye Sowe stated, "It is important for States to take measures to domestic international treaties they adhere to. Today's decision is very important not only for the promotion of women's rights in Mali and Africa, but especially for the visibility and effective use of the Maputo Protocol which so far has been underutilized by women's rights actors and stakeholders in Africa" (IHRDA 2018). For her part, APDF president Bintou Coulibaly Diawara stated, "We pay homage to our founding president, the deceased Fatoumata Siré Diakité, who was on the front lines of this fight. This verdict is above all a reassurance that we are defending a noble cause. We take this opportunity to thank all of the human rights organizations that have shouldered us through this mission" (Maliactu.net 2018). For now, the ACHPR has ruled that Mali must go back to the drawing board to revise its marriage code. The president of IHRDA clearly sees the case as a precedent for using the instrument to remake state law, while the president of APDF immediately acknowledged the team effort of human rights organizations inside and outside Mali who worked to secure the ruling. The goal of APDF is now to turn the effort back toward the legislative process in Mali.

## Conclusion

In tracing a broad history of marriage codes and law in Mali from 1962 to the present, this chapter shows the different moments when marriage has mattered to the state in the postcolonial era and how this has been articulated from a legislative standpoint. Efforts to reform marriage and family law codes were part and parcel of the democratizing process, but, more to the point, they were part—and continue to be part—of a neoliberal project. However, human rights strategies may be tools in the kit of nongovernmentality, but this does not mean that they cannot also be generated from within the state to be used to reconstruct the state (Mann 2015).

Actors for reform after 2009 in Mali are focused on the possibilities of using human rights–based frameworks as instruments for neoliberal statecraft, despite the opposition they faced in 2003. In Mali activists who seek to level the ground for inheritance, age of consent, and the moral language of marital obligation (i.e., mutual respect rather than obedience) are making straightforward human rights–based arguments in their efforts to reshape the state. This is a strategy that shows continued investment in human rights–based approaches to legal reform and social justice. For now, despite the shortcomings and limitations of human rights–based approaches, this continues to be the avenue for those who seek to have a seat at the political table in an era when the state is up for negotiation.

## Note

1. I use the term "marriagecraft" to suggest that marriage, like a state, is an institution to be strategically managed and fashioned in the service of a larger political project and that the work of making marriage relies on a particular set of technologies that change over time.

## References

*ACtHPR Monitor*. 2017. "Not a Charter Article in Sight: The Case of APDF and IHRDA v. Mali." June 7. http://www.acthprmonitor.org/not-a-charter-article-in-sight-the-case-of-apdh-and-ihrda-v-mali.
African Union. 2003. Protocol to the African Charter on Human and Peoples' Rights on the Rights of Women in Africa. July 11. http://www.refworld.org/docid/3f4b139d4.html.
Allman, Jean. 2009. "The Disappearing of Hannah Kudjoe: Nationalism, Feminism, and the Tyrannies of History." *Journal of Women's History* 21 (3): 13–35.
Awid. 2011. "The New Family Code of Mali and Why Its Promulgation Has Been Delayed." April 20. https://www.awid.org/news-and-analysis/new-family-code-mali-and-why-its-promulgation-has-been-delayed.
Banens, Alice. 2018. "African Court Issues Its First Judgement on Women's Rights." Intlawgrrls: Voices on International Law, Policy, Practice. September 13. https://ilg2.org/2018/09/13/african-court-issues-its-first-judgment-on-womens-rights/.
Bleck, Jaimie, and Kristin Michelitch. 2015. "The 2012 Crisis in Mali: Ongoing Empirical State Failure." *African Affairs* 114 (457): 598–623.
Brown, Hayes. 2012. "Violence against Women Spreading in Northern Mali." *Think Progress*, October 9. https://thinkprogress.org/violence-against-women-spreading-in-northern-mali-1e14495c92b3/.

Bunting, Annie, Benjamin N. Lawrance, and Richard L. Roberts. 2016. "Something Old, Something New? Conceptualizing Forced Marriage in Africa." In *Marriage by Force? Contestation over Consent and Coercion in Africa*, edited by Annie Bunting, Benjamin N. Lawrance, and Richard L. Roberts, 1–42. Athens: Ohio University Press.

Burrill, Emily. 2015. *States of Marriage: Gender, Justice, and Rights in Colonial Mali*. Athens: Ohio University Press.

Cornwall, Andrea, and Maxine Molyneux. 2006. "The Politics of Rights—Dilemmas for Feminist Praxis: An Introduction." *Third World Quarterly* 27 (7): 1177.

Da Jorio, Rosa. 1997. "Female Elites, Women's Formal Associations, and Political Practices in Urban Mali (West Africa)." PhD diss., University of Illinois.

———. 2002. "When Is 'Married' Married? Multiple Marriage Avenues in Urban Mali." *Mande Studies* 4:31–44.

Diawara, Manthia, André Magnin, Brigitte Ollier, Malick Sidibé, and Robert Storr. 2017. *Malick Sidibé: Mali Twist*. Paris: Fondation Cartier.

FIDH (Fédération internationale des ligues des droits de l'homme). 2011. "Le nouveau Code de la famille malien: Droit fondamentaux bafoués, discriminations consacrées." December 8. https://www.fidh.org/fr/regions/afrique/mali/Le-nouveau-Code-de-la-famille.

———. 2017. "Choosing Justice in the Face of Crisis." December 8. https://www.fidh.org/en/region/Africa/mali/mali-choosing-justice-in-the-face-of-crisis.

Geiger, Susan. 1996. "Tanganyikan Nationalism as 'Women's Work': Life Histories, Collective Biography, and Changing Historiography." *Journal of African History* 37:465–78.

Hirsch, Afua. 2013. "Mali Elections Won by Ibrahim Boubacar Keita." *The Guardian*, August 13, 2013.

Hodgson, Dorothy. 2002. "Women's Rights as Human Rights: Women in Law and Development in Africa (WiLDAF)." *Africa Today* 49 (2): 3–26.

Human Rights Watch: Mali. 2018. https://www.hrw.org/world-report/2018/country-chapters/mali.

IHRDA. 2018. "IHRDA, APDF Obtain Favourable Judgement against Mali in First Case before the African Court Applying Provisions of Maputo Protocol." May 11. https://www.ihrda.org/2018/05/press-release-ihrda-apdf-obtain-favourable-judgment-against-mali-in-first-case-before-the-african-court-applying-provisions-of-maputo-protocol/.

Jensen, Steven L. B. 2016. *The Making of International Human Rights: The 1960s, Decolonization, and the Reconstruction of Global Values*. Cambridge: Cambridge University Press.

Kamau, Winifred. 2009. "Law, Pluralism, and the Family in Kenya: Beyond Bifurcation of Formal Law and Custom." *International Journal of Law, Policy, and the Family* 23 (2): 133–44.

Konare, Adam Ba. 1993. *Dictionnaire des femmes célèbres du Mali (des temps mythico-légendaires au 26 mars 1991)*. Bamako: Jamana.

Lazreg, Marnia. 1990. "Gender and Politics in Algeria: Unraveling the Religious Paradigm." *Signs: Journal of Women in Culture and Society* 15 (4): 755–80.

LeCocq, Baz, Gregory Mann, Bruce Whitehouse, Dida Badi, Lotte Pelckmans, Nadia Belamat, Bruce Hall, and Wolfram Lacher. 2013. "One Hippopotamus and Eight Blind Analysts: A Multivocal Analysis of the 2012 Political Crisis in the Divided Republic of Mali." *Review of African Political Economy* 40 (137): 343–57.

Le Monde Afrique. 2012. "Crise au Mali: Plus de 268,000 réfugiés et déplacés depuis mi-janvier." April 19.

Maliactu.net. 2018. "Code malien des personnes et de la famille: Suite à une plainte de l'APDF la Cour Africaine des droits de l'Homme et des peuples ordonne sa revision." May 21. https://maliactu.net/mali-code-malien-des-personnes-et-de-la-famille-suite-a-une-plainte-de-lapdf-la-cour-africaine-des-droits-de-lhomme-et-des-peuples-ordonne-sa-revision/.

Mann, Gregory. 2015. *From Empires to NGOs in the West African Sahel: The Road to Nongovernmentality*. Cambridge: Cambridge University Press.

Mazower, Mark. 2013. *No Enchanted Palace: The End of Empire and the Ideological Origins of the United Nations*. Princeton, NJ: Princeton University Press, 2013.

New Humanitarian. 2009. "Back to the Drawing Board for the New Family Code." September 1. http://www.thenewhumanitarian.org/report/85960/mali-back-drawing-board-new-family-code.

Roberts, Richard. 2005. *Litigants and Households: African Disputes and Colonial Courts in the French Soudan, 1895–1912*. Portsmouth, NH: Heinemann.

Shulz, Dorothea. 2003. "Political Factions, Ideological Fictions: The Controversy over Family Law Reform in Democratic Mali." *Islamic Law and Society* 10 (1): 132–64.

Soares, Benjamin. 2006. "Islam in Mali in the Neoliberal Era." *African Affairs* 105 (418): 77–95.

———. 2011. "Family Law Reform in Mali: Contentious Debates and Elusive Outcomes." In *Gender and Islam in Africa: Rights, Sexuality, and the Law*, edited by Margot Badran, 263–90. Leiden: Brill.

Vogl, Martin. 2012. "Malian President Grilled by Angry Army Wives on TV." *San Diego Union-Tribune*, February 9, 2012.

Vogl, Martin, and Rukmini Callimachi. 2012. "Thousands March in Mali Streets to Support Junta." *San Diego Union-Tribune*, March 28, 2012.

Whitehouse, Bruce. 2012. "The Force of Action: Legitimizing the Coup in Bamako, Mali." *Africa Spectrum* 47 (2/3): 95.

Wing, Susanna D. 2011. "Legislating Marriage: Globalization and Family Law Reform in West Africa." In *Frontiers of Globalization: Kinship and Family Structures in Africa*, edited by Ana Marta González, Laurie DeRose, and Florence Oloo, 109–32. Trenton, NJ: Africa World Press.

———. 2013. "Briefing: Mali: Politics of a Crisis." *African Affairs* 112 (448): 476–85.

Zoglin, Katie. 2009. "Morocco's Family Code: Improving Equality for Women." *Human Rights Quarterly* 31 (4): 964–84.

# 2

 Early Marriage and the Debates over Gender-Based Rights in Niger

ADELINE MASQUELIER

"We all have our own cultures," Sheikh Abdou Salam, a Koran teacher and village chief, is quoted as saying in a *Wall Street Journal* article on the costly consequences of turning girls into brides before they are physically mature (Thurow 2005). Salam married off his daughter when she was eleven. Soon she was pregnant. Following four days of labor, the baby died, and the mother developed a three-inch-wide fistula. Marrying girls early, Salam explained, prevents the enormous shame of out-of-wedlock pregnancy. Salam, the article made clear, had since realized that marrying his daughter so young was a mistake. Whether it latches onto the figure of the hyperfertile African woman in need of birth control or the sacrificed virginity of the "child bride," the early marriage narrative relies on a vision of passive, powerless womanhood requiring protection from male violence. By circulating the image of the suffering African woman across global audiences, the narrative characterizes human rights intervention as "necessary and morally secure" (Scully 2011, 18). In this scenario, culture—the locus of oppressive traditions—is invariably portrayed as the culprit. Saving women from the abuses of patriarchy thus requires first and foremost effecting cultural changes.

In Niger the importance attached to women's reproductive roles and the pressure to contain female fertility within the boundaries of marriage often translate into a shortened girlhood for young women. Many girls experience youth as a brief interval between the onset of puberty and the advent of marriage. In fact, Niger leads the world when it comes to the practice of *mariage précoce* (early marriage): roughly 75 percent of Nigerien girls are married before the age of eighteen, and about 50 percent of them are married before they turn fifteen (DHS Program 2012). Of late, women's rights activists, humanitarians, and other "liberal" actors, operating on the assumption that Niger's development is tied to women's emancipation, have worked to rescue girlhood from what they perceive as oppressive patriarchal norms. "When young girls become wives, it is socially sanctioned sexual abuse," argued Betty McCollum, a congresswoman from Minnesota who in 2007 introduced legislation seeking to reduce the incidence of early marriage worldwide (*Washington Post* 2012). Girls' rights activists who claim that early marriage is a socially approved form of sexual abuse follow a long-standing European American convention of framing "stubborn" traditions in the Global South as impediments to the work of advocacy and gender justice. In endemically poor regions of the globe, so the story goes, "social norms" provide a veneer of legitimacy to practices such as early marriage that are harmful to women.

In the ongoing battle against early marriage, girls' rights advocates rely heavily on the narrative of victimhood provided by obstetric fistula, a birthing injury that is caused by prolonged, obstructed labor and that results in chronic urinary and fecal incontinence. Girls who marry early will likely become pregnant before they are physically mature and face higher risks of complication during delivery, including obstructed labor, so activists claim.[1] In recent years, fistula sufferers have received extraordinary media attention, much of it centered on their supposed stigmatization.[2] Their stories, translated into generic images of suffering, effectively serve as a rallying cry for global activism (Hannig 2017; Heller 2018).

The narrative of the vulnerable child bride on which the humanitarian industry relies to draw attention to the problem of obstetric fistulas is largely fabricated, however (Heller and Hannig 2017). Growing evidence suggests that the prevalence of obstetric fistulas has often more to do with lack of access to obstetric care than with age (Landry et al. 2013). Nevertheless, girls' rights activists draw the spotlight on early marriage, which they blame on local "custom," to account for the high incidence of obstetric fistulas in countries such as Niger.[3] By framing adolescent girls as an "at-risk" category, the discourse on obstetric fistulas is a prime instance of how human rights–based advocacy treats culture as a problem that requires "fixing" before progress can be achieved.

To delay marriage and motherhood, global humanitarianism advocates schooling. In the process, it conveniently dismisses the moral arguments many Nigeriens, drawing on Islamic law and other sources, deploy in the defense of "proper" social reproduction. In Niger, an overwhelmingly Muslim country where growing religious fervor in recent years has translated into renewed concerns over personal and communal purity, people's conception of female morality is rooted in marriage and maternity.[4] As such, it clashes with the image of vulnerable girlhood painted by global advocacy.

In this chapter I explore the fraught question of early marriage in Niger to consider how interventions in the name of girls' rights frame culture as an obstacle on the path to gender justice, foreclosing any possibility of genuine dialogue between advocates and opponents of gender-based reforms. Moving beyond the debates over the limits of rights as a "universal" concept, I discuss how girls' rights activists' notion of female vulnerability is inconsistent with the understanding of many Nigeriens, including Islamists, of what is "right" for girls. The model of girls' rights promoted by activists is based on a narrow definition of empowerment that is not easily reconciled with what it means to have status, enjoy respectability, and claim power over others when one is young and female in Niger. While I focus here on an issue that has divided women's rights activists and Islamists, I should note that their views are not always polarized.[5] In 2005 the two constituencies came together to draft a bill on repudiation (Kang 2015).

In what follows I first examine how the rhetoric of rights produced by global advocacy is articulated around the demonization of culture and the promotion of education as a tool of emancipation. I then consider the legal and moral arguments centered on marriage put forth by opponents to rights-based interventions. Finally, I discuss how a controversial family law project allowed proponents and challengers of early marriage to stake out their positions. Critical to my approach is a concern for the tension between "'the culture of rights' and 'the rights of culture'" (Hodgson 2011, 2) that has emerged in discussions of early marriage.

## The Problem of Culture

The practice of human rights, Sally Engle Merry writes, is hampered by an understanding of culture that "smuggles nineteenth-century ideas of backwardness and savagery into the process" together with assumptions of racial inferiority (2006, 226). In Niger, aid workers and international donors routinely describe culture as the main challenge to securing girls' rights to remain girls. Girls who are married before they are done growing up, the argument goes, are victimized by age-old insular traditions that preserve the status quo and prevent development. In cautionary tales about fistula, so-called traditional practices thus emerge as the main obstacle to successful birthing and healthy maternity. Commenting on the prevalence of early marriage in Niger, former prime minister Hama Amadou suggested that people's traditions and culture were "too strong" (Thurow 2005, A1) and therefore problematic. By characterizing culture as pathological, these narratives lay the outlines of a "geography of blame" (Farmer 1992) that engulfs most of rural Niger. In so doing, they conceal significant structural inequalities in the field of reproductive health.[6]

In human rights narratives, women almost invariably emerge as both the vessels and victims of tradition.[7] Indeed, scholars have noted how gender is often the lens through which human rights register the stubbornness of tradition (Scully 2011). As Sheikh Abdou Salam's testimony, with which I opened this chapter, exemplifies, popular fistula accounts typically include an elder's acknowledgment that it is "poverty and ignorance which move us to marry off our daughters too early" (Issa 2004). While girls emerge as casualties of abusive practices, culture frequently serves as a proxy for religion: "ignorant" Muslims generally invoke Islamic tradition to justify early marriage.

Whereas culture is constructed as the impediment to human progress, human rights, on the other hand, are unproblematically perceived to be universal, acultural, and unchanging. Yet the language of human rights has a historically and culturally specific trajectory. Take early marriage. International actors first identified child marriage as a problem in 1904, yet no steps were taken to address it until 1962, when the United Nations formulated the treaty known as the Convention on Consent to Marriage, Minimum Age for Marriage, and Registration of Marriages. Among the countries that ratified the convention, few set the minimum age at the current international standard of eighteen years (Kim et al. 2013). Significantly, the marriage convention did not bring to the forefront the health concerns linked to early marriage that inform current girls' rights debates. Attention to the potentially devastating consequences of early marriage is thus relatively recent.

If the moral argument deployed by human rights activists to eradicate the *mariage précoce* has earned limited traction in Niger, it is largely because it often competes for legitimacy with an Islamic model of society that defends early marriage as morally suitable for girls and for their families. Niger's transition to democracy in the early 1990s ushered in the rise of a lively public sphere and with it the emergence of sharp debates about what it meant to be Muslim. With the rise of an anti-Sufi reformist Muslim movement known colloquially as Izala, Muslims were urged to educate themselves about the content of the Koran and eschew practices that were supposedly not part of Islam.[8] The intensified questioning about Muslim identity in turn translated into an unprecedented focus on women's rights and responsibilities. With the signs of Islamic piety the focus of increased scrutiny, women's bodies became ever more critical sites of ideological struggles about purity, morality, and respectability.[9]

Though human rights positions itself as having a monopoly over the definition of what is moral, it is in reality but one kind of moral discourse. For many Nigeriens, marrying girls early is socially and morally preferable to the path to empowerment advocated by rights activists. In the next two sections I trace the broad contours of the debate over early marriage in Niger through a consideration of two strategies pursued by international organizations to promote women's empowerment and stimulate national development: fertility control and girls' education. Both issues hinge on the postponement of the age of marriage for girls. They are critical to the model of human progress deployed across the country through a variety of well-funded initiatives. In this model, girls stay in school until they turn eighteen. This allows them to delay marriage and childbearing, thereby shortening their reproductive lifespan and reducing their fertility.

## Protecting Girls, Lowering Fertility

In the UN Convention on the Rights of Children, early marriage is defined as the union of children or adolescents under the age of eighteen. According to UN estimates, fifteen million girls worldwide are married each year before their eighteenth birthday (UNICEF 2016). In 2015 governments around the world adopted the UN Sustainable Goals, including a target to end early marriage by 2030. As discourses of rights fueled by historically specific visions of progress are deployed with renewed intensity across the Global South, governments focus on early marriage as a "scourge" that must be urgently eradicated.[10]

As a troubling exemplification of the "traffic in women" (Rubin 1975), early marriage is said to rob girls of their aspirations, agency, and economic capital. Conscripted too young in the service of wifehood and motherhood, girls are denied the right to forge their own futures. Lacking the opportunities progressive societies bestow on their female children, they cannot fulfill their promise and end up contributing marginally to national economies. By limiting girls' prospects, early marriage thus amounts to an "enormous loss of human potential" (*The Lancet* 2017). This is a "tragedy" for not only the girls but also their countries (Human Rights Watch 2016). A recent report estimates that ending early marriage in countries such as Niger could generate millions of dollars in additional earnings each year (Wodon et al. 2017).

Early marriage also has demographic implications. Girls who marry early are likely to have a longer reproductive span than those who wait until their "majority" to have children. Not only do they supposedly face greater risks of sustaining injury or dying, but they are also more likely to face poverty. On the other hand, international donors argue, delays in marriage are associated with greater educational achievement and lower fertility. Lower fertility, in turn, is said to increase women's life expectancy and enhance their ability to provide for themselves and their children. Whether framed in economic costs or as a violation of rights, the global discourse on early marriage invariably casts the despoiled child bride as the centerpiece of a narrative in which development in the Global South depends on the drastic curtailment of fertility.

Calling attention to the harmful consequences of teen pregnancy, the World Health Organization has placed the minimum-age-of-marriage laws at the forefront of its efforts to reduce teenage childbearing. Niger, which boasts the highest fertility rates in the world, has received a great deal of attention on the part of international organizations whose stated goal is to protect women's rights in the name of development and nation building.[11] Over the years, international donors have provided substantial funding to organizations promoting the adoption of family law reforms on the basis that modernizing Niger's legal system will advance gender equality and spur economic development.

For those who debate the future of the world's population, countries with high fertility rates are mortgaging their futures.[12] Consequently, everything must be done to curb population growth in countries such as Niger. The notion that economic progress is linked to fertility control has translated into an increased focus on education for girls. Against the backdrop of heightened global attention to gender abuse, "child marriage" has emerged as a major impediment to development. In Niger, it became the focus of numerous sensitization and educational programs, especially after the government launched its Campaign to End Child Marriage in 2014.

*Mariage précoce*, many Nigeriens will tell you, is dangerous to adolescent girls' health. Children in primary school learn songs warning parents not to turn their daughters into *fistuleuses* (fistula sufferers) by marrying them too early. Older students perform skits in which girls develop fistulas after being forced into *mariages précoces*. During music competitions funded by international corporations, hip-hop artists refer to fistulas in songs warning about the perils of early marriage. Notwithstanding Alison Heller and Anita Hannig's (2017) claims that the humanitarian narrative on fistulas does not resonate with social realities, many people, in urban areas especially, have embraced the notion that marrying girls early is bad for their health. In the past decade, urban young men often mentioned fistulas when the topic of early marriage cropped up in our discussions. Whether or not they knew a woman battling chronic incontinence, they were familiar with the narrative of the child bride who develops a fistula during childbirth because her anatomy has not fully matured. The fact that, despite mounting attention to the problem, rates of early marriage remain high in Niger, especially in rural areas, signals the limits of the human rights approach for combatting gender inequalities.

### The Promise of Education

In the global effort to narrow the gender gap, renewed emphasis has been placed on promoting education as the ticket to a more stable future. Citing research demonstrating that girls with no education are more likely to marry young, lack agency, and live in poverty (World Bank Group 2014), girls' rights advocates cast education as the demonstrated pathway to women's emancipation. Schooling empowers girls by enhancing their capacity to aspire while improving their ability to earn an income and contribute to their families' sustenance. It also impacts marital patterns by postponing the age of first marriage for girls.[13] The rights-based framework has limitations, however, particularly in a country such as Niger, where secondary schools are seen as potentially risky environments for adolescent girls.

Niger has one of the lowest literacy rates in the world. Although primary education is now mandatory between the ages of seven and fifteen, school enrollment and attendance rates remain dismally low.[14] In the past decade, a number of campaigns have promoted girls' education in Niger as a catalyst for economic growth (see figure 2.1). If women are to contribute to the country's development, girls' rights advocates argue, they must be sent to school. Folded in this argument is also a plea for gender equity. Since education is a human right, no girl should be deprived of it. The problem is that, far from relying on a universal set of values, the language of human rights is burdened by certain assumptions about agency, autonomy, and maturity that do not always translate easily across time and space, especially when it comes to the status of women. Such a language depends on a set of gendered codes, based on "'approved' bodily practices, 'proper' sexual relationships, and normative family formations" (Hodgson 2011, 4) that may clash with gendered ideologies in other times and places.

Development experts typically paint a rosy picture of education. In experts' school-to-the-rescue model of development, children are groomed so that they can eventually contribute to what is envisioned as a progressive future. In Niger, girls' education is often described as the yardstick for measuring the country's

Figure 2.1. Poster advocating girls' education in Dogondoutchi, Niger: "I am taking my daughter to school, it is my duty. Follow my lead!"

development. Students in primary school learn that "when a girl goes to school, the whole country matures." Adolescent schoolgirls frequently cite this adage when describing the futures they foresee for themselves. Yet despite sustained efforts on the part of the government and its international partners to improve gender equity through education in recent years, schools are rarely adapted to the specific needs of adolescent girls (see Rachel Silver, this volume, for a similar disconnect between rhetoric and reality in Malawi). In the end, far from constituting an "unstoppable social engine" (Stambach 2000, 46), the formal school system ultimately reproduces existing gender inequalities.[15]

There is growing awareness that for girls to enjoy the benefits of education, the language of development must be customized to local realities. Efforts to tailor schooling to the social and structural constraints girls face nevertheless remain limited. A teacher assigned to a rural village tried to convince a father to keep his daughter in school rather than marry her off by outlining the "bright future" that awaited her once she completed her studies. Ignoring the fact that there was no secondary school in the village and that enrolling the girl in the nearest establishment some fifty kilometers away might expose her to sexual harassment and other dangers (and constitute a financial burden for the family, who would be forced to cover the cost of her room and board in town), he saw the father's decision to pull his daughter from school as proof of the villagers' "backward ways."

What cases such as this suggest is that the school system does not respond to the moral standards of local communities. Imported models of female empowerment stress the value of education by suggesting that the national body and the bodies of schoolgirls ideally mirror each other as they "develop." Paradoxically, the maturity of girls is precisely what places them at risk in school, where the absence of disciplinary oversight has created fertile grounds for sexual harassment and assault by male teachers. Sexual violence in school is allegedly a frequent occurrence.[16] Many parents, wary of the dangers their adolescent daughters may be exposed to, prefer not to send them to school. Rather than protecting girls from sexual abuse, schools often turn out to be hunting grounds for sexual predators.

Muslim religious elites, who have been vocal in their condemnation of adolescent girls' education, single out schools' failure to segregate genders as a factor contributing to the sexual harassment and abuse of female students. They advocate marriage as the proper alternative schooling. In November 2012, after a coalition of Islamic associations condemned a bill aimed at protecting the rights of girls to attend school until eighteen, the National Assembly overwhelmingly rejected it.[17] By encouraging parents to keep teenage girls in school, the bill, its detractors claimed, ignored Islamic teachings. Although many parents dream of stable professional futures for their daughters, their aspirations often collide with moral requirements that girls be married before they can shame their families by conceiving children out of wedlock. Pregnant girls are often pressured to marry their lovers. At the very minimum, the child's father is expected to pay for expenses related to the naming ceremony, amounting to a public acknowledgment of paternity. I heard about unmarried girls who had abortions, committed suicide, or threw their newborn child down a well.[18]

Added to the perception that it is inappropriate for girls to attend school once they are married (though this is slowly changing), the expectation that they must sacrifice homework to fulfill domestic duties puts them at a further disadvantage. Their academic performances may suffer. For these and other reasons, many girls often drop out of school before they reach fifteen. Parents sometimes invoke poor grades before removing adolescent daughters from school and marrying them off. Peer pressure is another factor: many girls literally cannot wait to get married. Through marriage and domesticity, they step into women's ordained position as wives (and, later, mothers), earning the social respectability that schooling cannot provide.

Girls who remain in school often face intense scrutiny. Perversely, their visibility (especially if they do not veil) enhances their vulnerability to accusations of moral impropriety. Occasionally, their struggle to reconcile conflicting normative ideals—on the one hand, the "modern" educated woman, on the other, the respectable housewife—finds expression in the language of possession. In recent years, schoolgirls throughout the country have been targeted by violent spirits who create havoc in the classroom. Susceptibility to spiritual attacks is reportedly rooted in impiety, immodesty (the girls dress "sexily"), and a deficient Islamic education (Masquelier 2018). Muslim religious leaders capitalize on these incidents to draw attention to society's moral failings, using the victims' plight to stress the need for moral reform. The girls themselves face a conundrum as they are enjoined to simultaneously embrace education's promising future and embody the virtues of tradition. Schooling for adolescent girls often comes at a cost, at once financial and moral, that some girls cannot afford to pay.

## Marriage and Islamic Law

Challenging the rhetoric of female empowerment based on continued education and delayed marriage, opponents to rights-based interventions articulate a notion of the moral good around marriage, motherhood, and what Nigeriens take to be Islamic tradition. Though officially secular, Niger has long been Islamic in its political culture. While successive constitutions have asserted a division between religion and the state, Islamic "custom" effectively regulates family life. The centrality of Islamic law in the realm of justice is a legacy of the French colonial legal structure. French administrators established two separate court systems, one based on French civil law and the other based on customary law, which was understood to be largely guided by Islamic legal principles (Cooper 2010). Today Islamic law, officially erased from the constitution, coexists uneasily with civil law and customary law. If criminal law no longer relies on Sharia, much of civil life is regulated by custom, defined largely as Islamic and operating in varying degrees of conformity with Maliki legal tradition (Cooper 2010).[19] Land, marriage, and family disputes are therefore adjudicated by customary law. When it comes to the rights of women to marry, seek custody of their children, and inherit, local interpretations of Islam are often highly selective. Thus, while Maliki tradition allows women to claim physical custody of their children (boys until weaned, girls until marriage) in the event of a divorce, in practice, children are understood to belong to the patriline.

In theory, the age of marriage is subject to legal regulations in Niger. It is officially fourteen for girls and sixteen for boys, as mandated by the colonial-era Mandel Decree (Boye et al. 1991).[20] In practice, however, there is no exact age of consent for marriage or sexual activity. The decree is virtually ignored outside the capital (Cooper 2010). There, it is not uncommon for girls to marry at thirteen or even twelve. Once they have grown breasts, girls are assumed to be ready for marriage. Islamic tradition is sometimes invoked as justification for early marriage. In particular, people cite the example of the Prophet Muhammad, who married Aisha when she was six or seven. Some Muslim religious leaders condemn these practices, arguing that they are based on "custom," not Islamic law, and that the Koran does not encourage early marriage. They stress that since consent is a necessary condition for marriage under Islamic law and "underage" girls cannot consent, they must not be thrust into wedded life. Muslim religious elites who oppose *mariage précoce* are in the minority, however. Most of them encourage parents to marry off their daughters at puberty.

Maliki law sets the age of majority for women and men at roughly seventeen and requires the consent of both the bride and the groom before they can be married. Therefore, a girl under seventeen cannot theoretically marry. However, her guardian can enter into a marriage contract on her behalf (Cooper 2010). Since her consent does not need to be witnessed, and she does not have to be present to express consent, it is relatively easy to marry her off against her will. Once married, she passes from her father's tutelage to her husband's. As a young woman subject not only to her husband's authority but also to her mother-in-law's, she enjoys limited rights. She cannot refuse to engage in conjugal sex, and civil law insufficiently protects her from violence, including spousal rape.[21]

Concerns about the containment of female sexuality are thus not exactly new in Niger—marriage has long been a means of reining in women's sexuality. It is nevertheless worth noting that at a time when the control of women, their mobility, and their sexuality has emerged as a critical modality through which to remoralize society, there is an added urgency to find husbands for girls before they "spoil."[22] From this perspective, far from harming girls, early marriage protects them by ensuring that their fertility is channeled toward the production of lawful progeny—a source of joy, pride, respectability, and financial stability for women.

After her three oldest daughters each conceived a child out of wedlock (two of them eventually married the children's fathers, rescuing the family's honor), a widow I knew arranged her youngest daughter's marriage. Though she had previously criticized neighbors for marrying off "little girls," she dreaded another shameful pregnancy that would further taint her own reputation (a daughter's deeds are said to reflect her mother's character). She had acted, she told me, in her daughter's best interest. The future husband came from a reputable family.

He was kind and made a decent living. After meeting him four times, Zeinabou, her fifteen-year-old daughter, agreed to the marriage. She was thrilled to leave her mother's mud-walled home for more prosperous lodgings, complete with running water and electricity.

Zeinabou's case is far from unusual. I met many fifteen-year-old girls who agreed to marry their suitor (even if that meant leaving school) or dreamed of doing so as soon as possible. I also met girls in their twenties who despaired over their status as "old maids." In some communities, fifteen-year-old girls who are not married are subject to merciless teasing (*Mariage précoce en Afrique de l'Ouest* 2017).

In the eyes of local actors pushing for reforms, these girls are victims who must be rescued from patriarchal violence, not agentive beings navigating the local landscape of moral regulations. The absence of robust legislation to replace the outdated Mandel Decree has fostered a situation that opens the door for abuse. As activists see it, *mariage précoce* violates two basic human rights: a woman's right to choose when and whom she marries and her right to sexual consent. Note that for many girls' rights activists, "early marriage," "child marriage," and "forced marriage" are interchangeable concepts. In Niger, however, child marriage is not a useful concept, for there is no consensus on what age category the term covers, and the kind of marriage a bride enters does not depend on her age. It is not age but maternity that pushes a girl over the threshold of womanhood. What this means is that a fifteen-year-old mother is a woman, whereas a twenty-year-old childless student remains a girl in the eyes of society. In humanitarian narratives, young girls are almost invariably married against their will to men two or three times their age. This is at best an oversimplification. If many girls are forced into marriage in Niger, others resist their parents' choice of a husband for them or the idea of marriage altogether until they complete their studies. In the end, most of them, including those who marry early, have a say in the process, even if they are also hemmed in by social expectations shaping the definition of respectable womanhood.

In the past, youth contracted "family marriages" arranged by elders. As a means of building alliances between lineages, matrimony was too serious a matter to be left to young, inexperienced people. A typical marriage was between paternal or maternal cousins, ensuring that the wealth exchanged between the bride's and the groom's kin remained "in the family." Today youth insist they want to marry for love, thereby deliberately positioning themselves in contrast to older generations for whom marital relationships were subject to collective surveillance (Masquelier 2009a). They cannot marry without parental consent, but, increasingly, they choose their own spouses. Ironically, while the new marriage model, which is based on emotional closeness and companionship, comes closer to the definition of marriage favored in the Global North, it is allegedly less stable than its "traditional" counterpart, which is anchored within a network of kinship ties that act as stabilizing forces. Changes notwithstanding, marriage remains embedded in social realities, the anthropological literature on the politics of matrimony has shown. By demonizing early marriage, this is precisely what humanitarian discourse has failed to acknowledge.

## The Perils of Fertility

In Niger the primary objective of marriage is procreation. Children are an expression of wealth and the "surest measure of the success of a marriage" (Cooper 1997, 151). Young women are pressured to produce a child within the first year of marriage.[23] Large families are a source of prestige, and it is by producing children that a woman secures her position in her husband's household. Fertility is a woman's greatest asset. Given men's preference for sons, women must often conceive until they give birth to male babies. In polygynous households where they compete with cowives for their husband's attention, women experience additional pressure to produce many children. It is by capitalizing on her fertility that a woman effectively outperforms her cowives, if she has any. As is the case elsewhere in Africa, the pressure to be prolific weighs heavily on women (Bledsoe 2002).[24]

Meanwhile, birth control is a contentious issue. Many Nigeriens told me God was the final arbiter when it comes to family size. Unschooled rural women often claim that interfering with the divine plan by curbing women's fertility is forbidden. Their better-educated urban counterparts, on the other hand, may admit to using contraception. Health workers speak of birth spacing, which ensures babies are not weaned prematurely, rather than birth control so as not to offend pious Muslims' sensibilities. Muslim religious leaders largely condemn practices aimed at limiting birth, though some concede that the failure to space births may raise infant mortality. While many people believe that some methods of birth spacing, such as abstinence, are religiously acceptable, others perceive coitus interruptus as a form of infanticide.[25] Claims by conservative Muslim leaders that the Koran is the ultimate source of truth have discouraged some women from adopting modern contraception, since it is not mentioned in the Koran. In the end, which form of birth spacing people consider religiously acceptable varies significantly. There is also a great deal of ambivalence surrounding the use of modern contraceptives in Niger.[26]

Such ambivalence points to the frictions produced when previously intimate matters regarding fertility and reproduction become the concern of foreign actors and institutions. Paradoxical as it may seem, given Niger's high fertility rate, infertility is a significant problem for many women—and something that policy makers largely ignore (Moussa 2012). Infertile women often attribute their reproductive disorders to a spirit's intervention or to witchcraft originating in a cowife's jealousy (Masquelier 2001). To ensure successful pregnancies, shield themselves from jealous cowives, and preserve marital stability, many women seek remedies from a range of medical practitioners. From these women's perspective, efforts to control the size of families make little sense.

That some Nigeriens perceive campaigns to promote family planning as violent intrusions into their reproductive lives should therefore come as no surprise (Cooper 2013). If anything, in an era of fiscal restrictions and shrunk health services, the fact that external donors are generously funding programs aimed at limiting family sizes is likely to arouse suspicion in some quarters.[27] One could argue that external actors' promotion of fertility control is but a contemporary form of imperial intervention—yet another attempt by the Global North to foist its vision of a sustainable future on the Global South (Cornwall and Molyneux 2008). The womb, scholars have shown, was an important site of political struggle in colonial contexts (Hunt 1999; Thomas 2003). Rather than focusing on what actually matters on the ground, policies dictated by external actors anxious to curb the fertility of countries such as Niger arbitrarily impose their vision of progress and their strategies for achieving it. Tangled as they are in the liberal rhetoric on women's empowerment, these strategies for curbing population growth are directly implicated in the construction of what Pamela Scully calls a "gendered field of justification for intervention" (2011, 27).

## Political Activism

Since independence in 1960 there have been a number of attempts in Niger to secure the minimum age of marriage for girls through the implementation of new legislation. Though none of these attempts have succeeded, the discussions that arise each time a bill to reform family law is introduced are illuminating. They afford us a glimpse of the multifaceted landscape of activism. In this final section, I focus on the debates over family law as a forum where opponents and defenders of early marriage claim competing positions. Space limitations prevent me from discussing in detail local activism in Niger. Let me simply note that there are numerous Nigerien organizations advocating against early marriage.

In 1999 the Nigerien government ratified the Convention on the Elimination of All Forms of Discrimination Against Women (CEDAW). A year later,

Niger became one of the first Muslim-majority democracies in the world to adopt a gender-quota law. Nevertheless, the country has an inconsistent record of women's rights policy adoption. It has yet to ratify the African Union's regional treaty on women's rights (also known as the Maputo Protocol), which calls on governments to enact appropriate national legislations guaranteeing that eighteen is the minimum age of marriage for women. And recent efforts to revive the debate about the Code de la Famille—a piece of domestic legislation that protects women's and children's rights in matters of child custody, marriage, divorce, and inheritance—have yet to produce a reform in family law. Consequently, Niger is one of the few countries in the world lacking a family code.

The earliest calls for family law reform date from the first years of independence, when the Union des Femmes du Niger (UFN) asked President Hamani Diori to adopt legislation that would improve women's rights to child custody and curb men's rights to repudiate their wives at will. Rather than heeding the UFN's call for women's rights, Diori officially adopted the colonial legal structure, which relied on customary law on matters relating to marriage, divorce, and inheritance (Kang 2015). During the administration of Seyni Kountché (1974–87), attempts to draft a family code failed twice. Following the liberalization of state politics in the early 1990s, women mobilized once again for the adoption of a family code. Supporters of the reform argued that the current judicial system left space for abuse and often led to arbitrary rulings (Kang 2015). Nevertheless, the reform was rejected. In 1994, when yet another attempt was made to adopt a family code, a massive mobilization of civil society led to the measure's defeat. Opponents declared that the reform was "anti-Islamic" and supported by the "forces of evil" (Kang 2015, 60). Bowing to conservative activists' demands, the government refused to adopt the bill. Later drafts were rejected because opponents claimed the bill would replace divine law. In 2010 the draft legislation was renamed Statut Personnel du Niger to dissociate the proposed reform from the ill-fated Code de la Famille. Opponents vilified the new bill as a "satanic" text, and it met the same fate as its predecessors.

Critics have blamed Islamists for Niger's failure to adopt new legislation on women's and children's rights. We must not be too quick to attribute this outcome solely to the intervention of "conservative" Muslims opposed to advancing gender equality and women's rights, some scholars have warned. The factions agitating for or against reform are shaped by a diversity of actors whose strategies have varied over time. The prospect of a code has occasionally united coalitions of unlikely bedfellows against those who would deny the supremacy of Islamic law in family matters. While ostensibly pitting feminists against Islamists, the debates centered on the family code therefore cannot be reduced to a simple opposition between "conservatives" anxious to preserve the status quo and "liberals" committed to promoting women's rights (Alidou 2005; Burrill, this volume).

I should point out that none of the rejected bills aimed to radically reform gender relations. For instance, by setting the minimum age of marriage at sixteen for women and eighteen for men, the early 1990s bill did not challenge regional trends (Kang 2015). Yet because each successive bill was presented as a threat to the status quo, it succeeded in uniting ordinarily warring factions concerned that the reforms would undermine entrenched practices (such as a man's right to have four wives) loosely based on Islamic family law.[28] Those who mobilized against the proposed reforms effectively leveraged the state's ambiguous relationship with religion. They argued that the proposed bills were antireligious texts driven by feminist principles that would corrupt Islamic tradition and compromise the integrity of Nigerien families (Kang 2015).

Since Islamic law gives rise to a wide range of interpretations, it does not predict the kinds of practices people engage in. Using the moral authority of Islamic tradition, anticode activists can easily accuse women's activists of pushing anti-Islamic reforms that threaten "authentically" Nigerien practices. This has created a specific challenge for Muslim women who are committed to their faith yet also anxious to secure legal protection for themselves and other women in Niger. Some of them have paid a high price for their involvement in the campaign to promote the adoption of the code. In 1994 a curse was issued against three female activists by a Muslim preacher, thereafter effectively silencing women who had spoken publicly in favor of family law reform.

A common explanation proffered by opponents to the family code is that the rights-based protocol upon which the proposed reform is grounded is secular and therefore unsuitable for Niger. Others insist that Islamic law is perfect and thus perfectly suited to the needs of God's creatures. To claim it needs improvement is therefore presumptuous—a demonstration of hubris. Yet others have argued that poverty is the number one problem facing Niger and that as long as it remains an issue, the code should be a low priority. Turning the discourse of women's rights on its head, they see the adoption of legal reforms as necessarily following rather than preceding the rise of development and prosperity. In the words of a civil servant, "Once there is some development, we can talk about the family code. Right now, the circumstances are not propitious." Granting women the legal right to own and inherit property while they still enjoyed male financial support, he surmised, only made sense in times of prosperity when such a privilege did not threaten men's ability to provide for dependents. In the current moment of precarity, however, focusing solely on improving women's situation amounted to a form of gender discrimination.

Conclusion

Within the logic of global humanitarianism, rights and culture often clash. All too often, gender rights advocates operate as if they can claim ownership of what is "right" for women across space and time. In Niger, the figure of the vulnerable child bride has emerged as a prominent trope in recent efforts to deploy the language of rights in the service of advocacy and development. Drawing on the register of victimhood, rights-based discourse on early marriage frames culture as a source of oppression. Culture is blamed for birthing injuries sustained by girls "too young to be mothers." The humanitarian sector has no jurisdiction over the boundaries of rights, however. As scholars have argued, gender-based rights, far from being a stable category, are "always in question, subject to alternative and sometimes competing interpretations, 'vernacularizations' appropriations, and contestations" (Hodgson 2011, 14). In Niger, debates over early marriage point toward a moral alternative to the emancipatory path—based on schooling—laid out by rights activists and development experts. It involves marrying girls early for their own sake.

In this chapter I examined the controversy surrounding early marriage through a consideration of the moral arguments both sides have deployed to define the "good" and defend their positions. I discussed the gender ideologies and legal frameworks informing both activists' demonization of early marriage and their opponents' defense of it. There have been several attempts in past decades to legislate women's rights in the family and secure the minimum age of marriage for girls as part of a broader set of initiatives aimed at challenging gender inequality. These efforts to empower women failed largely because rather than working with the moral frameworks within which early marriage is embedded, women's rights activists treated these as obstacles to progress.

Though the language of humanitarianism continues to demonize culture as a site of oppressive patriarchy, there have been attempts by international agencies to view "traditions" in a more positive light. In this respect, the lexicon Nigerien aid workers and activists employ to talk about women's empowerment is instructive. In Niger, people speak of *équité* rather than *égalité* on the basis that women aspire to "fairness" (they enjoy rights while occupying roles and positions different from those of men) rather than "equality" (in the sense of sameness), a principle that contradicts Koranic teachings (Henquinet 2013). In rural areas, my male and female interlocutors often defined men as the standard against which women's deficiencies were measured. When queried about gender equality, they uniformly struggled with the concept.[29] In their view, productivity was gendered: men, as producers, were responsible for women's subsistence, and women, in turn, were dependent on men (or they claimed to be when it was to their advantage to do so). Therefore, it was more accurate to speak of gender complementarity. Subsumed under the concept of equity, gender complementarity provides a useful register for discussing gender roles and rights beyond the narrow confines of global humanitarianism.

In the way it accommodates both female domesticity and male provision, the concept of complementarity provides perhaps the moral alternative to household economies that leave women vulnerable. While it implies that women have rights, including the right to inherit, it is compatible with Islam, since it allows for the uneven distribution of wealth between male and female heirs. As such, it provides something of a model for how to draft the terms of an inclusive dialogue that accounts for not only rights but also culture. If debates surrounding marriage, education, maternity, and girlhood in Niger are to make any headway, there must be a recognition on the parts of international actors working on behalf of girls that the formulation of rights is shaped by gender ideologies, as well as by cultural conceptions of agency, morality, and justice.

## Notes

I am indebted to all the Nigeriens who discussed their views of early marriage with me. Research for this chapter was supported by grants from Tulane University. Some of the writing was accomplished thanks to a fellowship from the Aarhus Institute of Advanced Studies. I thank Lydia Boyd, Emily Burrill, and the two anonymous reviewers for their incisive comments and helpful suggestions.

1. Adolescent girls' pelvises are said to be too immature to allow for the passage of a fully developed fetus (Wall 1998).

2. In activist discourse, stress is put on the leaking bodies of fistula patients abandoned by husbands and shunned by communities.

3. Niger is said to have the highest rate of obstetric fistulas in the world.

4. Roughly 95 percent of Nigeriens identify as Muslim.

5. For an account of the hardening of positions with respect to issues centered on gender, family, and reproduction in Niger in the past three decades or so, see Cooper 2019.

6. Ironically, it is in areas targeted by initiatives to end early marriage where medical care is most lacking and where women experiencing complications during childbirth cannot benefit from emergency obstetric intervention (Heller 2018).

7. The figure of the African woman has been a convenient site onto which to articulate a gendered vision of emancipation that challenges local social hierarchies while providing moral justifications for foreign interference (Boddy 2007).

8. This anti-Sufi movement is officially known as Jamâ'at Izâlat al-Bid'a wa Iqâmat al-Sunna (Society for the Removal of Innovation and Reinstatement of the Sunna) (see Masquelier 2009b; Loimeier 1997).

9. For many Nigeriens, the application of Sharia (Islamic law) is essentially about the control of sexuality. It translates into the prosecution of adultery and the repression of prostitution.

10. In 2014 the African Union unveiled its Campaign to End Child Marriage. Launched in partnership with UNICEF and the United Nations Population Fund (UNFPA), the two-year initiative encouraged African governments to launch their own national campaigns and develop national strategies to address the "harmful" impact of early marriage.

11. The fertility rate is 7.6 live births per woman (*Annuaire Statistique du Niger* 2014).

12. The rate of Niger's population growth is 3.1 percent (DHS Program 2012).

13. Education is said to empower women by enhancing their ability to make choices regarding family formation (to decide when and whom to marry, when and how many children to have, and when to leave a marriage).

14. According to 2017 data, 60 percent of girls went to primary school and 17 percent attended secondary school (UNESCO n.d.). These rates are significantly lower than those for boys.

15. My discussion does not include Koranic education.

16. Some observers have argued that girls' increasing exposure to sexual violence is tied to their growing presence in the classroom. In other words, facilitating girls' access to education has paradoxically enhanced their chances of being sexually assaulted.

17. In December 2017 the Nigerien government adopted a decree to expand "the protection, support, and accompaniment of girls during their schooling" (Maurel 2018).

18. Niger has some of the world's most restrictive laws on abortion.

19. Maliki law is one of the four schools of jurisprudence within Sunni Islam. It relies on the Koran and hadiths (record of the words and deeds of the prophet Muhammad) as primary sources.

20. The Mandel Decree promulgated by the French in 1939 in their African colonies sought to reduce the incidence of child marriage, thereby affording women—perceived to lack juridical rights—some legal protection. Aside from setting a minimum marriage age, it made the consent of both the bride and the groom a necessary condition for the validity of a marriage.

21. Most cases of sexual violence are not reported. Victims of spousal rape often do not seek legal recourse, fearing retribution and loss of economic support (Anwar 2009).

22. Though preventing out-of-wedlock pregnancy is the major reason for marrying girls early, some parents also aim to preserve their daughters' virginity until marriage. Virgin brides receive additional gifts (a cow, jewelry) from their husbands after the marriage is consummated. Other parents invoke religious arguments. A household head said that by stamping over the footsteps of his daughter of marriageable age (i.e.,

keeping his "mature" daughter at home and unmarried), a man denied himself the blessings earned through daily prayer and ultimately ruined his chances of entering paradise (*Mariage précoce en Afrique de l'Ouest* 2017).

23. With limited access to modern contraceptives, young brides often begin their childbearing soon after they are married.

24. Men too are constrained by normative definitions of masculinity, which are rooted in marriage and paternity. Newly married men face enormous pressure to produce children. They anxiously await the first pregnancy of their (first) wives, taken as a demonstration of the men's virility (and fertility) and yet another step on the path to full maturity.

25. Historically, birth spacing was ensured through abstinence. Husbands and wives waited until their child was weaned to resume sexual relations. In recent years, many couples have adopted the Muslim practice of abstaining from sex for forty days, a practice that has contributed to the rise of the natality rate.

26. Modern contraceptives became legally available in Niger in 1988. Because they were available only to women who had secured their husbands' approval, many wives I knew at the time could not procure them unless they resorted to subterfuge. In the 1990s, campaigns to combat the AIDS epidemic legitimized public discussion of sexuality (and the use of condoms) but they also had the unintended consequence of associating contraception with sexually transmitted disease and illicit sexuality (Cooper 2019). Meanwhile, because externally powered health initiatives are often suspect, rumors that contraceptives are harmful (women told me that Depo-Provera shots, a convenient, widely used method of contraception, caused infertility) are widespread.

27. The suspicion extends to other programs, notably the recent WHO-sponsored campaign to eradicate polio. In the early twenty-first century, rumor had it that the oral polio vaccine distributed to children under five was part of a Western plot to sterilize Muslims (Masquelier 2012).

28. Activists who have mobilized against family law reform are often well-educated, middle-class Nigeriens. Many of them are women (Alidou 2005).

29. The fact that Eve was fashioned out of Adam's rib is often invoked to suggest that women cannot stand on the same footing as men.

## References

Alidou, Ousseina D. 2005. *Engaging Modernity: Muslim Women and the Politics of Agency in Postcolonial Niger*. Madison: University of Wisconsin Press.

*Annuaire Statistique du Niger*. 2014. Niamey: Institut National de la Statistique.

Anwar, Zainah, ed. 2009. *Avis de recherche: Égalité et la justice dans les familles musulmanes*. 2009. Rapport des participants du Niger. https://www.musawah.org/resources/wanted-equality-and-justice-in-the-muslim-family-french/.

Bledsoe, Caroline H. 2002. *Contingent Lives: Fertility, Time, and Aging in West Africa*. Chicago: University of Chicago Press.

Boddy, Janice. 2007. *Civilizing Women: British Crusades in Colonial Sudan*. Princeton, NJ: Princeton University Press.

Boye, Abd-el Kader, Kathleen Hill, Stephen Isaacs, and Deborah Gordis. 1991. "Marriage Law and Practice in the Sahel." *Studies in Family Planning* 22 (6): 343–49.

Cooper, Barbara M. 1997. *Marriage in Maradi: Gender and Culture in a Hausa Society in Niger, 1900–1989*. Portsmouth, NH: Heinemann.

———. 2010. "Secular States, Muslim Law and Islamic Religious Culture: Gender Implications of Legal Struggles in Hybrid Legal Systems in Contemporary West Africa." *Droit et Cultures* 59:97–120.

———. 2013. "De quoi la crise démographique au Sahel est-elle le nom?" *Politique Africaine* 130 (2): 69–88.

———. 2019. *Countless Blessings: A History of Childbirth and Reproduction in the Sahel*. Bloomington: Indiana University Press.

Cornwall, Andrea, and Maxine Molyneux, eds. 2008. *The Politics of Rights: Dilemmas for Feminist Praxis*. London: Routledge.

DHS Program, USAID. 2012. *Niger: Standard DHS, 2012*. https://dhsprogram.com/what-we-do/survey/survey-display-407.cfm.

Farmer, Paul. 1992. *AIDS and Accusations: Haiti and the Geography of Blame*. Berkeley: University of California Press.

Hannig, Anita. 2017. *Beyond Surgery: Injury, Healing, and Religion at an Ethiopian Hospital*. Chicago: University of Chicago Press.

Heller, Alison W. 2018. *Fistula Politics: Birthing Injuries and the Quest for Continence in Niger*. New Brunswick, NJ: Rutgers University Press.

Heller, Alison, and Anita Hannig. 2017. "Unsettling the Fistula Narrative: Cultural Pathology, Biomedical Redemption, and Inequities of Health Access in Niger and Ethiopia." *Anthropology & Medicine* 24 (2): 81–95.

Henquinet, Kari. 2013. "Translating Women's Rights in Niger: What Happened to the 'Radical Challenge to Patriarchy'?" In *Worlds of Human Rights: The Ambiguities of Rights Claiming in Africa*, edited by Bill Derman, Anne Hellum, and Kristin Bergtora Sandvik, 219–43. Leiden: Brill.

Hodgson, Dorothy L. 2011. "Introduction: Gender and Culture at the Limit of Rights." In *Gender and Culture at the Limit of Rights*, edited by Dorothy L. Hodgson, 1–14. Philadelphia: University of Pennsylvania Press.

Human Rights Watch. 2016. *The Education Deficit*. https://www.hrw.org/report/2016/06/09/education-deficit/failures-protect-and-fulfill-right-education-through-global.

Hunt, Nancy Rose. 1999. *A Colonial Lexicon: Of Birth Ritual, Medicalization, and Mobility in the Congo*. Durham, NC: Duke University Press.

Issa, Ouseini. 2004. "Health-Niger: Enlisting Men in the Fight against Fistula." Inter Press Service, November 23. http://www.ipsnews.net/2004/11/health-niger-enlisting-men-in-the-fight-against-fistula/.

Kang, Alice J. 2015. *Bargaining for Women's Rights: Activism in an Aspiring Muslim Democracy*. Minneapolis: University of Minnesota Press.

Kim, Minzee, et al. 2013. "When Do Laws Matter? National Minimum-Age-of-Marriage Laws, Child Rights, and Adolescent Fertility, 1989–2007." *Law & Society Review* 47 (3): 589–619.

*The Lancet.* 2017. "When Childhood Is Stolen." *The Lancet* 389 (10086): 2264.

Landry, Evelyn, et al. 2013. "Profiles and Experiences of Women Undergoing Genital Fistula Repair: Findings from Five Countries." *Global Public Health* 10:1–17.

Loimeier, Roman. 1997. *Islamic Reform and Political Change in Northern Nigeria.* Evanston, IL: Northwestern University Press.

*Mariage précoce en Afrique de l'Ouest.* 2017. Enquêtes de référence: Régions de Niamey et Zinder. Accessed February 28, 2018. https://www.girlsnotbrides.org/wp-content/uploads/2018/04/rapport-NIGER.pdf.

Masquelier, Adeline. 2001. *Prayer Has Spoiled Everything: Possession, Power and Identity in an Islamic Town of Niger.* Durham, NC: Duke University Press.

———. 2009a. "Lessons from *Rubí*: Love, Poverty, and the Educational Value of Televised Dramas in Niger." In *Love in Africa*, edited by Jennifer Cole and Lynn M. Thomas, 204–28. Chicago: University of Chicago Press.

———. 2009b. *Women and Islamic Revival in a West African Town.* Bloomington: Indiana University Press.

———. 2012. "Public Health or Public Threat? Polio Eradication Campaigns, Islamic Revival, and the Materialization of State Power in Niger." In *Medicine, Mobility, and Power in Global Africa: Transnational Health and Healing*, edited by Hansjörg Dilger, Abdoulaye Kane, and Stacey Langwick, 213–40. Bloomington: Indiana University Press.

———. 2018. "Schooling, Spirit Possession, and the 'Modern Girl' in Niger." In *Femmes d'Afrique et émancipations: Entre normes sociales contraignantes et nouveaux possible*, edited by Muriel Gomez-Perez, 299–323. Paris: Karthala.

Maurel, Marie. 2018. "Les filles, éternelles oubliées de l'éducation au Niger." *Le Monde Afrique*, February 5.

Merry, Sally Engle. 2006. *Human Rights and Gender Violence: Translating International Law into Local Justice.* Chicago: University of Chicago Press.

Moussa, Hadiza. 2012. *Entre absence et refus d'enfant: Socio-anthropologie de la gestion de la fécondité féminine à Niamey, Niger.* Paris: L'Harmattan.

Rubin, Gayle. 1975. "The Traffic in Women: Notes on the Political Economy of Sex." In *Toward an Anthropology of Women*, edited by Rayna R. Reiter, 157–210. New York: Monthly Review Press.

Scully, Pamela. 2011. "Gender, History, and Human Rights." In *Gender and Culture at the Limit of Rights*, edited by Dorothy L. Hodgson, 17–31. Philadelphia: University of Pennsylvania Press.

Stambach, Amy. 2000. *Lessons from Mount Kilimanjaro: Schooling, Community, and Gender in East Africa.* New York: Routledge.

Thomas, Lynn. 2003. *Politics of the Womb: Women, Reproduction, and the State in Kenya.* Berkeley: University of California Press.

Thurow, Roger. 2005. "The Promise: Married at 11, a Teen in Niger Returns to School." *Wall Street Journal*, June 13, 2005, A1.
UNESCO. n.d. "Niger: Education and Literacy." Institute of Statistics. Accessed September 27, 2019. http://uis.unesco.org/country/NE.
UNICEF. 2016. *Annual Report 2016*. https://www.unicef.org/publications/index_96412.html.
Wall, Lewis L. 1998. "Dead Mothers and Injured Wives: The Social Context of Maternal Morality and Morbidity among the Hausa of Northern Nigeria." *Studies in Family Planning* 29 (4): 341–59.
*Washington Post*. 2012. "Niger Leads World in Childhood Marriage." July 9.
Wodon, Quentin, et al. 2017. *Economic Impacts of Child Marriage: Global Synthesis Report*. International Center on Women's Research and the World Bank. http://documents.worldbank.org/curated/en/530891498511398503/pdf/116829-WP-P151842-PUBLIC-EICM-Global-Conference-Edition-June-27.pdf.
World Bank Group. 2014. *Voice and Agency: Empowering Women and Girls for Shared Prosperity*. http://www.worldbank.org/content/dam/Worldbank/document/Gender/Voice_and_agency_LOWRES.pdf.

# 3

 Where Are the Women?

## Gendered Experiences of Land Resource Management in the Time of Climate Change in Southern Burkina Faso

ELISABETH KAGO ILBOUDO NÉBIÉ

In recent decades, national and international development projects have promoted the emancipation of women, especially as it relates to their access to land, which is vital to women's livelihoods. One example of this emancipatory project is the application of gender quotas: international development institutions often request a particular gender quota for specific projects or fund women's projects for integrated and sustainable management of natural resources. Yet local social systems often exclude women even in instances when project guidelines deem their participation mandatory. Quotas and parity policies do not guarantee that men and women have equal access to decision-making processes regarding local natural resource management.

This chapter explores the tensions between a more kin-based system of right to land versus the state-based or international-donor framework that dominates the current shift in land management in the context of climate change. The case study examined in this chapter shows that rights-based frameworks are insufficient to promote gender parity because they typically do not translate to local practice, especially in rural areas where customary laws and values regulate gender relations above and beyond any formal laws and policies. In this way, the findings of this study echo the work of other scholars, including those included in this book (e.g., see Rachel Silver's chapter on the education rights of pregnant girls in Malawi). Rights-based approaches are, in practice, often constrained by broader social and political attitudes that interpret political capital in terms of local moral norms and customary laws.

In Burkina Faso, despite the fact that climate change and land degradation have resulted in dramatic changes in household and labor configuration, we see continued resistance to women taking on formal leadership roles in land management and property allocation decisions. Through an examination of the case of Sondré-Est, a vast pastoral zone territory in the Center-South region of Burkina Faso, this chapter shows how one community grappled with gender-based quotas in local committee leadership to address land management issues in a context of climate change adaptation. State leaders and politicians use rights-based frameworks at times to reconfigure legislative and decision-making processes at different levels of the state. In the case of Burkina Faso and land management, the application of gender-based quotas has not succeeded in bringing more women to the table. This chapter shows the way that state rights-based initiatives are circumscribed, especially when they have limited or no support from traditional institutions.

Over the past three decades, in the southern regions of Burkina Faso, farmers and herders have adapted their livelihood practices to accommodate rainfall variability and demographic pressure on scarcer natural resources. Climate change and subsequent shifts in land management increase gender-based vulnerabilities in a number of different ways. Women are often responsible for collecting firewood and water, two critical resources for daily life that are threatened by climate change. Climate change often presses men to engage in labor migration for new forms of work, leaving women to run households and care for children. Furthermore, women and children make up the majority of the world's impoverished population, a factor that will likely only become more pronounced as climate change becomes a more urgent global issue (Fortmann and Rocheleau 1997; Tompkins and Adger 2004; Canziani et al. 2007; Blomstrom et al. 2009; Pérez et al. 2015). Fortunately, some responses to these climate change adaptations have resulted in an increase in women's leadership in household decision-making, especially following men's labor migration (Cordell, Gregory, and Piché 1996), but this has not translated to women taking on leadership in community land management. Participation in rural land resource management is gendered, with men taking on the vast majority of management roles (Fortmann and Rocheleau 1985; Porro and Stone 2005). While earlier scholarship and policy on climate change and environmental change focused only on how women were victims of environmental crises, scholarly focus and policy recommendations have shifted to examining how women can be efficient environmental managers and leaders (Braidotti et al. 1994). Cases from Latin America and East Africa demonstrate that gender-diverse groups consistently perform better than single-gender groups in all management functions of the forest, for example (Mwangi, Meinzen-Dick, and Sun 2011).

The management of natural resources and pastoral infrastructure in the Sondré-Est zone of Burkina Faso has been heavily gendered, typically privileging work associated with men (e.g., cattle herding, cultivation). Sondré-Est was created in the 1970s to resettle pastoralists displaced by major droughts, demographic pressures, and a lack of arable land in Central and North Burkina Faso. As part of the state initiative to promote pastoralism in this new area, officials created the local umbrella management committee known as the Comité de Gestion (COGES, Local Management Committee), whose purpose is to manage and protect resources in Sondré-Est. Male leaders excluded women from management, even though women are interested in serving on the committee and are increasingly performing tasks typically regarded as "men's work" (e.g., cultivation). Moreover, while historic avenues surrounding women's formal rights to land are changing in the current context of increasing state control over land management, women's actual access to land in rural settings has not increased.

### Gender-Based Quotas and Social Expectations: Possibilities and Limitations for Participation

Over the past two decades, women have gained unprecedented access to livelihoods, resources, and decision-making processes as a result of gender quota policies (Tripp and Kang 2008). These policies often result from the mobilization of local and international women's groups, political incentives, and the priorities of international organizations. In some developing countries, gender-friendly policies are used to help political regimes maintain power and a positive reception from the international community (Burnet 2008). In Burkina Faso, the involvement of the state in rural land control, the promotion of individualized land tenure, and the decreasing power of traditional chiefs have opened more opportunities for women and vulnerable groups (e.g., transhumant Fulße herders) to access land. Over the past four decades, beginning before the peak period of gender quota adoption in the mid-1990s, the government of Burkina Faso has adopted two major policies that influenced women's access to land and then their position in management: the Réorganisation agraire et foncière (RAF, Agrarian and Land Tenure Reform) during the presidency of Thomas Sankara in 1984 and the Gestion des Terroirs Villageois (GTV, Village Land Use Management) approach during Blaise Compaoré's regime in the 1990s (Marchal and Quesnel 1997).

The RAF considered all land as property of the state and allocated control to government officers over traditional leaders (Faure 1995; Marchal and Quesnel 1997). The Marxist-Leninist political ideology that defined Sankara's administration (1983–87) played a significant role in advancing women's rights to land in the country, as one of the tenets of this ideology states that all are equal under the state. In his speech commemorating Women's Day on March 8, 1987, Sankara (1990) famously declared that private property and capital accumulation principles allowed men to own slaves, land, and women. Sankara perceived development as an unreachable goal without the freedom of women. The integration of women in resource access and decision-making processes was one of his major concerns. He saw the revolution he led as a process that would bring men and women to rethink social relations and eliminate the exploitative system sustaining gender inequalities. During his presidency, the state nationalized land, promoted economic self-sufficiency, and challenged the power of traditional leaders. This revolution advanced women's rights and mobilized the masses to slow down environmental degradation in times of political and ecological crises (Batterbury and Warren 2001).

In 1991 Compaoré's regime overturned Sankara's Marxist policies and opened Burkina Faso to foreign aid. Under Compaoré, neoliberal structural adjustment programs played a critical role in the refashioning of international policies. His government revised the 1984 RAF to encourage private landownership, with the reformed RAF allowing farmers to obtain land titles following a simple administrative procedure (Faure 1995). During Compaoré's tenure, international organizations also promoted the GTV as a participatory development approach in the country. The GTV approach involves national officers' transfer of control over resource management to local management committees (Batterbury 1998). Land management decisions under this approach became decentralized and were no longer made exclusively by men. The GTV committees include all groups present in the village, including customary village leaders and underrepresented groups such as women, girls, young men, herders, and migrants (Kevane and Gray 1999). In Sondré-Est, for example, the Burkina Faso government is testing COGES as part of the country's GTV approach to development. Many described COGES as an "improved" version of the Comité Villageois de Développement (CVD, Village Development Committee), an administrative and centralized institution created by the government but led by local leaders under the supervision of the prefect (state representative).¹ COGES moves beyond state management, introducing more independent and decentralized management of the zone by local leaders and integrating women. These actions comply with the principles of the GTV approach.

Yet women are still underrepresented in COGES. Despite a longer history of state-supported land reform in Burkina Faso, in rural areas, land belongs to or is accessible to clans or village communities, which are led by men. Drawing on the cases of Mossi farmers and Fulße herders, Mark Breusers (2010) argues that men's identity and their kin group history legitimize their claims to land in a particular village. He explains that among Mossi farmers, seniority status within a kin group, ethnicity, and time of arrival in a village determine the strength of land access and control. The earth priest grants or withdraws access to land to kin groups that arrived after the "actual" autochthons and that are referred to as "strangers." In local discourses, it is accepted that if a lowland farm occupied by a stranger produces more, the autochthons can withdraw this land from the stranger's use in the name of their "birth right" on the land. In contrast, Breusers adds, the Fulße herders, who rely on seasonal mobility of livestock, perceive any uncultivated land as free to use by everyone (even without permission), unless they are told otherwise by autochthons. Their mobile lifestyle implies a nonattachment to land. Therefore, even though sedentary communities' frequent use of one plot of land over a long period of time can lead to some kind of "autochthonization" over multiple generations, the Fulße are excluded from these entitlements because of their mobility.

Natural resource management, which is linked to land tenure and access rights, is therefore also gendered. In most of Burkina Faso's ethnic groups, women do not inherit land; instead, they borrow it from male relatives, and the women's husbands are informed (Stamm et al. 2003). Michael Kevane and Leslie Gray (1999) describe a Mossi proverb from Burkina Faso stating that women create their fields at night, meaning that household bargaining is conducted in the private space of households at night between husband and wife (and cowives to some extent). In this way, dealings in the private space influence women's access to land and labor. Women must bargain with men, who are the only people entitled to own (and therefore deal in and operate) land (Kevane and Gray 1999). Women's rights to farm a plot of land are determined by marital or kinship status with men as mothers, sisters, wives, or daughters. As land becomes scarce, women's rights to use it weaken, as men are given priority (Kevane and Gray 1999).

In Burkina Faso, women face a double burden of patriarchal norms that emerge from faith-based expectations, such as how Islam is interpreted by religious leaders to uphold men's dominance, as well as cultural expectations that prescribe a hierarchy of gender roles in work and family organization. A gender analysis of the Fulße community, which is mainly Muslim, illustrates this situation (VerEecke 1989). One view is that any respect or protection that women might engender stems from their willingness to be submissive to their husbands. In this sense, their esteem results from a womanliness symbolized by domestic competence, servitude, and obedience (VerEecke 1989). Furthermore, a woman's social status is derived from her husband, who might accrue status and honor through age, honesty, knowledge, cattle ownership, and generosity. These cultural norms and practices fly in the face of the history of top-down policies that promote equal access to land.

Today in Burkina Faso, some reformers see continued state-based strategies and solutions that enforce gender diversity in political decision-making, such as gender quotas, as a potential antidote to social and cultural expectations of women's submission. Through an examination of COGES at work in Sondré-Est, we see some of the shortcomings of top-down quota policies in rural settings. Women elected through gender quota policies do not necessarily hold the interests of women and the underrepresented in high regard, and the impact of gender quota policies on the measurable improvement of women's conditions has sparked debates among researchers and the general public (Franceschet, Krook, and Piscopo 2009; Burnet 2011). Some researchers argue for the importance of going beyond attention to numbers, because quota policies might increase women's political presence but can potentially undermine merit as a criterion of selection and reinforce stereotypes about women's inferiority in politics (Franceschet and Piscopo 2008). Women who are filling "quota seats" tend to be just as qualified (in terms of formal education) as men (Franceschet, Krook, and Piscopo 2009).

According to some scholarly and policy critiques, some of these quota policies have backfired; while they emphasize higher numbers of participation by women, they do not necessarily support programs for increasing political literacy and other education-oriented approaches to increasing women's involvement in political decisions at different levels. Having more women in government did not automatically lead to greater democracy and better defense of women's interests. In Rwanda, the Forum of Women Parliamentarians (FWP) is often cited as a gender quota success story (Burnet and RISD 2003), but this gender-based political organization did not take any specific policy position on Rwanda's 2004 Land Law, although studies have found that rural women viewed land rights as central to their livelihoods. FWP women leaders stated that land was an issue for all Rwandans and not only for women. If the case of Rwanda is instructive for Burkina Faso, we see that quotas did not guarantee rural women's participation and the improvement of their living standards:

poor state supervision and follow-up after the launch of rural projects showed very little top-down political will or desire behind these initiatives. Thus, it is not only that formal laws value women's participation compared to traditional and religious norms; it is also that they are not really invested in changing social practice.

This is not to say that gender quota policies have not had lasting cultural and social impacts. Overall, these policies have improved the economic power of urban women, but some studies show that they have increased rural women's workload and worsened their exploitation (Burnet 2011). Urban women have gained the greatest benefits from these policies, with increased access to lucrative jobs and better purchasing power. While women take on more responsibilities and duties outside the home, men have not taken on more of the domestic responsibilities to support women's increased and diversified workload. Subsequently, some women elected to office have to deal with conflicting household and public duties, a dynamic widely understood as the "second shift" of women's unpaid domestic work after paid work hours have concluded (Hochschild and Machung 1989). According to Jennie Burnet (2011), the increased participation of women at the local level has helped to legitimate women as political agents and increased respect for them, which is a powerful and lasting outcome. However, some rural women face the challenge of explaining the meaningful benefits of their political involvement to their husbands, as it is a type of work and commitment that may not bring substantial financial gains. This has increased the workload of rural women who cannot afford to pay for household and child-care assistance. In contrast, rural men leaders reap social benefits (e.g., networking, increased prestige) and often receive gifts (e.g., beer, crops, or money) from citizens in gratitude for their services. When we examine the context of Sondré-Est, we see that gender quotas do not translate to increased leadership by women on local land management committees; furthermore, we see that ethnic identity and other cultural markers play a large role in determining women's participation in decision-making processes on the committee level, with distinct dynamics playing out between pastoral herders who have recently settled in the area and the autochthonous farmers who claim a longer tenure on the land.

## Locating Sondré-Est in a Time of Climate Change

Research on land use and climate change in Sondré-Est has revealed unanticipated insights into the gendered aspects of land management decisions and the challenges to gender quota policy applications at the heart of this chapter. One of the objectives of this study, which was part of the Local Governance and Adapting to Climate Change in Sub-Saharan Africa project under the leadership of the International Livestock Research Institute and the World Agroforestry Center, was to examine the governance of land resources in the Sondré-Est Pastoral Zone and its surroundings. The research team conducted a total of forty-three semistructured individual interviews (44 participants, including 40 men and 4 women participants) and eleven focus groups (220 participants, including 106 men and 114 women) intermittently over a period of twenty months. Questions were administered in the Mooré (the Mossi native dialect; the Mossi, largely involved in agriculture, are the major ethnic group in the country), Fulfuldé (the Fulße native dialect), and French (the official language of Burkina Faso) to local pastoral and agropastoral communities, as well as government officials and development workers in the study area. To make up for the smaller number of women who participated in one-on-one interviews, the research group formed discussion and focus groups conducted in the Fulfuldé language, which stimulated women's participation in discussion and created greater incentives for them to become involved. This difference in discussion and knowledge sharing sheds light on the gendered nature of local decision-making processes, which inform political outcomes at various levels.

Created in 1983, Sondré-Est is a domain of 16,460 hectares with 15 percent of land reserved for housing and 85 percent for grazing. It is located about thirty kilometers north of Manga, the capital of Zoundwéogo Province in the Center-South region of Burkina Faso (see figure 3.1). No census was conducted during fieldwork, but the total population was about 3,100 (1,457 males and 1,643 females) in 2006. Called Sondré-Est because of its location to the east of the Mossi village of Sondré, the zone's vegetation includes both savannah and gallery forest (see figure 3.2). The zone is divided into four residential areas, or "sectors," with no clearly marked boundaries. Pastoralism is the major activity in Sondré-Est, with seasonal movements of cattle in and out of the pastoral zone during the dry season in a literal quest for greener pastures. Key resources in the pastoral zone include pastures, forest products, and infrastructure such as dams, pumps, and vaccination parks. Secondary activities include agriculture and the commercialization of livestock and dairy products at nearby markets.

Overall, the zone is ethnically homogeneous because the state of Burkina Faso only invited Fulße herders to come and settle in various areas of the zone. The Fulße, one of the largest pastoral groups in West Africa, are also known as Fulani, Peulh, Fula, Felatta, or Haalpullar (Bruijn and Van Dijk 2003). They are predominantly Muslim, and their identity and social prestige are closely

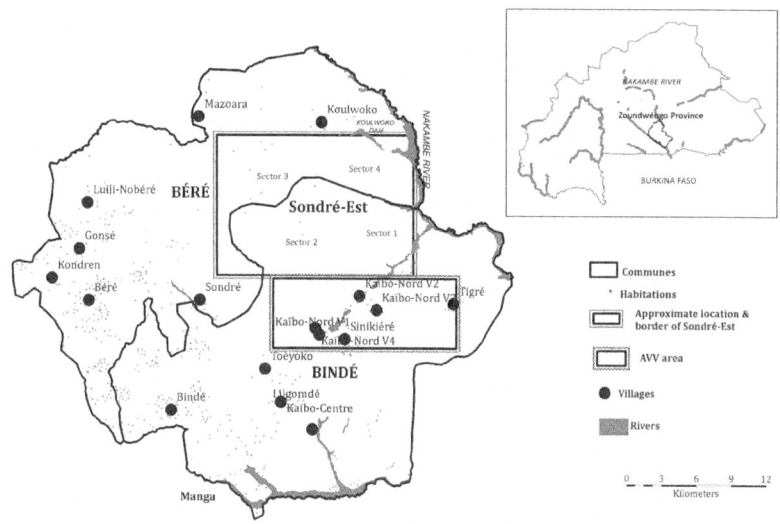

Figure 3.1. Map of Sondré-Est. *Source*: Institut Géographique du Burkina 2015.

Figure 3.2. A typical household in Sondré-Est.

linked with cattle ownership. Livestock also include sheep, goats, chickens, guinea fowls, and donkeys. The Fulße mainly raise cows and small ruminants for milk and markets and for paying bride wealth, or dowries. While Fulße frequently sell small ruminants to fund household subsistence and health expenses, they only sell cattle as a last resort to fund major expenses such as a pilgrimage to Mecca. During my fieldwork in 2016–17, I estimated the livestock population in Sondré-Est to be between ten and eleven thousand animals. Fulße men and women own cattle that they inherit from their parents, especially their mothers and maternal relatives. The commercialization of dairy products in local and urban markets is the major economic activity of women Fulße and helps stabilize households. In the dry season, when men migrate with household cattle, Fulße women take on leadership and decision-making responsibilities in the household. These include tending household livestock and launching farming activities until men return.

For their part, the autochthons of Sondré-Est's surrounding areas are the Mossi and Bissa, and the groups have not historically commingled in settlement practices and customs. Previously, the territory fell under the chief of Sondré's dominion, who transferred ownership and control over to the government to create the pastoral zone. The Aménagements des Vallées des Volta (Planned Settlement of the Volta Valleys), commonly known as the AVV resettlement program, and transhumance mechanisms have since brought in more Mossi, Yadsé, and Fulße communities who live in Kaïbo-Nord V2 (see figure 3.1). These communities were not invited or allowed to settle in the zone because of the formal purpose of the zone as a herding area.

While the borders of Sondré-Est were deliberately imagined and planned, the different communities who have settled in the area, as well as the autochthonous community, have increasingly challenged and encroached upon these boundaries (see figure 3.3). On the one hand, Mossi agriculturalists claim the pastoral zone's land, water, and forest resources based on customary land tenure rights. On the other hand, other nonresidents, more precisely, Fulße herders from riparian villages, are making inroads into the zone with no clear entitlement claim other than their intent to take advantage of pastures. These nonresident herders share ethnic or kin ties with the zone's current residents, whose customs prescribe that members of the Fulße community share access to water and pasture with the newly arrived members who also identify as Fulße (Tonah 2003). This cultural element of resource sharing within the broader ethnic identity group has contributed to an increase in the Fulße population in the area at a faster rate than other groups. As a result of the population shift, the state introduced a local COGES into Sondré-Est to help Fulße herders efficiently manage their resources, especially in times of rainfall variability and declining

Figure 3.3. The western border, delineated by a dirt road and contested by the village of Sondré.

natural resources. COGES members work to enforce the residents' rights over Sondré-Est, a critical task with the goal of supporting sustainable land use and long-term prosperity in a context of decreasing arable land and rapid climate change.

## Gendered Management of Resources in the Sondré-Est Pastoral Zone

Study results indicate that while most residents of Sondré-Est express satisfaction with increased accountability measures for resource use, which have resulted in decreased tensions between herders and farmers, there is still dramatic gender disparity in leadership and a blind spot in understanding how women and men are experiencing land use differently. Created in October 2015 as the only operational zone-wide management committee, COGES regulates the use of resources in the pastoral zone. In the pastoral zone, access to and allocation of resources depends on a user's residency status. Natural resources and infrastructure within the pastoral zone are solely reserved for herder residents. Exploitation of resources by both residents and outsiders requires fees paid to COGES. Men, who own far more cattle than women, use most of the pastoral resources (dams and vaccination parks), while women mainly use water pumps and forest products for household consumption. Residents pay annual membership per person rather than per household. COGES leaders directly collect nonresident fees at water points and vaccination parks before allowing the use of resources. Each sector has a COGES that supports individual residents and groups in managing resources at the sector level. The central COGES, as shown below, has been created out of the four committees of the four sectors. The committees have a total of twenty-four leaders (six per sector), who are democratically elected for a period of three years and can only serve two terms in a lifetime. They are assigned to work for the common interest of all community members.

Through COGES, members of the herding community argued that they have improved the management of local natural resources. First, when a resource is owned by a specific sector, money gained from its exploitation goes into the budget of that sector. When the budget of the central COGES is insufficient to cover infrastructure repairs, the extension agent generates a repair quote and forwards the matter to the ministry in charge of animal resources. Second, when riparian agriculturalists and herders now enter the zone, they know they should first speak to COGES leaders to acquire permission to collect wood or use water points inside Sondré-Est.

This system has decreased conflicts with outsiders, but inside the pastoral zone there are unequal power relations between men and women regarding how the population manages livelihood resources. During one of our focus groups with Fulße women in Sondré-Est, one woman explained, "Men think that being in the committee is not a woman's activity" (focus group, sector 1, May 23, 2016). Another woman added, "Protecting resources is crucial, but we can't do anything about it apart from paying COGES membership fees. We are not integrated into COGES management. If we were integrated into COGES, we could help men tackle this issue" (focus group, sector 1, May 23, 2016). However, women of Sondré-Est have so far not been able to take any concrete action to change the status quo, as they are up against many daily obstacles to participation. One of these obstacles is the perception that women's leadership and women's work are not of the so-called public sphere. For example, while conducting research for this study, most interviews with women took place within house compounds, contrary to interviews with men, who often met with the researcher at the business center of the pastoral zone.

The different participation patterns of men and women in this study highlighted the virtual absence of women from the political sector, within which men predominated and therefore had a greater voice in community resource management. The household expectations that women should be working within the domestic compound explains and reinforces their dismissal from certain community-level projects, especially when external project managers cannot directly talk to them. Men, for their part, explained the absence of women from some of the discussions as weather related (in the rainy season, floods in certain sectors of Sondré-Est prevent people, especially women who have to walk long distances, from moving from one place to another), as due to lack of transportation, or as due to the perception that "Fulße women are shy and reserved." These stereotypes of women's nature and the unequal access to resources that would allow women to participate in formal processes located in the zone's business center (e.g., women's lack of reliable transportation or their need to remain at the home compound to prepare food and to protect themselves, their children, and their household assets during inclement weather) are just some of the obstacles that women face when it comes to participation in the decision-making processes in Sondré-Est and the surrounding areas. One solution to this would be for project managers to relocate the site of project discussions, but this has not been proposed as an alternative.

Key obstacles to women's involvement in resource management committees are historical precedent and gendered expectations concerning how women and men "provide" for their families in different ways. Historically, men have been more involved in resource governance than women in the region, and mostly men attend COGES meetings. Overall, adult men—who are almost always the heads of households—and older residents are more familiar with COGES because they are seen as the ones who are responsible for women and youth, who depend on men, and are therefore seen as the primary decision makers. Broadly (and unsurprisingly), leaders who participate in COGES or other zone-related management committees possess more information about COGES than commoners, and that knowledge was not always transmitted to nonparticipants, the majority of whom were women. For example, most female participants in the focus group discussions had heard of an institution that was recently created to manage resources in the pastoral zone, but few were even familiar with the name "COGES" or knew its basic functions. Thus, we can conclude that there was little to no knowledge transfer within the group, particularly between genders.

The government required the election of at least two women per sector COGES and encouraged their participation in the central COGES, but the government has done little to enforce the application of the gender quota, and it has not actively sought feedback or information from COGES about gender quota outcomes or the process through which the committees achieved a gender balance in their leadership. Our experience in Sondré-Est revealed that only two women, one in sector 1 and the other in sector 4, were actually members of their sectors' committees. What is more, these women held positions (e.g., communication officer) that were less coveted by men, positions that were still seen as being in service to the group rather than leadership roles. Since the launching of the COGES project in 2015, state representatives have not attended COGES meetings to find out if gender parity is respected. This failure on the part of state representatives to attend a COGES meeting is a great example of the lack of top-down political will and upholds the perception that gender quotas and gender parity might be listed as governance goals but that there is little effort made to ensure their success.

The two women who were part of the committees in their sectors had distinctive and unusual backgrounds. Their status as "exceptional women" has allowed them to occupy leadership positions, unlike other women in their communities. One of them was a literate woman married to a former leader of the pastoral zone, while the other woman was older and influential in her community by virtue of local connections. Differences of age, educational status, and husband's position could explain why these women were more outspoken and had greater chances to integrate into their sectors' committees compared to younger, middle-aged, and largely illiterate Fulße women. Though these two women were well respected in their respective sectors and eligible to serve, male leaders did not allow them to sit on the central committee, where decision-making regarding the zone is centralized.[2] State policies promote women's access to land and their participation in the management of land resources, but these top-down policies clash with the locally and culturally accepted concepts of gender. These local concepts do not perceive the public sphere as a space for women. The perception of what women's space ought to be and the dismissal of women as resource managers result from different prescriptions that reinforce the domination of women at the hands of men.

In Sondré-Est, women understandably have issues voicing their needs in public settings. Rural literacy levels (Burge and Haughey 2002) favor men over women and reduce women's power and participation in community management and decision-making processes. Owing to their status and literacy, men are the interlocutors with external organizations and play the role of gatekeepers for women. Most external organizations promoting agricultural and pastoral services and natural resource management assistance automatically target men, while those focusing on health, education, nutrition, and family planning issues target women. Even when men support the involvement of women, men still play the role of intermediaries. Some have interpreted male mediation as harmless by assuming that helping men is the same as helping women because all resources are shared between men and women in the household (Pérez et al. 2015). However, households have diverse and even contradictory goals based on their members, and one cannot assume that individual choices reflect the entire household's goals (Goldstein and Udry 2004). Women's restricted access to key organizations and to the political sphere implies that their specific needs are less likely to be heard; there are resulting consequences to their adaptive capacity (Brooks, Adger, and Kelly 2005).

## Where Are the Women?
## In Internal Village Groups

In the context of their marginalization from COGES and other state-backed political organizations, local women's associations serve as alternative venues that women rely on to achieve their goals. Even though local women's groups do not take up issues of land, they are focused on issues of women's economic empowerment. In the pastoral zone, most women's groups promote the commercialization of dairy products, which is women's main economic activity. Traditionally, Fulße women do not cultivate, because women individually involved in cultivation decrease their husband's prestige in the eyes of the community. However, the observed benefits of fodder cultivation in boosting annual milk production have pushed some women to create a female group known as the Muyan, which is exclusively dedicated to fodder cultivation.

In the past decade, nongovernmental organizations such as Plate-Forme d'Actions à la Sécurisation des Ménages Pastoraux (PASMEP, Action Platform for Securing the Livelihoods of Pastoral Households) that promote the resilience of pastoral households in general and that of women in particular have supported Fulße women's organizations such as Muyan. PASMEP introduced and subsidized the construction of an improved modern storage facility locally referred to as a *fénil*. As an indoor storage space, the *fénil* improves fodder management, as fodder is stored—sometimes locked—in a hidden environment and protected from natural phenomena (sun, wind, humidity) and theft. In order to benefit from PASMEP's subsidies, one needs to be a group member. Within each group, a specific number of people (two or three) are selected to receive PASMEP's subsidy. Eligibility depends on each pastoralist's ability to fund 50 percent (87,500 CFA francs) of the building in a timely fashion.

In Sondré-Est, *fénils* are typically owned by men, but a few women who are members of Muyan were also able to get subsidies. Gaining land tenure permission from husbands to build a *fénil* at home has not been raised as a major challenge for women, as it becomes a valuable asset for the entire household. Still, the owner of the *fénil*, regardless of gender, decides on its management and regulates its use by others in the household. This increases women's respect in the household and community, as their husbands and cowives request space in their *fénil* to store fodder, or they borrow fodder from women owners to feed livestock.

Responses to the effects of climate change on declining land resources have caused changes to the existing social order. Responses such as the migration of men have increased women's workload and leadership in household decision-making and their ability to command leverage. However, this has not yet translated into how women are represented in community resource management leadership and decision-making. Women are typically perceived as viable and efficient decision makers at the household level but not at the community level. In Fulße communities in particular, this discrepancy is a result of ethnic and religious prescriptions. To be viewed and respected as a good mother, wife, and daughter revolves around women's performance within their household, but this has not carried over into women's formal leadership roles in the public sphere. Thus, we see real tensions between the so-called public sphere, where men are more "visible," and the private sphere, which is viewed as women's space. This could explain the dismissal of women from participation in community land management debates. Unfortunately, gender quota policies have not rectified these differences of perception and expectation.

This study has shown a disconnect between state policies and customary values. Even though the state and international organizations promote laws and policies that aim for gender parity, the last word on whether these laws come into effect on the ground belongs to local community decision makers. The case study of COGES shows that rights-based frameworks are insufficient to promote gender parity because they typically do not translate into local practice, especially in rural areas where customary laws and values regulate gender relations above and beyond any formal laws and policies. Although colonial and postcolonial development initiatives viewed traditional land management systems as barriers to development and environmental protection, local communities do not always seek a Western type of land tenure security (Breusers 2010). Breusers's study of the Mossi and Fulße shows that their traditional land management systems are flexible and suitable for geographic mobility, which is a key component of their livelihood systems (e.g., shifting agriculture and extensive livestock herding). In these communities, land control and access are not differentiated by both gender and ethnicity. These gender and ethnic restrictions further complicate women's access to land resources and management.

While most activists sincerely mobilize for the adoption of gender quotas to mitigate these challenges, in some instances, top-down state laws instrumentalize women and local organizations' focus on them to fulfill gender quotas to comply with donors' requirements. In such cases, government officials are more preoccupied with checking boxes to fill in administrative paperwork than with actual project implementation and meetings in targeted communities. The result is that few do much work to confront reality on the ground. There is no overt resistance to what the state requires in terms of gender parity in resource management because local organizations are willing to create a bureaucratic fiction in which they argue that they will do what the Burkina state requires to benefit from opportunities.

This study questions the state's interest in promoting gender equity. It is apparent that there are instances when the state uses gender quotas as a mechanism to fulfill donor requirements. Since this parity does not translate in practice, customary laws may be considered to be stronger than top-down state laws. The importance of this study lies in the fact that it questions the state's ability to regulate its constituents at the local level. The existence of quotas and parity policies does not ensure that men and women have equal access to decision-making processes. On paper, both the state and local communities create a local fiction. I have experienced this fiction based on fieldwork and the case studied here. These parties say what they will do (and women, influenced by contemporary discourses on the benefits of gender parity, express their desire to also be involved in land management), but in reality, they do not do it because of their cultural and religious values regarding men's and women's roles in society and because of the possible negative impacts of quotas policies on marriage and family harmony. As a result, women rely more on internal village groups, such as women's associations (e.g., Muyan), to cope with, manage, or adapt to stress in their daily lives. These local and female support groups open women's access to food, labor, and cash and alleviate their productive and reproductive responsibilities, at the same time allocating women recognition as leaders in their communities. Time will tell if these strategies, which are generated in local communities, will connect with top-down incentives to reconfigure space for women's participation in formal decision-making.

## Notes

1. Officially, the CVD remains, but it has been largely supplanted by COGES in pilot communities such as Sondré-Est.

2. One of the women (the oldest one) was sick on election day. The other one attended, but men refused her candidacy.

## References

Batterbury, Simon. 1998. "Local Environmental Management, Land Degradation and the 'Gestion des Terroirs' Approach in West Africa: Policies and Pitfalls." *Journal of International Development: The Journal of the Development Studies Association* 10 (7): 871–98.

Batterbury, Simon, and Andrew Warren. 2001. *The African Sahel 25 Years after the Great Drought: Assessing Progress and Moving towards New Agendas and Approaches*. Amsterdam: Elsevier.

Blomstrom, Eleanor, Sarah Cunningham, Nadia Johnson, and Cate Owren. 2009. "Making NAPAs Work for Women." In *Climate Change Connections: Gender, Population and Climate Change*. UNFPA and WEDO.

Braidotti, Rosi, Ewa Charkiewicz, Sabine Hausler, and Saskia Wieringa. 1994. *Women, the Environment and Sustainable Development: Towards a Theoretical Synthesis*. London: Zed Books.

Breusers, Mark. 2010. "Searching for Livelihood Security: Land and Mobility in Burkina Faso." *Journal of Development Studies* 37 (4): 49–80.

Brooks, Nick, Neil Adger, and Mick Kelly. 2005. "The Determinants of Vulnerability and Adaptive Capacity at the National Level and the Implications for Adaptation." *Global Environmental Change* 15 (2): 151–63.

Bruijn, Mirjam, and Wim van Dijk. 2003. "Changing Population Mobility in West Africa: Fulbe Pastoralists in Central and South Mali." *African Affairs* 102 (407): 285–307.

Burge, Elizabeth, and Margaret Haughey. 2002. *Using Learning Technologies: International Perspectives on Practice*. London: Routledge.

Burnet, Jennie. 2008. "Gender Balance and the Meanings of Women in Governance in Post-genocide Rwanda." *African Affairs* 107 (428): 361–86.

———. 2011. "Women Have Found Respect: Gender Quotas, Symbolic Representation, and Female Empowerment in Rwanda." *Politics & Gender* 7 (3): 303–34.

Burnet, Jennie, and RISD. 2003. "Culture, Practice, and Law: Women's Access to Land in Rwanda." In *Women and Land in Africa: Culture, Religion and Realizing Women's Rights*, edited by L. Wanyeki, 176–206. New York: Zed Books.

Canziani, M., O. Parry, J. Palutikof, P. van der Linden, and C. Hanson, eds. 2007. *Climate Change 2007: Impacts, Adaptation and Vulnerability; Contribution of Working Group II to the Fourth Assessment Report of the Intergovernmental Panel on Climate Change*. Cambridge: Intergovernmental Panel on Climate Change.

Cordell, Dennis, Joel Gregory, and Victor Piché. 1996. *Hoe and Wage: A Social History of a Circular Migration System in West Africa*. Boulder, CO: Westview Press.

Faure, Armelle. 1995. *Private Land Ownership in Rural Burkina Faso*. International Institute for Environment and Development. Issue paper no. 59. https://pubs.iied.org/7308IIED/?a=A+Faure.

Fortmann, Louise, and Dianne Rocheleau. 1985. "Women and Agroforestry: Four Myths and Three Case Studies." *Agroforestry Systems* 2 (4): 253–72.

Franceschet, Susan, Mona Lena Krook, and Jennifer Piscopo. 2009. "The Impact of Gender Quotas: A Research Agenda." Paper presented at the Midwest Political Science Association National Conference, Chicago.

Franceschet, Susan, and Jennifer Piscopo. 2008. "Gender Quotas and Women's Substantive Representation: Lessons from Argentina." *Politics & Gender* 4 (3): 393–425.

Goldstein, Markus, and Christopher Udry. 2004. "Gender, Power and Agricultural Investment in Ghana." Paper, London School of Economics.

Hochschild, Arlie, and Anne Machung. 1989. *The Second Shift: Working Families and the Revolution at Home.* New York: Viking.

Institut Géographique du Burkina Faso (IGB). 2015. *Document de Spécifications Externes de Contenu de la Base Nationale de Données Topographiques (BNDT), Version 1.0.* Paris: IGN France International.

Kevane, Michael, and Leslie Gray. 1999. "A Woman's Field Is Made at Night: Gendered Land Rights and Norms in Burkina Faso." *Feminist Economics* 5 (3): 26.

Marchal, Jean-Yves, and André Quesnel. 1997. "Dans les vallées du Burkina Faso, l'installation de la mobilité." In *La ruralité dans les pays du Sud à la fin du XX$^e$ siècle*, edited by J. Gastellu and J. Marchal, 595–614. Paris: Orstrom.

Mwangi, E., R. Meinzen-Dick, and Yan Sun. 2011. "Gender and Sustainable Forest Management in East Africa and Latin America." *Ecology and Society* 16 (1): 17.

Pérez, Carlos, E. Jones, Patricia Kristjanson, Laura Cramer, Philip Thornton, Wiebke Förch, and C. Barahona. 2015. "How Resilient Are Farming Households and Communities to a Changing Climate in Africa? A Gender-Based Perspective." *Global Environmental Change* 34:95–107.

Porro, Noemi, and Samantha Stone. 2005. "Diversity in Living Gender: Two Cases from the Brazilian Amazon." In *The Equitable Forest: Diversity, Community and Resource Management*, edited by C. J. P. Colfer, 242–55. Washington, DC: Resources for the Future and CIFOR.

Sankara, Thomas. 1990. *Women's Liberation and the African Freedom Struggle.* New York: Pathfinder Press.

Stamm, Voker, Jean Sawadogo, Saidou Ouedraogo, and Denis Ouedraogo. 2003. *Micropolicies on Land Tenure in Three Villages in Bam Province, Burkina Faso: Local Strategies for Exchanging Land.* International Institute for Environment and Development. Issue paper no. 124. https://pubs.iied.org/9310IIED/?k=denis.

Tompkins, Emma, and Neil Adger. 2004. "Does Adaptive Management of Natural Resources Enhance Resilience to Climate Change?" *Ecology and Society* 9 (2): 10.

Tonah, Steve. 2003. "Integration or Exclusion of Fulbe Pastoralists in West Africa: A Comparative Analysis of Interethnic Relations, State and Local Policies in Ghana and Côte d'Ivoire." *Journal of Modern African Studies* 41 (1): 91–114.

Tripp, Aili, and Alice Kang. 2008. "The Global Impact of Quotas: On the Fast Track to Increased Female Legislative Representation." *Comparative Political Studies* 41 (3): 338–61. https://doi.org/10.1177/0010414006297342.

VerEecke, Catherine. 1989. "From Pasture to Purdah: The Transformation of Women's Roles and Identity among the Adamawa Fulbe." *Ethnology* 28 (1): 53–73.

# 4

 Sex, Schooling, and the Paradox of the Readmission Policy in Malawi

RACHEL SILVER

*Madalitso was in her final year of primary school when she discovered that she was pregnant. Hoping to sit for the culminating exams, she hid her pregnancy until a teacher suspected her, called her into the office, and expelled her. In Malawi, pregnant students are not allowed to attend school. Madalitso waited only three months after Precious was born before returning to school, leaving her daughter at home to be cared for by her mother. Since the school banned the baby's presence, Madalitso's mother would bring Precious near the school, and Madalitso would slip out of class to breastfeed. After repeating the last year of primary school, Madalitso sat for her primary school leaving exams and secured a place in secondary school, where she attended without anyone knowing her status as a mother. She dreamed of becoming a nurse and carefully avoided any relationships—with boys or girls who had boyfriends—that could distract her from her goals.*[1]

In 1993 Malawi became the first country in southeastern Africa to institute a Readmission Policy, which bans the permanent expulsion of pregnant girls from school. The policy, deeply controversial at the time, emerged during an era of sweeping change as the country simultaneously adopted a "global policy package" of political democratization, neoliberalization, and free primary education (Kendall 2007). Legalizing school return for young mothers offered one means through which to enact the newly enshrined right to schooling. Pregnancy was no longer "the end of everything" for adolescent girls like Madalitso.

Still, nearly twenty-five years later, the question of what to do with schoolgirls who become pregnant remains a flashpoint in the region. In July 2017 Tanzanian president John Magufuli announced to a crowd of students on his reelection campaign trail that "after getting pregnant, you are done" (Ratcliffe 2017).[2] Concerned that a student mother would both distract and negatively influence her peers, he suggested that NGOs run schools for parents if they like but stop seeking to sway the government on issues of sex and schooling. His statement met with swift condemnation from human rights groups.

Though Malawi maintains its more open stance toward maternal reentry, the same questions—how to approach student sexuality, how (or if) to safeguard the right to education for girls whose school lives often extend past puberty, and how to manage the encroachment of international NGOs and funders into areas of governance and policy making (Mkandawire 2010; Odora Hoppers 2014)—animate life for diverse Malawian actors.[3]

Student pregnancy is a significant issue in Malawi, given high rates of adolescent sexual activity and low rates of contraceptive availability and usage among youth. According to the Health Policy Project, more than 12 percent of youth age ten to fourteen and 52 percent of youth age fifteen to nineteen reported having had sex, with less than half using contraception in their first encounter (HPP 2015). The *Malawi Demographic and Health Survey* notes that 29 percent of adolescents age fifteen to nineteen have begun having children (Government of Malawi 2016). Pregnancy accounts for 40 percent of school dropouts among Malawian girls, according to one estimate (Sanga 2016).

Despite its symbolic significance as a guarantor of rights, Malawi's Readmission Policy has largely failed to get girls back to school. Madalitso's story is exceptional. As a result, in 2016 the country's Ministry of Education, Science and Technology (MoEST) called for a formal review of the policy to make it more effective and widely disseminated. This chapter focuses on a new version that was finalized in 2018.

I show that Malawi's Readmission Policy is a paradox, tenuously balancing an access-based human rights approach to education with a more broadly conservative approach to youth sexuality and reproductive health (SRH) in a way that renders the policy limited in practice. The Readmission Policy is palatable and even popular among different actors because it promotes the widely celebrated project of girls' education while continuing to stigmatize student sexuality. In Malawi, debates among educational elites in and outside of government over the policy's review reveal core tensions between universal rights ideals and localized moral panic around a perceived loss of control over girls' sexuality.[4] They also reflect broader contestation over the relative authority of the Malawian state (Silver 2019).

Within the MoEST, a commitment to girls' educational rights, codified in the Readmission Policy, stands in for a parallel commitment to girls' rights to SRH information and services. Young mothers are permitted to return to school amid a broader landscape of policy and practice that focuses heavily on abstinence and forbids the provision of contraception or comprehensive sex education in schools (see Eunice Musiime and Leah Eryenyu's chapter in this volume for discussion of debates around comprehensive sex education in Uganda). In the policy review process, a range of stakeholders across NGOs, funding bodies, and research institutions pointed out this contradiction and sought to reimagine a more holistic approach to pregnant students. Yet MoEST officials upheld their conservative stance. They asserted moral and political authority over Malawian schools in a context where funders and NGOs have long encroached on spaces formerly restricted to government policy makers (Kendall 2007; Mkandawire 2010; Silver 2019).

In many ways, however, the Readmission Policy's paradox—that pregnant schoolgirls' right to education is protected while their SRH rights are not—is what makes it work, even as the majority of girls do not return to school. According to David Mosse, in international development, "ideas that make for 'good policy'" are those that "legitimiz[e] and mobiliz[e] political and practical support," whether or not they are successfully implemented (2004, 663).

The Readmission Policy recognizes student pregnancy and allows continued funding for girls' education and human rights to flow into the country. At the same time, it aligns with powerful conservative interest groups, including US-based evangelical Christians and, increasingly, US aid organizations. The US President's Emergency Plan for AIDS Relief (PEPFAR) program, for instance, has brought to the region tremendous resources for HIV prevention and treatment efforts with an explicit focus on abstinence-based prevention strategies (Boyd 2015). USAID is among Malawi's largest funders, and PEPFAR money reaches the education sector via SRH programming targeting youth.

By retaining a morally conservative view of student SRH, then, Malawi's Readmission Policy signals an ideological consensus among conservatives, local and global. Yet it fails to attend to structural issues barring girls from preventing early pregnancy and places the burden of responsibility for support of young mothers' education, including childcare, onto individuals and families.

## The Limits of Malawi's Readmission Policy

*Fatsani became pregnant at the end of her third year of secondary school. She went home for the long holiday but failed to return for what would have been her final year. Fatsani knew that her mother could not support her baby and seven younger siblings if she remained a student. She also knew that, having been pregnant, she was no longer eligible for the bursary she had previously received from a local girls' education organization to cover school fees and supplies. Fatsani remained at home, helping her mother tend their small garden and doing* ganyu (*piecework*). *Several months later, Fatsani's former head teacher visited her at home, informing Fatsani and her mother of the Readmission Policy and inviting Fatsani to claim her right to reenroll in school. The teacher explained that two large, internationally funded girls' education projects had started up in the area and that he had been trained to track and return girls like Fatsani to school. Fatsani did reenroll after this visit but dropped out again several months later due to lack of school fees and hunger.*

Malawi's Readmission Policy was born out of the sustained activism of elite stakeholders within the Ministries of Education and Gender and grassroots advocates who worked as part of the eight-year, $82 million USAID-funded Girls Attainment in Basic Literacy and Education (GABLE) project in the 1990s. The exact origin story varies according to the teller, but certain key elements feature in each telling: a feminist minister of education; advocacy from within the National Commission for Women and Development and Chitukuko Cha Amayi, the women's wing of the ruling Malawi Congress Party; funding from GABLE; interest from a USAID staff member with close connections to Malawian women's movements; and a widespread network of Malawian activists who partnered with sympathetic community-based leaders to contest barriers to girls' education.

Nahid Mazloum (2000) and Olivia Liwewe (2012) add that in the early 1990s, the Ministry of Health (MoH) expressed concern to the MoEST over the number of schoolgirls having abortions. According to these accounts, the MoH suggested providing contraceptives to school-going youth and considered the legalization of abortion. The MoEST, rejecting both, chose the Readmission Policy as a response to the MoH's concern. It was in many ways revolutionary—the first among several similar policies in the region to allow girls who became pregnant a second chance at schooling. As in Fatsani's case, however, the policy has been largely unsuccessful in getting girls to return to and stay in school (Samati 2013). There are several reasons for this failure.

To begin, Malawi's Readmission Policy is bureaucratically onerous. According to its 2006 guidelines, school reentry requires a pregnant teenager to write a letter withdrawing from school while pregnant, wait a year to seek reentry after the birth, and reapply for enrollment by again writing a letter to the MoEST and the local school head teacher. MoEST officials recommend that a girl reenroll at a school different from the one she originally attended in order to avoid stigma. This stipulation has significant implications for young rural women, who often already face long walks to their catchment primary or secondary school.

According to Maria Mayzel, Faith Kachala, and Brad Kerner (2010), the policy is not implemented evenly in practice, with teachers and administrators adjudicating school return on an ad hoc basis. Young fathers, who are also supposed to be expelled—though without conditions for return—are rarely, if ever, made to leave school (Mazloum 2000; Liwewe 2012). Nor does the policy address the challenges facing young mothers who seek reentry, including issues with infant feeding and a lack of financial resources or childcare options to make their schooling feasible. Only one pregnancy, and one readmission, is allowed.

Madalo Samati (2013) highlights the policy's failure to take on the cultural dimensions of gender inequality, take account of girls' lived experiences, and take seriously the need for local ownership and sustained financial resources for implementation. Bagele Chilisa (2002), Violet Wekesa (2011), and Elaine Unterhalter (2013) contend that reentry policies like Malawi's are not gender transformative, as they fail to attend to the ways in which multiple spheres of patriarchy intersect while feminizing blame for pregnancy and responsibility for childcare. The Readmission Policy, therefore, is an approach that, while meaningful in principle, does not address girls' material realities, and it positions school completion as all that stands between young mothers and their idealized "bright futures" (Frye 2012; Kendall and Silver 2014).

Young people's lives were increasingly precarious at the time of my research.[5] Malawi was in a formally declared state of emergency, its food crisis so severe that more than a third of the country's population faced starvation (Lukupe 2016). The twinning of the 2015 El Niño floods and 2016 La Niña droughts, both exacerbated by climate change, ruined harvests and resulted in diminished yields for several consecutive years. Households across Malawi could not feed themselves. Skyrocketing maize prices exacerbated this problem. Malnutrition became acute and widespread, and a range of hunger-related side effects were rampant: higher school absenteeism and drop-out rates, as well as increased gender-based violence and transactional sex. Student mothers and nonmothers alike struggled to attend school under these conditions, and they often did so on empty stomachs.

Why, then, in a context of humanitarian crisis, did Malawian actors *and* international funders sustain a commitment to girls' education broadly and to the Readmission Policy specifically? At the time of my research in 2016, the girls' education industry in Malawi was booming, with fifty-five organizations running 571 girl-focused educational interventions across a country of just eighteen million people (Runganaikaloo 2016; World Bank n.d.). To answer this question, Malawi's Readmission Policy must be made sense of as part of a larger conversation about the role of schooling in regulating sexuality and the centrality of girls' education to funders' agendas.

## The Promise and Perils of Girls' Education

For decades now girls' education has been a cornerstone of the global Education for All (EFA) initiative and the Millennium and Sustainable Development Goals (MDGs/SDGs), which rationalize a focus on girls by pointing to the high public returns to state investment in their primary schooling (see, e.g., Psacharopoulos 1987). The human capital approach to girls' education, which emphasizes potential economic productivity through delayed reproduction, dovetails with a focus on human rights (Vally and Spreen 2012; Bajaj 2014) and gendered concerns around public health and overpopulation (Subbarao and Raney 1995; Herz and Sperling 2004). For human rights practitioners, a focus on access to primary schooling fits seamlessly into obligations outlined in the 1948 Universal Declaration of Human Rights.

A rights-based approach to education centers the individual as a rights-bearing subject who is entitled to quality schooling without discrimination and reflects the globalization of a set of ideas around democracy and individual entitlements (Bajaj 2014). For population actors, schooling has long been heralded as a key means through which to ensure more sustainable population growth by delaying first birth and by teaching girls to have smaller, healthier families (Caldwell 1982; Cleland and Van Ginneken 1988; Jejeebhoy 1996). Schooling is also framed as an antidote to "harmful social practices," like early marriage and sexual initiation, which are said to constrain girls (see, e.g., UNESCO 2014).

Student pregnancy represents a failure of this scheme, with young pregnant women embodying schooling's aborted promise (Moeller 2018). Yet the relationship between schooling, sexuality, and pregnancy is more complex than originally imagined (Grant and Hallman 2008). Monica Grant (2015) has found that the median age of first birth in Malawi has not, in fact, changed despite vast increases in female enrollment and retention in education (see also Psaki et al. 2014). Schoolgirl pregnancy cannot be disarticulated from cultural practices and economic imperatives like early marriage (Lloyd and Mensch 2008); schools may expose girls to new forms of sexual coercion and gender-based violence (UNESCO 2014); and other factors, including poverty, parental educational attainment, and future schooling expectations, can influence decision-making around dropout or engagement in sexual activity (Mpando 2002). Girls do not make fertility choices in a vacuum, and decisions about family size and timing are often made by men in line with culturally legitimized distributions of gendered power (Jeffery and Jeffery 1998; Nii-Amoo Dodoo and Frost 2008).

Finally, projects that seek to shape or curb adolescent female sexuality are particularly fraught in contexts like Malawi, where historic understandings of a woman's worth were linked to fertility. As numerous anthropologists and historians have shown, in societies across southeastern Africa, it was (and often still is) through marriage and childbearing that young women could claim adult status, including, in matrilineal areas, access to land. Children were pathways to prosperity, wealth, and power. Christian missions and colonization brought to the region new efforts to regulate youth sexuality, with the womb a site of sociopolitical struggle (White 1990; Thomas 2003) and formal education a key strategy for enacting gendered social change (Stambach 2000; Vavrus 2003). Colonial attempts to control an African female sexuality understood as excessive and dangerous (Burke 1996; Chernoff 2003) echo in postcolonial regulations around gender.

Given how girls' education has figured into broader historic projects, a human rights approach to student pregnancy, which guarantees an individual girl a "second chance" to access schooling, has been called upon by a range of interest groups as an open-ended, relatively neutral means through which to advance diverse agendas.[6] It is one of a handful of policy stances that rests comfortably within a network of international norms and local mores. While this framework is not explicitly instrumental in the way of human capital and population approaches, it brings the same perceived instrumental benefits.

As Monisha Bajaj (2014) argues, international human rights are "productively plastic," allowing myriad actors to organize across multiple spheres (the global, national, and local), even if the meanings under which they operate are in fact quite different. The project of girls' educational equity broadly and school reentry specifically encompasses actors with quite divergent views on student rights and student sexuality. We see this in the processes and interactions that constitute "uneven policy implementation" in rural communities. We see this in the range of actors and institutions interested in funding girls' education, from the United Nations Population Fund (UNFPA) to Christian missionaries to the Nike Corporation (Moeller 2018). And in Malawi we see this in the frictions that emerge among educational elites over what to include in a new Readmission Policy.

Steve Stern and Scott Straus contend that "human rights are constituted ineluctably by a paradoxical intersection between the universal and the specific" (2014, 4). Local actors in particular settings claim or deny global or universal rights, and the local and global can be in tension. I turn now to explore how elite-level stakeholders within and outside the MoEST navigated these tensions in the process of policy making on student sexuality. MoEST actors, in particular, reinforced the paradox of Malawi's Readmission Policy, which represented at once a progressive, rights-based approach to girls' education and a morally conservative substitute for comprehensive SRH services and education.[7]

## "Second Chances" and Student Sexuality in Malawi

Schools in Malawi walk a fine line in their engagement with youth sexuality. On the one hand, there is the Readmission Policy. By granting young mothers the right of reenrollment, MoEST actors acknowledge that youth are having sex. Yet the policy itself is punitive. The original version of the Readmission Policy is a single-page circular titled "Discipline Policy on Girls Education." It places stipulations on sexually active girls' educational rights, requiring a one-year withdrawal period from school and allowing only a single return. The Readmission Policy allows girls a second chance to access education as a form of redemption, a chance to be "born again" in their school lives. If they "fall pregnant" twice—a passive phrasing I heard over and over, from teacher rooms in village schools to MoEST hallways—they are finished with government school, formally excluded from a space that was supposed to belong to unmarried and presumably virginal youth.[8] As a director of one prominent NGO explained, "This Readmission Policy is supposed to work for a girl who had a baby almost like by accident. So this was an accident. Let her come back to school." Malawi's Readmission Policy, therefore, opened access, but it also regulated girls' sexual engagement. It largely ignored young fathers, and it ended with a cautionary note: "It must be stressed that the modern approach to the discipline of girls does not, under no circumstances whatsoever, constitute softening of preventative measures/rules and regulations schools have in place for girls and boys. School rules/regulations should continue to be enforced with the vigour they deserve."

Despite the disclaimer, the policy and the modernity it was said to represent met with fierce resistance in communities and among some elite actors, reflecting a broader moral panic about the loss of control over girls' sexuality from teachers and parents, chiefs and clerics alike. This panic must, at least partially, be understood in the context of the HIV/AIDS pandemic. Still, the earliest document reveals a tension between a view of girls' education as a legitimate human rights claim and the socially conservative nature of the MoEST and many communities with respect to girls' sexuality.

Indeed, the single readmission rule was but one effort in a broader policy landscape originating from the MoEST and aiming to regulate girls' sexuality. First, young single mothers could return to government schools; married women could not. This unwritten but widely enforced policy points to assumptions about young women's sexuality and the limits to their independence within marriage. I was not able to find any documentation barring the enrollment of married students in government schools, but the rule was echoed in every interview I conducted and followed strictly at every school I visited. One high-level MoEST official explained in the case of young mothers: "When they're being readmitted, we do not expect them to be coming from a boy's house or a man's house. No. They should be single!" She went on to share that if a girl was suspected of being married, the school would send a representative to her marital home, where she would be given a choice to permanently leave the marriage and return to her parental home or withdraw from government school.[9]

This rule had significant implications for families. If a girl could not return to school from a marital home, then her parents had to bear the burden of caring for both the young woman and her child. Her female relatives, by default, had to assume responsibility for the child while she was in school. And the child's father was placed in a passive role, dissolved of official responsibility to care for the mother or the child.

In line with the restrictions on marriage was a broader set of disciplinary policies regarding heterosexual relations that were again not written down at the MoEST but were widely acknowledged and codified in the disciplinary policies of individual schools. These included common "no's": no kissing, no "pairing," no carrying of contraceptives at school, no inappropriate boy/girl relationships. Students found doing any of these were to be expelled. One school's rules and regulations, for instance, included the following: "Immoral and indecent behavior is not allowed; do not be involved in pairing in the school," along with "wear school uniform all the time" and "be punctual for all school activities." At another school the rules dictated that "sexual relationships are not allowed," which the head teacher personally supplemented by banning students from the forested hill behind the school, where he had previously found students having sex. He named this hill "The Don't" and expelled any student found there for any reason. As a MoEST representative explained brusquely, "Whenever we catch [students] making, having sex, we expel them from school. We don't suspend them—we boot them out of the system. They will *never* find a place in our system."

The strong antisex stance in school rules mirrors the abstinence-only approach taken by the MoEST more broadly. Malawi's official curriculum has a compulsory subject, Life Skills, designed to provide information about SRH. Life Skills originated in the late 1980s as UNICEF's and the MoEST's response to HIV/AIDS, taking an abstinence-only stance. Since then, the curriculum has been officially revised to adopt an "ABC," or abstinence-plus approach. Although officially ABC stands for "abstinence, be faithful, use a condom," I was told by several stakeholders that in practice it meant "abstinence, but if you have to, condoms." Condoms were seen as best used within marriage for child spacing or for those who lacked appropriate self-control. A teacher explained to me: "There are people who regard sex as food; they cannot do without. They always want to have sex. It is they [who] are advised to use condoms."

Life Skills classes that I observed were imbued with moralizing tropes. One teacher told her female students that they were "married to their education." Relations with boys could wait; attempting to combine schooling and a sexual relationship was untenable (see Stambach 2000). MoEST officials at the national level likewise spoke of a firm ministerial commitment to abstinence, describing themselves as a "unified front" against those, usually in the MoH or in public health and population NGOs, who would promote the provision of contraception at schools (see also Eunice Musiime and Leah Eryenyu's chapter in this volume). They saw their mission as exclusively educational and held firm on what was known as the "one-hundred-meter rule," which banned the distribution of any family planning services within one hundred meters of the school grounds. Life Skills was to provide the information that needed to be provided; schools were not for service provision *or* for referrals.[10] In practice, however, Life Skills teachers often omitted or amended lessons on contraception.

Of course, these rules, from expulsion for kissing to the banning of most preventative health measures related to sex, set up an obvious contradiction when juxtaposed with the Readmission Policy and with student demographics. Nancy Kendall and Zikani Kaunda point to the "misalignment that exists between the current realities of youth educational progress, school-based sex education messages, contraceptive availability for youth, average age of sexual initiation, and average age of first childbirth, to the structure of schooling and childcare in Malawi" (2015, 34–35). Or as an interviewee noted: "If you find a boy and a girl kissing, or doing any indecent behavior, they're excluded [expelled] from school. Not even withdrawn but excluded for indecent behavior. And you find someone is pregnant—it means she did *more* than kissing.

She is coming back. But because of being a signatory to charters and whatever, the Readmission Policy is a cause that is all [around]."

## Readmission Policy Review and the MoEST

In its original form, the Readmission Policy was an exception to the MoEST's rules on (female) student sexuality. It was justified in the name of rights. The policy's review opened up the possibility for reengaging sexuality in an analysis of youth, but officials within the MoEST upheld their abstinence-focused stance.

Within the MoEST, I interviewed officials in a range of relevant departments on what a new Readmission Policy should look like and watched them manage the policy review process. These were the key players in government necessary for this reform to take place. They were less likely to spend time in "the field"—development code for the mostly rural areas targeted by NGO programming—than to sit and plan policy with funders or NGO directors. Each person with whom I spoke agreed that young people had a right to access education and that part of ensuring such a right meant allowing mothers the option of reenrollment in school. Each MoEST official with whom I spoke also acknowledged the contradiction between readmitting mothers and stigmatizing sexuality but maintained it nonetheless.

They admitted, if regretfully, that students were having sex, even if such an acknowledgment represented a moral failing of society broadly and of young people specifically. Youth sexuality was a shame; it should not be happening. One secondary education official told me: "I think we are a sex society. We think about sex, nothing else. You think about sex, and you spoil everything! We are in a mess as a country." MoEST actors acknowledged and lamented the high rates of nonconsensual sex in Malawi, including predation by teachers. This focus on sexual violence and girls' vulnerability to male predators was one means through which they could mentally and morally square the need for a reentry policy with their broader understandings of the purposes of schooling for children and the immorality embodied in student pregnancy.

Indeed, MoEST officials viewed the role of education as imbuing young people with a moral code, training them to be "reliable citizens in Malawi" and to understand the chronology of a proper life course. Early sex, according to this viewpoint, happened parallel to and in spite of in-school messaging. As noted, the MoEST had created a Life Skills curriculum to arm students with *information* about sex for their future married lives, but that was all. Nonetheless, government actors knew that this information was often not provided in practice; they also knew that rape happened and that "good girls" made mistakes. Girls who erred should therefore be allowed redemption; for these actors, pregnancy—whether the result of force or of a mistake—should no longer end lives. A young mother's return to school represented a signal of her willingness to eschew premarital sex and embrace a born-again identity as a secondary virgin that resonated strongly with an evangelical ethos embraced across Malawi. However, girls still should not get a free pass. A mother could be given a second chance, and all steps should be taken to ensure that she actually be allowed back at the school level. But MoEST actors wanted the Readmission Policy to remain a disciplinary measure to some extent. No one in this group was looking to remove the one-year waiting period to return, which was justified in several ways, from the health of the new mother to the health of the child. And if a girl erred twice, then that was on her. Her formal school career was done.

Furthermore, despite being public proponents of the Readmission Policy and "second chances," MoEST officials were quite frank about the limitations that they felt were appropriate for the Malawian context regarding student sexuality and the role of schooling. Specifically, these stakeholders formed a hard line of resistance against providing SRH services in schools and against abortion. They argued that advocates of condom provision in schools were either naive about the context and its limitations or were trying to promote ways of being that were simply unacceptable in Malawi. MoEST officials contrasted Malawi with other societies like the United States and Great Britain, which they saw as morally lax and sexually permissive, in addition to better resourced. According to one official, "When we are looking at [the Readmission Policy], we should also look at where our country stands. . . . We cannot equate our country to a country that has a clinic at the school, to a country that has all the laws and order, and to a country that will allow girls to get pregnant as many times as they wish as long as the uterus is there."

As such, the visibility of pregnancy, babies, and breastfeeding around schools was to be restricted; we saw this in how Madalitso managed school-going. SRH service provision—for adults—remained the province of the MoH and its clinics, and the Readmission Policy could remain a paradox. As one MoEST representative noted with amusement, "People smoke *chamba* [hash]. Doesn't the country know that people smoke *chamba*? It's illegal, but people still smoke. So [this issue is] the same. Those children will continue [having sex], but you can't let government say that 'let's give children contraceptives!'" For these actors, preaching abstinence and then providing condoms represented a far greater hypocrisy than allowing the return of young mothers to school.

In sum, MoEST actors wanted a more robust policy that acknowledged the need for certain forms of support for returning girls—psychosocial, for instance.

They acknowledged sexual violence and provided "good girls" one redemptive chance. But they believed strongly in restricting the mission of Malawian schools to produce the right kind of "moral Malawian" and therefore in the inappropriateness of truly comprehensive sex education or condom provision in educational settings. MoEST actors used the Readmission Policy, permissive on one hand, punitive on the other, to answer one human rights claim and to resist another. By taking seriously young mothers' right to educational access, the MoEST aligned itself with the rights-based approach of the EFA initiative and the SDGs. By remaining pro-abstinence, the MoEST reflected the sexual conservatism of US evangelical movements, politics, and aid funding (see Boyd 2015).

## "A Band-Aid on a Broken Arm": Nongovernmental Actors and the Readmission Policy

Outside of government, stakeholders in public health and education were quick to discuss the shortcomings of the MoEST's approach in the face of high rates of youth sexuality, pregnancy, and HIV/AIDS. These actors included directors of Malawian NGOs who spent time with funders and government officials advocating for pregnancy policy review or for new approaches to youth sexuality; project managers and fieldworkers who implemented programming in villages; local academics, called upon as consultants to monitor and evaluate programs; and Malawian representatives of bilateral or multilateral funding bodies. As a group, they took a range of responses to controversial issues like contraception in school but were unanimous in wanting change from the MoEST. They acknowledged the need to provide girls with more comprehensive SRH information and were more likely to have spent extensive time at the school and community levels than their government counterparts.

Many had trouble with the contradiction that they felt the Readmission Policy represented. One project manager gave me his assessment of the complex landscape of MoEST policies related to sexuality.

> I find [a] contradiction. Because realistically if you are teaching about condoms... then it means you expect that somebody should use [condoms]. . . . And similarly, we have heard of successes, where maybe a thirteen-year-old girl who was married for several months or several years goes back to school! Somebody who is used to having sex in a family. The probability [is] that they will have sex [again]—maybe with the same man who married her or another man. So basically, the Readmission Policy on teen

mothers does contradict with the main education policy, which doesn't allow distribution of condoms.

Those who worked to implement NGO programming related to girls' education and sexual/reproductive health, including the above interviewee, were quick to say that youth were having sex and that there was no point in denying it or pretending that it was only a matter of transactional sex or rape. Certainly, both were problems, but many young people had sex because they were curious, or because they liked it. Many activists said that it was strange and limiting for the MoEST to allow girls who had babies back to school while denying interventions or teachings that might change sexual habits and protect youth from pregnancy. Many thought greater access to condoms would make sense. Some expressed frustration about the strictures within which they had to work. One NGO worker noted straightforwardly: "There's generally an idea that sex is bad, which I've always found awkward."

Critics of the MoEST's de facto abstinence-only policy drew on empirical evidence in public health to argue that access to condoms, comprehensive sex education, and safe and legal abortions would save lives and that merely allowing school reentry was dangerously insufficient. Student sexuality was not necessarily something to condemn; it just was. Unwanted pregnancies happened, unsafe abortions happened, and people died, they explained, in part because of the MoEST's stubborn refusal to engage what they well knew was happening on the ground. The Readmission Policy was, in the words of one academic with whom I spoke, "a Band-Aid on a broken arm."

By continuing to focus on the policy, to review it, and to funnel resources toward it instead of toward other approaches, the MoEST operated according to what a director of one family planning organization called an "ostrich style of management, whereby you rightly know there is a problem, but you pretend everything is okay." The same director explained:

> We have tried to reach out to [the MoEST], but the education sector is still adamant. They feel, they say, their schools are not brothels. That's the word they use—our school is not a brothel, so we can't allow you. If a boy is found with a condom, he's expelled from school. I say, What? What wrong have they found with a condom? I want to protect myself! They said no, if it's an STI [you get], we will treat you, if it is pregnancy [you get], you will come back after being pregnant.

These activists were not naive about moral and religious conservativism in Malawi; they were Malawians, and they too attended church or mosque. Still, they believed strongly in a public health approach and that youth sexuality—

consensual, for exchange, or forced—was a fact to be pragmatically addressed. Schools made sense as the most logical and practical point for the provision of services to youth. The current stance of promoting youth-friendly services at health clinics was fine but limiting.[11] Not using schools as a point of service provision represented the failure to leverage a key resource that could help curb unsustainable population growth, disease, and unwanted pregnancy. These were the problems to be concerned with, not student sexuality itself.

These actors impressed upon MoEST officials that the right of young people to access contraception and comprehensive SRH information was *as important as* their right to education. But most were not in the rooms where policies related to student sexuality, including the Readmission Policy, were being made. Those who were included in key meetings convened by the MoEST could express their opinions. But they would not author education policy. They would be called upon to implement it. Similarly, Malawian representatives from bi- and multilateral funders could offer input. But non-Malawian officials at funding agencies were quite circumscribed in sharing their views because they knew that, whatever their personal beliefs, their presence in the country depended on the government's approval, even if the government was disempowered vis-à-vis this group in almost every other way.[12] The MoEST, after all, managed access to schools.

Elsewhere, I explore what Malawi's Readmission Policy can tell us about the politics of partnership in development (Silver 2019). I argue that, through subtle interventions and strategic delays throughout the policy reform process, MoEST officials resisted the ability of funders and NGOs to fully dominate development interactions.

Here, I explore the political economy of rights. Readmission Policy reflects synchronicity between the values of MoEST actors—translated into policy—and those of both liberal rights regimes *and* ideological conservatives. There is a lot of money and shared interest in protecting educational rights. At the same time, key funders in Malawi, including the United States, are quite sexually conservative in their policies. Since the beginning of the Trump administration, the United States has dramatically restricted its protocols for international aid and family planning. President Trump reinstated a strengthened Global Gag Rule within a week of taking office, withdrew US funding for the United Nations Population Fund, and has repeatedly proposed drastic cuts to PEPFAR.[13] These actions are part of a broader effort to limit women's access to SRH services at home and abroad.

Readmission Policy, then, became one key space—a point of agreement—in which funders like USAID and MoEST officials could safely engage the fact of youth sexuality. Its proponents could acknowledge that sex was happening, but by taking a reactive stance, they could avoid engaging with any of the more sex-positive or proactive responses to youth sex. At the same time, they could continue to focus on educational access—a politically safe, unanimous priority. The policy, supported in different ways by funders such as USAID, DFID (Department for International Development, a British government department), UNFPA, and UNICEF, among others, offered an avenue through which these agencies could partner with the MoEST, address the issues of HIV/AIDS and pregnancy, and meet internal funding goals without losing access or becoming controversial.

In the end, the MoEST rewrote the Readmission Policy in a way that continued to foreground the right to education and hold the line on youth sexual rights. The new version explores the option of more comprehensive sex education, though the MoEST lacks the funding and political will to implement what would be a dramatic change of approach, particularly as many teachers already opt not to teach ABC. Accordingly, the 2018 policy represents a palatable approach to young people's SRH for MoEST actors and conservative funders. It exemplifies Mosse's (2004) understanding of "good policy" in development—sustainable if unimplementable. Susan Watkins and Ann Swidler similarly focus on "working misunderstandings," or those approaches, themes, and practices in development that "work in the sense that they satisfy the varied agendas of the major actors sufficiently to sustain their day-to-day cooperation" (2012, 197). They describe, for instance, how in Malawi's AIDS industry, there are certain "themes that make everyone happy" (201).

Readmission Policy in Malawi is a development project that "works," though perhaps without misunderstanding. It belongs to the MoEST. It draws on themes that make everyone happy: access to education for girls, (certain) human rights, and moral redemption. Yet it does not return girls to school in significant numbers. MoEST actors retained a version of the policy that gives young mothers the right to return to school but, by continuing to stigmatize sex, limits their ability to claim it.

## Conclusion

By standing in lieu of a more comprehensive approach to youth sexuality and alongside regulatory efforts, the Readmission Policy reveals the limitations of a rights-based approach to girls' education. Attention to its review demonstrates how one circumscribed, albeit important, effort to expand educational access may foreclose more transformative means through which to improve the lives of young women in Malawi.

The Readmission Policy remains a policy and funding priority in Malawi because it directly supports a girl's right to education, something that everyone from funders to government officials, NGO fieldworkers, teachers, and students can get behind. Young mothers can go back to school; their lives are no longer "finished." The Readmission Policy fits neatly alongside the EFA movement, the SDGs, the Malawian Constitution, and a broader global focus on the instrumental benefits of educating girls. It engages the fact of student pregnancy and transforms the lives of individuals like Madalitso without threatening to change anything structurally or materially. By excluding provisions related to students' sexual and reproductive rights, the Readmission Policy offers a broadly acceptable moral narrative, allowing funding for girls' education to flow into Malawi amid a more globally conservative climate. Within the country, the policy rests on a prevailing understanding within the government that schools are for children and that student sexuality is untimely.

Malawi's Readmission Policy is paradoxical, however, because it threatens the notion of school as a site of sanctified childhood—a notion that is still being carefully enforced in a range of other ways. Further, many young mothers in Malawi, like Fatsani, are precluded from remaining in school by extreme poverty. The Readmission Policy cannot and will not ever really *work* without a preventative piece and without meaningful material support for students who live in profound and increasing precarity.

## Notes

1. I have used pseudonyms throughout this chapter to protect participant confidentiality.

2. President Magufuli also suggested that men who impregnate schoolgirls be imprisoned for thirty years, during which time they could "put the energy they used to impregnate the girl into farming while in jail" (Ratcliffe 2017). Though characterized as extreme by many, his statement does acknowledge that it is often men outside of the school or male teachers rather than schoolboys who impregnate school-going girls, as the literature on student pregnancy most often suggests.

3. The term "donor" refers to multilateral, bilateral, nongovernmental, or private institutions that provide overseas development assistance. Given the extensive literature noting that aid funding does not remain in the recipient country, I follow Kendall and Silver (2014) to use the term "funder."

4. Of course, this particular panic is also globalized; transnational religious approaches to sexuality are localized in Malawi, while views about school reentry emerge from global rights frameworks.

5. I draw on Judith Butler (2009) to conceptualize precarity as an ontological and a material condition taking interlinked but distinct forms across class, race, gender, and geography.

6. Of course, the project of human rights is far from neutral in Malawi, having been entwined in political democratization and with economic liberalization (Englund 2006; Kendall 2007).

7. I draw on a year of multisited ethnographic research conducted primarily in 2016 that examined discourses, policies, and practices related to schoolgirl pregnancy as they were enacted across levels of social organization from the individual girl to the transnational education arena. Methods combined interviews with more than one hundred key stakeholders in diverse social locations, archival research, and extensive participant observation in a range of spaces, including ministry-level policy review sessions, NGO programming on girls' education, and a peri-urban secondary school. I pay particular attention here to educational elites in government and NGOs for their unique ability to shape the translation of global rights edicts into local practice (Luke and Watkins 2002).

8. The use of the passive voice to describe what happens to schoolgirls who become pregnant in Malawi mirrors the more widespread trope of the pregnant girl as vulnerable victim in mainstream development discourse. It also reflects the reality of inequitable power relations in many sexual relations in Malawi. Still, it erases the possibility of a young woman's agency in decision-making around sexuality and sits in tension with the general tendency to blame girls for pregnancy.

9. Married students could still enroll in "open schools," the largely unregulated, teacher-run programs held in government school buildings after regular school hours to prepare nontraditional students for national exams.

10. Schools were, however, used commonly across Malawi for the provision of other health services, such as vaccinations, deworming medications, and bilharzia treatment.

11. Notably, however, many service providers at MoH clinics refused to provide contraception to youth under the age of eighteen or to girls who had not yet had a child, exhibiting similar internal contradictions and understandings of child versus adult rights as MoEST officials. The distinction between child rights and adult rights is extensive in the international human rights arena, both animating and constraining the ways that rights can be claimed.

12. While aid money has been redirected from the Malawian government toward NGOs for decades (Mkandawire 2010; Cammack 2012), the Malawian government has faced particularly acute disenfranchisement by funders since the 2012 Cashgate Scandal, after which aid money has been almost entirely kept from state coffers. Cashgate is a corruption scandal that has engulfed the Malawian government since 2012, when it was discovered that government employees were embezzling millions of US dollars. Both the British and German governments have conducted audits to uncover the extent of theft, and funding to Malawi has been suspended or redirected from multiple sources in the ensuing years.

13. The Global Gag Rule refers to a policy first implemented in 1984 by the Reagan administration that suspended US financial support to any foreign NGO that advocated for or provided abortions. Since then, the policy has been rescinded and reinstated according to the standing president's political party. The Trump administration reinstated the Gag Rule in January 2017, significantly expanding the number and types of organizations subject to its restrictions. In Malawi, this will have life-or-death consequences for women.

## References

Bajaj, Monisha. 2014. "The Productive Plasticity of Rights: Globalization, Education, and Human Rights." In *Globalization and Education, Integration and Contestation across Cultures*, edited by Nelly P. Stromquist and Karen Monkman, 55–70. Lanham, MD: Rowman and Littlefield.
Boyd, Lydia. 2015. *Preaching Prevention: Born-Again Christianity and the Moral Politics of AIDS in Uganda*. Athens: Ohio University Press.
Burke, Timothy. 1996. *Lifebuoy Men, Lux Women: Commodification, Consumption, and Cleanliness in Modern Zimbabwe*. Durham, NC: Duke University Press.
Butler, Judith. 2009. "Performativity, Precarity, and Sexual Politics." *AIBR Revista de Antropologia Iberoamericana* 4 (3): i–xiii.
Caldwell, John. 1982. *Theory of Fertility Decline*. New York: Academic.
Cammack, Diana. 2012. "Malawi in Crisis, 2011–12." *Review of African Political Economy* 39 (132): 375–88.
Chernoff, John M. 2003. *Hustling Is Not Stealing: Stories of an African Bar Girl*. Chicago: University of Chicago Press.
Chilisa, Bagele. 2002. "National Policies on Pregnancy in Education Systems in Sub-Saharan Africa: The Case of Botswana." *Gender and Education* 14 (1): 21–35.
Cleland, John, and Jerome van Ginneken. 1988. "Maternal Education and Child Survival in Developing Countries: The Search for Pathways of Influence." *Social Science and Medicine* 27 (12): 1357–68.
Englund, Harry. 2006. *Prisoners of Freedom: Human Rights and the African Poor*. Berkeley: University of California Press.
Frye, Monica. 2012. "Bright Futures in Malawi's New Dawn: Educational Aspirations as Assertions of Identity." *American Journal of Sociology* 117 (6): 1565–624.
Government of Malawi. 2016. *Malawi Demographic and Health Survey 2015–2016 Key Indicators Report*. Zomba, Malawi: National Statistics Office.
Grant, Monica. 2015. "The Demographic Promise of Expanded Female Education: Trends in Age at First Birth in Malawi." *Population and Development Review* 41 (3): 409–38.
Grant, Monica, and Kelly Hallman. 2008. "Pregnancy-Related School Dropout and Prior School Performance in KwaZulu-Natal, South Africa." *Studies in Family Planning* 39 (4): 369–82.

Herz, Barbara, and Gene Sperling. 2004. *What Works in Girls' Education: Evidence and Policies from the Developing World.* New York: Council on Foreign Relations.

HPP (Health Policy Project). 2015. *Evaluation of Youth-Friendly Health Services in Malawi.* Washington, DC: USAID.

Jeffery, Patricia, and Robert Jeffery. 1998. "Silver Bullet or Passing Fancy? Girls' Schooling and Population Policy." In *Feminist Visions of Development: Gender, Analysis and Policy*, edited by Cecile Jackson and Ruth Pearson, 239–59. London: Routledge.

Jejeebhoy, Shireen. 1996. *Women's Education, Autonomy, and Reproductive Behaviour: Experience from Developing Countries.* Oxford: Clarendon Press.

Kendall, Nancy. 2007. "Education for All Meets Political Democratization: Free Primary Education and the Neoliberalization of the Malawian School and State." *Comparative Education Review* 51 (3): 281–305.

Kendall, Nancy, and Zikani Kaunda. 2015. "Transitions: Girls, Schooling, and Reproductive Realities in Malawi." In *Educating Adolescent Girls around the Globe: Challenges and Opportunities*, edited by Sandra L. Stacki and Supriya Baily, 23–39. New York: Routledge.

Kendall, Nancy, and Rachel Silver. 2014. "The Consequences of Global Mass Education: Schooling, Work, and Well-Being in EFA-Era Malawi." In *Globalization and Education, Integration and Contestation across Cultures*, edited by Nelly P. Stromquist and Karen Monkman, 247–66. Lanham, MD: Rowman and Littlefield.

Liwewe, Olivia. 2012. *Re-entry Policy: The Case of Malawi.* Lilongwe: Forum for African Women Educationalists Malawi.

Lloyd, Cynthia, and Barbara Mensch. 2008. "Marriage and Childbirth as Factors in Dropping Out from School: An Analysis of DHS Data from Sub-Saharan Africa." *Population Studies* 62 (1): 1–13.

Luke, Nancy, and Susan Cotts Watkins. 2002. "Reactions of Developing-Country Elites to International Population Policy." *Population and Development Review* 28 (4): 707–33.

Lukupe, Ganizani. 2016. "Education Cluster Food Insecurity Response Plan." Presentation at the Meeting of the National Girls Education Network, Lilongwe, Malawi, June 23.

Mayzel, Maria, Faith Kachala, and Brad Kerner. 2010. *Reaching Out to Teen Mothers in Malawi.* Lilongwe: USAID.

Mazloum, Nahid. 2000. *Readmission/Pregnancy Policy Status Report.* Lilongwe: UNICEF Malawi.

Mkandawire, Thandika. 2010. "Aid, Accountability, and Democracy in Africa." *Social Research* 77 (4): 1149–82.

Moeller, Kathryn. 2018. *The Gender Effect: Capitalism, Feminism, and the Corporate Politics of Development.* Berkeley: University of California Press.

Mosse, David. 2004. "Is Good Policy Unimplementable? Reflections on the Ethnography of Aid Policy and Practice." *Development and Change* 35 (4): 639–71.

Mpando, L. R. S. 2002. *Malawi Core Welfare Indicators Report.* Lilongwe, Malawi: National Statistics Office.

Nii-Amoo Dodoo, F., and Ashley Frost. 2008. "Gender in African Population Research: The Fertility / Reproductive Health Example." *Annual Review of Sociology* 34:431–52.

Odora Hoppers, Catherine A. 2014. "Globalization and the Social Construction of Reality: Affirming or Unmasking the 'Inevitable.'" In *Globalization and Education, Integration and Contestation across Cultures*, edited by Nelly P. Stromquist and Karen Monkman, 101–18. Lanham, MD: Rowman and Littlefield.

Psacharopoulos, George, ed. 1987. *Economics of Education: Research and Studies.* Oxford: Pergamon Press.

Psaki, Stephanie R., Erica Soler-Hampejsek, Barbara Mensch, Christine A. Kelly, Monica J. Grant, and Paul C. Hewett. 2014. "The Effect of Gender-Related Aspects of School Quality on Schoolgirl Pregnancy in Rural Malawi." Presentation at the Meeting of the Population Association of America, Boston, MA, May 1–3.

Ratcliffe, Rebecca. 2017. "After Getting Pregnant, You Are Done: No More School for Tanzania's Mums-to-Be." *The Guardian*, June 30, 2017.

Runganaikaloo, Dave. 2016. Email message to the author, April 4.

Samati, Madalo. 2013. "At the Interface of Policy and Cultural Change: Engaging Communities in Support of Girls' Education in Malawi." In *Improving Learning Opportunities and Outcomes for Girls in Africa*, edited by Xanthe Ackerman and Negar Ashtari Abay, 69–100. Washington, DC: Brookings Institution.

Sanga, Linice. 2016. "At the Interface of Policy and Cultural Change." Presentation at the National Stakeholders' Meeting, Lilongwe, Malawi, December 19.

Silver, Rachel. 2019. "Nothing but Time: Middle Figures, Student Pregnancy Policy, and the Malawian State." *African Studies Review* 62 (4): 110–33.

Stambach, Amy. 2000. *Lessons from Mount Kilimanjaro: Schooling, Community and Gender in East Africa.* New York: Routledge.

Stern, Steve, and Scott Straus. 2014. "Introduction: Embracing Paradox; Human Rights in the Global Age." In *The Human Rights Paradox: Universality and Its Discontents*, edited by Steve Stern and Scott Straus, 3–28. Madison: University of Wisconsin Press.

Subbarao, Kalanidhi, and Laura Raney. 1995. "Social Gains from Female Education." *Economic Development and Cultural Change* 44 (1): 105–28.

Thomas, Lynn. 2003. *Politics of the Womb: Women, Reproduction, and the State in Kenya.* Berkeley: University of California Press.

UNESCO. 2014. *Developing an Education Sector Response to Early and Unintended Pregnancy: Discussion Document for a Global Consultation.* Paris: UNESCO.

Unterhalter, Elaine. 2013. "Connecting the Private and the Public: Pregnancy, Exclusion, and the Expansion of Schooling in Africa." *Gender and Education* 25 (1): 75–90.

Vally, Salim, and Carol Ann Spreen. 2012. "Human Rights in the World Bank Education Strategy." In *The World Bank and Education: Critiques and Alternatives*, edited by Steve Klees, Joel Samoff, and Nelly Stromquist, 173–87. Rotterdam: Sense Publishers.

Vavrus, Frances. 2003. *Desire and Decline: Schooling amid Crisis in Tanzania.* New York: Peter Lang.

Watkins, Susan, and Ann Swidler. 2012. "Working Misunderstandings: Donors, Brokers, and Villagers in Africa's AIDS Industry." *Population and Development Review* 38 (1): 197–218.

Wekesa, Violet. 2011. "Bending the Private-Public Gender Norms." *ISS Working Paper Series / General Series* 515:1–51.

White, Louise. 1990. *The Comforts of Home: Prostitution in Colonial Nairobi*. Chicago: University of Chicago Press.

World Bank. n.d. "Malawi Data." Accessed July 21, 2017. data.worldbank.org/country/malawi.

# 5

 The Debate over
Comprehensive Sexuality
Education in Uganda

## Barriers to Vernacularizing
## Reproductive Rights

EUNICE MUSIIME AND LEAH ERYENYU

The ability to achieve sexual and reproductive health and rights, including being able to decide when and whether to have children, is critical for the health and well-being of all women. In Uganda, according to the Uganda Bureau of Statistics, one in every four teenage girls between fifteen and nineteen has been pregnant. The Population Secretariat indicates that of the 1.2 million pregnancies recorded in Uganda annually, 25 percent of these are teenage pregnancies. These more than three hundred thousand teenagers who get pregnant also account for the bulk of unwanted pregnancies, which end up categorized as unintended births or abortions (UNAIDS 2017).

Yet there is strong evidence that supports the efficacy of specific interventions that would help young people enjoy their sexual and reproductive health and rights. In particular, the International Conference on Population and Development and other international bodies have repeatedly called on governments to provide adolescents and young people with comprehensive sexuality education (CSE). CSE has been highlighted as a critical evidence-based intervention—alongside related policies like the expansion of quality sexual and reproductive health services and the creation of youth-friendly health facilities and environments—that would help stem the spread of HIV and address the health needs of adolescents and young adults, especially in high-risk regions like eastern and southern Africa.

The United Nations Population Fund's new Operational Guidance for CSE defines it as a rights-based and gender-focused approach to sexuality education, whether in school or out of school (UNFPA 2014, 6). This definition was developed in alignment with the International Conference on Population and Development's "Programme of Action" and the Commission for Population and Development resolutions of 2009 and 2012. It has evolved from international standards, including the United Nations International Technical Guidance on Sexuality Education, and is compatible with the most widely held views among donor organizations on the crucial aspects of human rights–based and gender-focused sexuality education.

While progressive legal and policy frameworks at the international, regional, and national levels support the expansion of CSE, there remains major opposition to and marginalization of CSE in sub-Saharan Africa, including opposition to educational approaches that seek to promote gender equality and human rights. Uganda provides an important window onto the debate over whether to adopt comprehensive sexuality education, especially because of the country's history of successful efforts to expand comprehensive sex education in the context of the HIV epidemic. When President Yoweri Museveni took power in Uganda in 1986, he gave priority to fighting the country's growing AIDS epidemic, spearheading a national response to HIV/AIDS that was characterized by an environment of openness, strong political commitment to AIDS awareness, and multisector government support for a wide array of prevention programs, including the expansion of a comprehensive sexual education program that was first introduced in 1995. Yet despite this history of support for CSE, sexual education remains deeply controversial in the country, and recent actions by Ugandan parliamentarians have highlighted new concerns about and resistance to CSE.

Over the past three years the debate over CSE has reached new heights in Uganda, culminating in a ban of comprehensive sexuality education by the parliament in August 2016.[1] The lawmakers argued that comprehensive sexuality education emphasizes values, practices, and behaviors that are against Ugandan customs and aspirations. The resolution by parliament halted dissemination of sexual education training materials until a new suitable policy, one that would be, in the words of parliamentarians, "values based," was put in place by the Ministry of Education and Sports. But it took more than two and a half years, until May 2018, for the ministry to develop a new framework.

This prompted the civil society organization Centre for Health Rights and Development (CEHURD) to sue the government before the high court in Kampala, Uganda, over the delay by the Ministry of Education to issue a new comprehensive sexuality education policy. In her sworn affidavit, Joy Asasira, the program manager for research and advocacy at CEHURD, stated that the delay by the ministry to put in place a policy on sexuality education had jeopardized young Ugandans' realization of their right to education and access to information.

Despite these efforts by activists advocating for the adoption of CSE, the resistance to CSE has been sustained and strong in Uganda, including numerous politicians and leaders in Uganda's religious communities. Those opposed to CSE have adopted a conservative approach exemplified by a preference for "abstinence-only" education. Abstinence-only sexual education has in recent years gained widespread support among Ugandan politicians, including the president of Uganda, Yoweri Kaguta Museveni, who proclaimed on the International Women's Day, March 8, 2012, that "our message is to put padlocks on your private parts until the time comes to open them when you have a husband." He also encouraged the public to be wary of some of the messages from foreign NGOs, a comment that highlights how sexuality education is framed by broader concerns about the influence of foreign, particularly Western, cultures and the threat such influences may pose to "traditional" Ugandan culture and gender norms (Okello and Okaba 2012). Museveni's remarks go to the core of the negative links between a patriarchal state that is intent on adopting a conservative approach to sexuality and dominant cultural and religious movements that likewise seek to propagate a particular version of piety and morality. Rights to reproductive health and sexual education are increasingly seen through a lens that characterizes such approaches as un-Ugandan, associated with a global nongovernmental realm dominated by Western cultural values. This ideology finds fertile ground in a deeply religious country where the majority subscribes to Judeo-Christian ethics that uphold "traditional" family values. Uganda's First Lady, who is also the minister of education and sports, is widely known as deeply religious. She had this to say about proposed guidelines that recommend providing teenagers with access to contraceptives: "We no longer have pride to say no. People are given contraceptives to use them and do what they want, have sex, take pills, conceive and abort. This is not our culture in Africa."[2] Her sentiments echo the fear that many Ugandan parents have about educating children about sex and about the ways sexual education is thought to lend itself to new and disruptive kinds of youth independence and agency.

The costs of ongoing restrictions on CSE is reflected not only in these high levels of HIV and pregnancies among the youth but also in the high numbers of unsafe abortions in Uganda. According to a study by the Guttmacher Institute and Makerere University (Prada et al. 2016), unsafe abortions were estimated at 314,000 in 2013. That year more than half (52 percent) of all pregnancies in Uganda were unintended, and approximately a quarter of these unintended pregnancies ended in abortion. Against this background, it is clear that the state and other stakeholders must rethink strategies for promoting adolescent sexual and reproductive health rights and that those strategies must be contingent upon creating a legal and policy environment that addresses deep-seated religious, cultural, and traditional norms.

This chapter uses the case of Uganda to explore the tensions between global and national perspectives and the ways these tensions shape the delivery of adolescent CSE and sexual and reproductive health rights (SRHR). Whereas international organizations and funders have long acknowledged the importance of adolescent CSE as an integral part of SRHR, state-level actors in Uganda continue to uphold the idea that an abstinence-only approach is a more culturally appropriate form of sexual education and in tune with religious norms. To analyze these contestations, we draw from Sally Engle Merry's (2006) theoretical framework on vernacularization to explore why, despite support from global stakeholders, comprehensive sexuality education has yet to gain national-level support in Uganda. In doing so, we examine how global human rights norms have taken shape and engaged with local cultural and political stakeholders at the national level in Uganda. The view in Uganda has largely been that the promotion of rights gives young people the unprecedented, unchecked power of choice, opening the door for them to directly violate the principles of Judeo-Christian and Ugandan traditional morality. The fears expressed by the First Lady that characterized contraceptives as providing opportunity for people to have sex and abort whenever they please lend credence to this conclusion. The bigger threat, of course, lies with the belief that promoting rights implies that people have the freedom to do whatever they want without responsibility, an argument that powerful figures within the church and state have used to characterize rights-based projects as social, moral, and political threats. The third part of the chapter therefore explores the way the state, religion, and culture have either enabled or disenabled the translation of international and regional instruments on sexual and reproductive health rights in Uganda. We include an analysis of the contested May 2018 National Sexuality Education Framework proposed by Uganda's Ministry of Education and Sports.

## Domesticating International Human Rights Laws and Norms

Feminist scholars have applied "vernacularization" as a theoretical framework to capture the important role that local agents play in making international human rights laws and ideas applicable in their local contexts. The work of vernacularization counters hegemonies of women's human rights discourse through practices such as building rights consciousness, consultations, and intersectional relationships between global and local stakeholders. Sally Engle Merry (2006), through her case studies of the translation of human rights ideas in campaigns targeting violence against women in countries as diverse as Fiji, India, and Hong Kong, found that the vernacularization of rights challenges deep-seated ideas of gender violence as a normal and natural social practice. Vernacularization recognizes that because human rights are experienced primarily in a local context, it is necessary to localize the meaning of "rights" and interrogate their communal operation (Ife and Fiske 2006; Merry and Levitt 2017). Thus, there is a need for activists to translate these rights within a local context in order to situate rights-based arguments alongside rather than in conflict with existing sociocultural norms.

There is growing evidence that efforts to promote women's human rights are viewed in many local communities as being in direct confrontation with the nation-state, as well as with local cultural norms. Those who attempt to advance a feminist agenda have been accused of being unpatriotic or complicit with the colonizers (Kapur 2002; Merry 2006). Accusations of having violated cherished traditions and national values have been leveled against activists for having the temerity to advocate for notions such as gender equality and women's bodily autonomy. It is no wonder that feminist scholars have demonstrated that women have a contentious relationship with national governments. Sealing Cheng (2011), in her study of the paradoxical effects of women's rights activism in South Korea, references Adrienne Rich's (1979) argument that the nation-state forces women into positions of complicity by demanding that they define themselves as either "loyal or disloyal" to the nation (1979, 275). Rich's analysis exposes the patriarchal underpinnings of nation-states where women and their bodies are seen as symbols of the nation. To advocate for women's liberation therefore becomes a threat to the nation, as the state loses the control it wishes to have over women's bodies, particularly their reproductive functions and sexuality.

By extension, the process of vernacularizing women's human rights—such as lobbying for new laws and their enforcement—is fraught with contradictions. As a consequence of the controlling relationship between a patriarchal nation-state and "its women," education and liberation around women's sexuality become highly contested arenas. In line with this, feminist analysis has revealed that many sex education curricula are delivered within a moralist framework that enshrines sex and sexuality within heterosexual marital relationships and exiles all other sexual identities and expressions as deviant (Jackson and Weatherall 2010, 169). This take on sex education is known among educators as the abstinence-only approach, in which refraining from sex outside marriage is the only option given to young people. Feminist and human rights advocates, both globally and within Uganda, argue that such messaging robs young people of critical information and ignores the realities of teen sexual behavior (Edwards 2016). The result of such approaches has been that male sexual needs and domination are perpetuated, thus hindering female sexual empowerment and recognition of other forms of sex and sexuality (Jackson and Weatherall 2010, 173).

Sex and sexuality, including desires and behaviors, are gendered social constructions that are transmitted, articulated, and sometimes redefined through everyday practices, religion, learning institutions, media, laws, and so forth (Baber and Murray 2001, 25–26). The feminist standpoint is therefore that sexuality education should supply students with skills and information that give them the ability to "maximize their own sexual health and satisfaction and minimize sexual exploitation of themselves and others" (23). A rights-based approach to sexuality education emphasizes the ways that sexuality is shaped by gender and cultural norms and advocates for an expansion of programmatic goals beyond reducing unintended pregnancy and sexually transmitted diseases to broaden the curriculum to include such content as gender norms, violence, and individual rights and responsibilities in relationships (Berglas, Constantine, and Ozer 2014).

This feminist approach is therefore primed for conflict with local arguments that celebrate "cultural" values as bulwarks against globally supported efforts to promote values like equality, women's agency, and youth rights. State actors have embraced values-laden discourse as a political tool, and most Ugandan political leaders have emphasized the importance of having the sexuality education curriculum adhere to the "cultural values" of Ugandan society. This ideology is apparent in several speeches and write-ups by the architects of Uganda's new sexuality education framework. The First Lady, in the foreword for the framework, bills it as "a home-grown framework that provides guidance on sexuality education to all young people . . . to protect their morals and ensure they can contribute appropriately to the nation's social and economic development" (Ministry of Education and Sports 2018, ii). During a meeting convened by Janet Museveni in 2017 to discuss the draft curriculum, Dr. Larry

Adupa, a consultant who worked on the framework, also emphasized the need for "parental involvement in sexuality education and the centrality of the family as a basic unit in society."[3] In this context, both the church and the state use the framework of the heteronormative, patriarchal family to stand in for "cultural values" and to counter global human rights frameworks for sexual education. As Uganda's debates surrounding sexual education reveal, rights-based frameworks for such projects remain deeply controversial and difficult to implement.

## The 2018 National Sexuality Education Framework and the Effort to Defend Ugandan "Values"

In response to the 2016 parliamentary ban on sexual education (in the absence of what were considered appropriate guidelines for such education), Uganda's Ministry of Education and Sports launched the National Sexuality Education Framework in May 2018 as the first-ever comprehensive national curriculum for sexuality education. The framework is considered a blueprint in guiding the teaching of age-appropriate, culturally and religiously sensitive sexuality education in schools. During the launch event, First Lady and Minister of Education and Sports Janet Museveni stated that the framework would provide holistic education that goes beyond the academic, as it empowers children with life skills and values and builds character. Representing the Inter-Religious Council, Rev. Can. William Ongeng, provincial secretary of the Church of Uganda, appealed to the government to work hand in hand with religious bodies in developing the content so that the country's values are upheld (Ahimbisibwe 2018b).

The 2018 national sexuality framework has been grouped into five categories. The early childhood group between the ages of three and five will be introduced to "knowing themselves," recognizing forms of unacceptable body touch, and developing sex refusal skills. The lessons directed to lower primary level children, between six and nine years old, will revolve around learning and discovering their talents, understanding unacceptable body touch, and appreciating the changes in male and female bodies during puberty. Upper primary, with pupils aged between ten and twelve years, are expected to define the purpose of one's life, maintain personal hygiene, and commit to sexual abstinence. The fourth group looks at lower secondary, with students between thirteen and sixteen years; the framework proposes that a child should be able to cope with risky behavioral vulnerability during puberty and be able to identify where and when to seek appropriate health services. The last group is made up of those children who are seventeen years old and above; the areas under the topic of "sexuality and relationships" to be covered include "committing oneself to sexual purity and abstinence," with the goal of imparting values that include "purity and morality, virginity, and faithfulness" (Ministry of Education and Sports 2018, 35). In sum, there is an emphasis on how to apply personal values in order to commit to premarital abstinence and marital faithfulness and to be able to appreciate the role that strong marriages and families play in national development.

In response to the new framework, Billie de Haas, assistant professor of population studies at the University of Groningen (the Netherlands), opined in an article from 2018 that "Uganda's new sex education framework will do more harm than good" because the new sex education framework is based on religious and cultural values that instruct abstinence-only teaching. Students are taught the virtues of premarital abstinence and marital faithfulness. They are also taught traditional gender roles for men and women and that masturbation and same-sex sexual relationships are not normal.

While controversial, the Ministry of Education and Sports' framework merely formalized what had already been the rule rather than the exception. Uganda has taken an abstinence-only approach in schools for a long time (De Haas 2018). It has incorporated sex education into primary and secondary schools' curricula for over fifteen years, and earlier versions of this curriculum had often emphasized abstinence over other approaches to sexual education. One prior effort to design a sexual education curriculum, the Presidential Initiative on AIDS Strategy for Communication to Youth, introduced by President Museveni in 2001, had received international criticism for only providing the abstinence option to students, as opposed to a curriculum that teaches use of condoms and other contraceptives as additional strategies for preventing HIV/AIDS transmission.

The "new" 2018 framework builds on these earlier approaches by simply refusing to acknowledge the reality of youth sexual behavior, which is that many young people are already sexually active. This is observable from the high rate of teenage pregnancies (25 percent) and unsafe abortions in the country. Pregnancy-related complications are some of the leading causes of death and disability among young Ugandan women (De Haas 2018). Based on their research on how sex education is perceived by students and sex education teachers in secondary schools in Kampala, De Haas and Inge Hutter (2017, 2018) assert that Uganda's abstinence-only approach is problematic for a number of reasons. It limits students' choices, and it prevents them from trusting, accessing, and using contraception. This in turn puts them at a higher risk of pregnancy, sexually transmitted infections, and unsafe abortions. The framework also appears aimed at sheltering students from understanding and questioning harmful gender roles, and it stigmatizes students who do not adhere to society's morally accepted norms and values.

Thus, De Haas and Hutter's argumentation reiterates what previous research on sexuality education in Uganda has found, namely, that there is a narrow view of accepted sexuality (which is expressed as heterosexual marital sex, preferably reproductive) and that there is a great disconnect between the current sexuality curricula and adolescents' lived experiences (Muhanguzi and Ninsiima 2011, 60; Rijsdijk et al. 2013, 416–20; Porter 2015). Arguably, this severely impedes the sexual health and rights of adolescents, primarily girls. Florence Muhanguzi and Anna Ninsiima's (2011, 58) research revealed that Ugandan sexuality education largely stressed girls' sexuality and downplayed boys'. This invoked a false image of sexuality problems being inextricably linked to girls' behavior, a notion that fueled sexual harassment of girls by boys, as it reinforced male dominance and male denigration of female bodies.

Because of this context, several nongovernmental organizations operating in Uganda have long supported the independent implementation of comprehensive approaches to sex education in Ugandan schools. These efforts aim to provide positive, accurate, and complete information about sexuality and to include discussions about gender and relationships. In the evaluation of one of these programs (The World Starts with Me), there was a reported improvement in class atmosphere and relationships between girls and boys.[4] Additionally, "myths concerning pregnancy decreased, perceived social norms towards delaying sex improved, and self-efficacy in dealing with sexual violence increased" (Vanwesenbeeck et al. 2016, 475).

However, studies have shown that even when teachers are given the tools to deliver CSE, the implementation remained fractured and limited, since teachers felt conflicted about delivering educational material that went against their often religiously informed moral values (Iyer and Aggleton 2014, 442–44; Tushabomwe and Nashon 2016, 338–40; Vanwesenbeeck et al. 2016, 475). This is not surprising, considering the fact that the religious block in Uganda has been one of the sources of greatest opposition to the country's efforts to advance CSE. In a study of public debate on sex and sexuality in Uganda, Barbara Bompani and S. Terreni Brown (2014) found that religious Christian discourses that conceptualize normative and normal sex as confined to heterosexual marriages with the aim of reproduction dominate Ugandan attitudes about appropriate sexual behavior. It is a view held especially by the socially and politically influential Pentecostal-Charismatic born-again Christian community.

While criticized by donors and researchers, the 2018 sex education framework has drawn widespread support from Ugandan religious leaders, especially Pentecostal-Charismatic Christians. By dint of their mass appeal, Pentecostal Christians have managed to shape attitudes about sexuality through their social and discursive power as the conceptualizers of clear dichotomies between "decency" (heterosexual marital sex) and "deviance" (everything else). The research by Bompani and Brown revealed that Pentecostal-Charismatic Christian values and morality dominate sexuality discourse to such a high extent that the rights-based approach is not considered a viable alternative on the subject. They also discovered that the media is so heavily influenced by this view that there is no reporting on "sexualities that do not conform to the hegemonic heteronormative discourse" (2014, 121).

The outsize power and influence of Pentecostal Christians are a recent phenomenon. Although smaller in number than the mainstream traditional Christian religions, Pentecostals count many political and financial elites among their members. The First Lady is a born-again Christian, and one of her daughters is a pastor at a Pentecostal church in Kampala. The proliferation of the churches coincides with the foray of the American evangelical movement into Uganda. Several Pentecostal Church leaders, supported by American funding and talking points, are known to have roused public support for Uganda's deeply controversial 2009 Anti-Homosexuality Bill, largely by drawing on similar rhetoric to that used during debates over comprehensive sexual education: a language of conservative "African" family values that celebrates heteronormative patriarchal family structures and that paints efforts at social change in the name of rights as a threat to such values. It was these same fears that compelled the Family Life Network, a Ugandan NGO that "promotes the restoration of values and morals," to petition parliament to ban CSE after a book appearing to depict a same-sex relationship between a teacher and a student was discovered at one school (Fallon 2017). (The same organization allegedly played a role in awakening antigay hysteria before the passage of the Anti-Homosexuality Bill.) It is no surprise, given this political environment, that the new sexuality framework stipulates one of the core values to be imparted as "man is created and purposed by God" (Ministry of Education and Sports 2018, 6).

Pentecostal Church leaders are not alone in their opposition to CSE. While there appeared to be cooperation between the church and the Ministry of Education and Sports in developing the framework, as evidenced by the statement of the First Lady's website in 2017 and Rev. Can. Ongeng's call for government to work with religious leaders to develop the framework's content in May 2018, it appears that the religious leaders did not ultimately get their way, and the relationship soured. Both the Catholic Church and Church of Uganda (CoU) leadership oppose the implementation of the new national framework for sexuality education in their schools unless the current content is changed to meet their long-held values. In July 2018 the *Daily Monitor* newspaper (Ahimbisibwe 2018a) reported that the plenary of the Assembly of the Catholic Bishops had issued a statement rejecting the framework, saying that while they appreciate a positive, age-appropriate sex education program that upholds moral and Christian values and reflects Ugandan culture, their input was ignored in the final sexuality education document. "In the final and published edition of the document, the contributions of the Catholic experts have been substantially ignored. As it stands now, the National Sexuality Education Framework, though containing some valid ideas and guidelines, fails to answer some crucial questions," the statement reads in part. The religious leaders were also opposed to the new framework's suggested start of sexual education at three years of age. In the same news report, Rev. Can. Ongeng articulated his opposition: "What [sexuality] can you discuss with a child of three years? What do you tell them about it?" (Ahimbisibwe 2018a). His counterparts at the Catholic Church shared the same position, insisting that the content in its current form will not be allowed unless it meets their standards.

The Ministry of Education and Sports has continued to hold consultations with the key stakeholders to ensure that a compromise is reached. This portends negatively for the advocates of CSE, who believe that a much-watered-down version will be adopted to accommodate the views of the religious and cultural leaders.

## Approaches and Barriers to the Vernacularization of Reproductive Rights and CSE

A human rights–based approach is about empowering people to know and claim their rights and increasing the ability and accountability of individuals and institutions that are responsible for respecting, protecting, and fulfilling rights. Although a rights-based approach to sexuality education has been increasingly discussed by Ugandans in the past decade, documented consensus regarding the goals, concepts, and underlying assumptions of this approach is lacking. Differences in the assumed meaning of a rights-based approach can limit its implementation and evaluation and impede opportunities to explore and critique a new model for sexuality education. This section discusses some of the ways "rights" are framed as an alternative to the "values" approach supported by many religious and political leaders and describes some of the reasons why "rights" remain a contested and controversial framework for CSE and reproductive health generally in Uganda.

In talking about rights, there is recognition not just of an individual's humanity but also of an individual's autonomy and attendant dignity and respect of their person. As articulated earlier, the conversation on rights in Uganda is fraught with the belief that it encourages permissiveness as it shifts power to individuals and loosens the state's (and traditional society's) control over them. The backlash against rights-based approaches to interventions is a reflection of the state's anxiety at losing power and control over its citizens as they assert themselves.

The structure of geopolitical power also creates conditions whereby some developing countries consider human rights as aspirational and utopian but not truly inherent or practical. There is a sense that rights are abstract concepts developed in the wealthy Global North and then imposed on the poorer South. Accountability on human rights becomes ritualistic and performative: representatives from aid-recipient states in the Global South must make periodic trips to New York or other seats of political and economic power to get their report cards. Human rights become things that these states must appear to be upholding, but in truth there is no political will or interest to do so. Remaining in the good books of the global elite means that states in the Global South can retain access to economic and political power and with it legitimacy, which in turn is required to maintain control at home. Human rights therefore become the trump card deployed by donor nations to control state behavior and make leaders in the Global South compliant. Comply and receive social and material capital; resist and get trade embargos. Adherence to human rights happens because the global order demands it, not because rights merit being upheld. In this context, the perception that human rights are a threat to sovereignty and, by extension, the values, culture, and identity of a people is never far off. It is not uncommon to hear people in Uganda say, "Will we eat rights?," apparently unaware that access to practical basic needs for sustenance constitutes a right in and of itself. Human rights are more often, by both ordinary people and state leaders, seen as tools of the global elite to manipulate donor-dependent countries rather than mechanism of liberation or positive social change.

The debate over the language and practice of SRHR and CSE has been defined by this kind of rhetoric, which characterizes "Western" values as lacking the finesse and humility with which Ugandans talk about sex. Comprehensive sexual education and reproductive health rights are easily characterized as "un-Ugandan" in this context and as opposed to "Ugandan values." The fight to restrict comprehensive sexual education is thus couched in terms of protecting Ugandan culture from the manipulation of Western donors and governments, which are viewed as imposing their own cultural values and attitudes regarding sexuality onto Ugandan society.

Yet despite this resistance to rights-based frameworks at the state level, civil society actors in Uganda have often used rights-based instruments to advance their own agendas and push back against the hegemony of state power. The 2016 parliamentary ban on CSE was challenged by several Ugandan nongovernmental actors, including the earlier mentioned effort by the group CEHURD to sue the government over the prolonged absence of sexual education guidelines. At an intergenerational dialogue organized that same year by Reach a Hand Uganda (RAHU), a youth-run nonprofit organization that emphasizes sexual health and rights, Maj. Rubaramira Ruranga, a board member of the Uganda AIDS Commission, voiced concern about the ban's effects on the country's fight against HIV/AIDS, hepatitis B, and early pregnancy. Peninah Tomusange, a Ugandan medical consultant at the United Nations Population Fund, said that the ban on comprehensive sexuality education in Uganda would affect sustainable development goals and potential achievement by 2030, adding that adolescents risk getting sick because of a lack of information on good health (Montalto 2017). CSE in these contexts is considered in terms of young people's right to self-realization, health, and reproductive choice. Furthermore, CSE is placed alongside a constellation of interventions that are understood to benefit Uganda's larger efforts at economic development. From the perspective of many international actors, as well as some local Ugandan activists, CSE is a policy shaped by broader efforts to use rights-based approaches to achieve goals of political and economic empowerment. More than a threat to cultural values, rights in these instances are discursive and legal tools that challenge and attempt to reform state power.

The debate over CSE reveals more about the complexity surrounding the deployment of rights-based frameworks to secure changes to sexual and gender-based policies in Uganda than it does a clear-cut solution to these ongoing conflicts. The Ugandan experience with the Marriage and Divorce Bill, which has languished in parliament for more than four decades without passage into law, presents another comparative study in unpacking the conflict and trade-offs in the vernacularization of rights-based frameworks. The bill first appeared in parliament as the Domestic Relations Bill in 1977. It reemerged years later, in the 2010s, as the Marriage and Divorce Bill. It was intended to "reform the law of marriage to reflect and conform to both the Constitution of Uganda, which is the supreme law in Uganda, as well as other regional and international human rights instruments that Uganda is signatory to" and to reform and consolidate the law relating to different types of marriages in Uganda (DRB Coalition 2011, 5). Some members of the public, including many religious leaders, objected not only to some of the controversial provisions within the bill but also to the name, because the combination of the two words (marriage and divorce) put them at conflict with each other. According to them, the bill suggested that women could marry and divorce at will and get rewarded for it through division of marital property at the marriage's dissolution (Otto 2017). Here the controversy played out as one that characterized "women's rights" (to marital property, child custody) as a threat to the strength of familial and marital bonds. Rights were characterized as having the ability to weaken relationships of interdependence, viewed as central to Ugandan processes of social and moral reproduction. This characterization cast the bill in a deeply unfavorable light and effectively dissolved any political capital the bill had amassed. The bill is now named the Marriage Bill, and there are indications that it could come back for tabling soon in parliament.

Arthur Larok (2018) opines that in Uganda, conservative civil society is becoming more influential, as exemplified by how conservative groups joined forces to defeat this proposed law, which would have accorded equitable rights to women over marriage and divorce. Larok states that their campaign against the Marriage and Divorce Bill was striking because Christians and Muslims united against the bill. Politicians from different parties in parliament united as well, and even some women legislators opposed the law. The defeat left Uganda's women's movement and allies shell-shocked as they sought to overcome yet another setback in a nearly five-decade struggle for gender equality. This specific example of conservative civil society's rising influence demonstrates several key lessons that are of broader relevance for the vernacularization of human rights. Efforts to promote gender equality are seen as a threat to institutions that consider themselves custodians of tradition and culture, causing anxiety in some sections of these institutions that accord them power and privilege.

Larok recommends that progressive movements engage with conservative groups by drawing on areas of convergence, which could either entice conservatives to shift their positions or weaken their collective resolve. The importance of a robust media and communications strategy to counter propaganda and deliberate disinformation cannot be understated. It is important that both genders be mobilized to actively take part in the equality and justice movement lest the struggle be stereotyped as women's selfishness—a framing that is always likely to attract negative reactions in a deeply patriarchal society. Moreover, rights-based claims to gender equity need to be framed as integral rather than external to Ugandan culture.

The current state of things indicates that there will not be much progress in getting policies on CSE and SRHR passed without changes in language. The obvious risk of compromise in language is that toothless policies (such as the present sexuality framework) are advanced. A delicate balance needs to be struck to ensure that the core essence of the legal and policy framework is preserved even as language is changed to address people's concerns with cultural sovereignty. However, a case can be made for developing a framework that can legitimize a culture of talking about sex, however piously, which can then be built on incrementally introducing more radical and responsive policies that meet young people's needs.

## Conclusion

While sexuality education remains controversial, there is growing evidence that a high standard of CSE has a positive impact on sexual knowledge, attitudes, communication skills, and behaviors. CSE has a great potential to provide young people with the necessary information about their bodies and sexuality; to reduce misinformation, shame, and anxiety; and to improve their abilities to make safe and informed choices about their sexual and reproductive health. Access to CSE may contribute to a reduction in early childbirth, unsafe abortions, sexual violence, and sexual ill health and to the promotion of gender equality and young people's overall SRHR. The benefits of CSE extend even further, as it could support youth, particularly girls, in a safe transition to adulthood and in achieving their full potential in education, earning capacity, and societal participation. Adequate access to CSE could thus contribute to the socioeconomic development of countries (Vanwesenbeeck et al. 2016, 472).

This chapter has highlighted the deeply embedded cultural, religious, and societal norms that work in tandem to uphold the abstinence-only approach that hinders CSE and legal and policy implementations that would attend to the SRHR of adolescents in Uganda. It has furthermore raised the importance of harmonization of different instruments to work together, be it in sexual and reproductive health services, CSE, legal instruments, and so forth, if we are to see a safer, healthier, and more gender equal future for Ugandan adolescents. The chapter also showed that a feminist lens is largely lacking in the vernacularization of international women's rights instruments. Ugandan legal scholar Sylvia Tamale (2014) affirms that African political struggles for sexual rights take place against the very powerful institutions of law, culture, and religion, and their terms of engagement remain contested. This means that activists have to devise creative ways of advancing their cause. For example, utilizing the framework of public health or development is found to be more strategic for some groups than espousing the language of "sexual empowerment."

Some African scholars, such as Abdullahi Ahmed An-Na'im (1992), have devoted considerable time to examining how religion and culture can be legitimately transformed to accommodate issues of human rights and constitutionalism. Given how many African people are entrenched in their traditional and religious beliefs, An-Na'im is convinced that any attempts to pursue reform must be adapted to local conditions. In other words, it is only through people's conviction and agency that social change can happen. An-Na'im argues that it is possible to integrate human rights and constitutionalism into culture and religion through a process of internal cultural transformation that is married to progressive religious interpretations. We must respect the fact that religion is a place where most Africans anchor their beliefs and values. As such, we should aim at reconstructing religion in a manner that makes it relevant to the needs of African people (particularly women), work to unlearn the dominant hegemonic religious culture, and relearn a new liberating one. Mobilizing religion as a source of rights will resonate with many African people. The challenge is for activists and scholars to develop effective praxis-oriented methods of engendering legal and social change in the quest for sexual citizenship in Africa.

## Notes

1. On August 17, 2016, the Parliament of the Republic of Uganda passed a resolution directing the Ministry of Education and Sports to ban the teaching and training of CSE in Uganda and halt dissemination of CSE training materials to schools in Uganda. On November 28, 2016, the minister of gender, labor, and social development issued a press statement to reemphasize the ban of CSE in Uganda in both school and nonschool environments (*CEHURD v. Attorney General*, Constitutional Petition No. 16 of 2011, https://www.globalhealthrights.org/africa/center-for-health-human-rights-and-development-cehurd-v-attorney-general/).

2. Uganda condemns sex education for ten-year-olds as "morally wrong" (Okiror 2017).

3. "First Lady and Minister of Education and Sports Mrs. Janet Museveni with the Members of the Inter-Religious Council of Uganda after Their Meeting at State House Nakasero on Wednesday," statement on the First Lady's website, September 15, 2017, https://janetmuseveni.org/first-lady-and-minister-of-education-and-sports-mrs-janet-museveni-with-the-members-of-the-inter-religious-council-of-uganda-after-their-meeting-at-state-house-nakasero-on-wednesday/.

4. Programs such as The World Starts with Me and others were in place before the suspension. Controversy surrounding the program was one of the reasons given for the suspension of CSE after the government alleged that its authors were "smuggling" homosexuality into their curriculum (Ahimbisibwe 2016).

## References

Ahimbisibwe, Patience. 2016. "At Least 100 Schools Tricked into Teaching Homosexuality." *Daily Monitor*, May 7. https://www.monitor.co.ug/News/Education/At-least-100-schools-tricked-into-teaching-homosexuality/688336-3192576-10r64ıy/index.html.

———. 2018a. "Church Rejects Sexuality Education in Their Schools." *Daily Monitor*, July 24. https://www.monitor.co.ug/News/National/Church-sexuality-education-schools-CoU-children/688334-4677858-121evf5z/index.html.

———. 2018b. "Government Drafts Policy on Teaching Sexuality." *Daily Monitor*, May 16. https://www.monitor.co.ug/News/National/Government-drafts-policy-teaching-sexuality/688334-4563788-jjjoqn/index.html.

An-Na'im, Abdullahi Ahmed. 1992. *Human Rights in Cross-Cultural Perspectives: A Quest for Consensus*. Philadelphia: University of Pennsylvania Press.

Baber, Kristine M., and Colleen I. Murray. 2001. "A Postmodern Feminist Approach to Teaching Human Sexuality." *Family Relations* 50 (1): 23–33.

Berglas, Nancy, Norman Constantine, and Emily Ozer. 2014. "A Rights-Based Approach to Sexuality Education: Conceptualisation, Clarification and Challenges." *Perspectives on Sexual and Reproductive Health* 46 (4): 63–72.

Bompani, Barbara, and S. Terreni Brown. 2014. "A 'Religious Revolution'? Print Media, Sexuality, and Religious Discourse in Uganda." *Journal of Eastern African Studies* 9 (1): 1–17.

Cheng, Sealing. 2011. "The Paradox of Vernacularization: Women's Human Rights and the Gendering of Nationhood." *Anthropological Quarterly* 84 (2): 475–505.

De Haas, Billie. 2018. "Uganda's New Sex Education Framework Will Do More Harm Than Good." *The Conversation*, July 1. https://theconversation.com/ugandas-new-sex-education-framework-will-do-more-harm-than-good-98634.

De Haas, Billie, and Inge Hutter. 2017. "Young People's Perceptions of Relationships and Sexual Practices in the Abstinence-Only Context of Uganda." *Sexuality, Society and Learning* 17 (5): 529–43.

———. 2018. "Teachers' Conflicting Cultural Schemas of Teaching Comprehensive School-Based Sexuality Education in Kampala, Uganda." *Culture, Health & Sexuality* 21 (2): 233–47.

DRB Coalition. 2011. *Memorandum on the Marriage and Divorce Bill 2009*. https://mifumi.org/wp-content/uploads/2017/01/MEMORANDUM-ON-THE-MARRIAGE-AND-DIVORCE-BILL2009-2011.pdf.

Edwards, Nichole. 2016. "Women's Reflections on Formal Sex Education and the Advantage of Gaining *Informal* Sexual Knowledge through a Feminist Lens." *Sex Education* 16 (3): 266–78.

Fallon, Amy. 2017. "NGOs Turn to Court to Unravel Uganda's Ban on Sexual Education." *Devex*, April 17. https://www.devex.com/news/ngos-turn-to-courts-to-unravel-uganda-s-ban-on-sexual-education-89979.

Ife, Jim, and Lucy Fiske. 2006. "Human Rights and Community Work: Complementary Theories and Practices." *International Social Work* 49 (3): 297–308.

Iyer, Padmini, and Peter Aggleton. 2014. "'Virginity Is a Virtue: Prevent Early Sex'; Teacher Perceptions of Sex Education in a Ugandan Secondary School." *British Journal of Sociology of Education* 35 (3): 432–48.

Jackson, Sue, and Ann Weatherall. 2010. "The (Im)possibilities of Feminist School Based Sexuality Education." *Feminism & Psychology* 20 (2): 166–85.

Kapur, Ratna. 2002. "The Tragedy of Victimization Rhetoric: Resurrecting the 'Native' Subject in International/Post-Colonial Feminist Legal Politics." *Harvard Human Rights Journal* 15 (1): 1–38.

Larok, Arthur. 2018. "The Conservative Alliance against Gender Justice and Equality in Uganda." In *The Mobilisation of Conservative Civil Society*, edited by Richard Youngs, 57–62. New York: Carnegie Endowment for International Peace.

Merry, Sally Engle. 2006. "Transnational Human Rights and Local Activism: Mapping the Middle." *American Anthropologist* 108 (1): 38–51.

Merry, Sally Engle, and Peggy Levitt. 2017. "The Vernacularization of Women's Human Rights." In *Human Rights Futures*, edited by Stephen Hopgood, Jack Snyder, and Leslie Vinjamuri, 213–36. Cambridge: Cambridge University Press.

Ministry of Education and Sports. 2018. "National Sexuality Education Framework." https://www.education.go.ug/files/downloads/NATIONAL%20SEXUALITY%20EDUCATION%20FRAMEWORK.pdf.

Montalto, Francesca. 2017. "The Need for Comprehensive Sexuality Education in Uganda." *Borgen Magazine*, September 8. http://www.borgenmagazine.com/comprehensive-sexuality-education-in-uganda/.

Muhanguzi, Florence Kyoheirwe, and Anna Ninsiima. 2011. "Embracing Teen Sexuality: Teenagers' Assessment of Sexuality Education in Uganda." *Agenda* 25 (3): 54–63.

Okello, Felix Warom, and Patrick Okaba. 2012. "Don't Teach Sex in Schools—Museveni." *Daily Monitor*, March 9. https://www.monitor.co.ug/News/National/688334-13 62342-9jiaqnz/index.html.

Okiror, Samuel. 2017. "Uganda Condemns Sex Education for 10-Year-Olds as 'Morally Wrong.'" *Guardian*, October 20, 2017.

Otto, Alex. 2017. "Marriage and Divorce Bill Changed." *Uganda Radio Network*, July 6. https://ugandaradionetwork.com/story/marriage-divorce-bill-changed.

Porter, Holly E. 2015. "'Say No to Bad Touches': Schools, Sexual Identity and Sexual Violence in Northern Uganda." *International Journal of Educational Development* 41:271–82.

Prada, Elena, Lynn M. Atuyambe, Nakeisha M. Blades, Justine M. Bukenya, Christopher Garimoi Orach, Akinrinola Bankole. 2016. "Incidence of Induced Abortion in Uganda, 2013: New Estimates since 2003." *PLoS ONE* 11 (11): e0165812.

Rich, Adrienne. 1979. "Disloyal to Civilization: Feminism, Racism, Gynephobia." In *On Lies, Secrets and Silence: Selected Prose 1966–1978*, edited by Adrienne Rich, 275–315. New York: W. W. Norton.

Rijsdijk, Liesbeth E., Rico Lie, Arjan E. Bos, Joanne N. Leerlooijer, and Gerjo Kok. 2013. "Sexual and Reproductive Health and Rights: Implications for Comprehensive Sex Education among Young People in Uganda." *Sex Education* 13 (4): 409–22.

Strode, Ann, Rofiah Sarumi, Zaynab Essack, and Priya Singh. 2018. "A Feminist Critique of Legal Approaches to Adolescent Sexual and Reproductive Health Rights in Eastern and Southern Africa: Denial and Divergence versus Facilitation." *Agenda* 32 (1): 76–86.

Tamale, Sylvia. 2014. "Exploring the Contours of African Sexualities: Religion, Law and Power." *African Human Rights Law Journal* 14 (1): 150–77.

Tushabomwe, Annette, and Samson Madera Nashon. 2016. "Interpreting Teachers' Perceptions of Contextual Influences on Sexuality Discourses within the School Curriculum: Lessons from Sex Health Education Teachers in Kampala, Uganda." *Canadian Journal of Science, Mathematics and Technology Education* 16 (4): 331–44.

UNAIDS. 2017. *UNAIDS Data 2017*. https://www.unaids.org/sites/default/files/media_asset/20170720_Data_book_2017_en.pdf.

United Nations Population Fund (UNFPA). 2014. *UNFPA Operational Guidance for Comprehensive Sexuality Education: A Focus on Human Rights and Gender*. New York: UNFPA. https://www.unfpa.org/sites/default/files/pub-pdf/UNFPA_OperationalGuidance_WEB3.pdf.

Vanwesenbeeck, Ine, Judith Westeneng, Thilly de Boer, Jo Reinders, and Ruth van Zorge. 2016. "Lessons Learned from a Decade Implementing Comprehensive Sexuality Education in Resource Poor Settings: *The World Starts with Me*." *Sex Education* 16 (5): 471–86.

# 6

 Family Violence in the Refugee Claims of Asylum Seekers from West Africa

CHARLOTTE WALKER-SAID

In early 2011 a Cameroonian woman was trafficked to Chicago, Illinois, from Douala, Cameroon, by her extended family members. She expected to begin salaried work as a nanny and housekeeper in Chicago for her relatives upon her arrival but instead was forced to work without pay for the next five years. Her experience became part of a federal trafficking case, as well as a civil suit against her traffickers for unpaid wages, that lasted from 2016 to 2017.[1] After going to the police and filing paperwork with US Citizen and Immigration Services—nearly five years after she had arrived in the United States—"Christine" received a T1 trafficking visa.[2] Christine also filed a protective order in the US District Court for the Northern District of Illinois against the Cameroonian American individuals who trafficked and exploited her and filed a civil suit against them for unpaid wages.[3] In 2017 Christine successfully won her civil suit against her traffickers and indenturers.

Christine had gathered a wealth of evidence that her traffickers had deceived and exploited her (as well as brought her to the United States illegally), but proving her claim rested on demonstrating that her relatives—her *own family*, as it were—misled and exploited her and that she did not owe them her labor as a familial obligation. In short, the court was asked to determine what were the duties and obligations of family membership and what constituted

125

unfair treatment in a family context in Christine's case. This was complicated by the fact that Christine demonstrated loyalty to her family as much as she showed she was victimized by them.

This chapter analyzes the phenomenon of "family violence" as it has been experienced by claimants, litigants, and asylum seekers from the West African country of Cameroon for whom I have testified as an expert witness in American courts of law. These claimants have forwarded claims of protection or redress on the basis of trafficking, forced marriage, intimate partner violence, and family-based violence (violence committed by relatives, such as female circumcision, discipline for homosexuality, and honor crimes), as well as rape, incest, concubinage, indentured servitude, enslavement, and widow inheritance—all of which constitute violations of individual rights and dignity by members of the individual claimant's family.[4] This chapter also demonstrates the paradoxes of family violence, in which those exploited by their kin and relations often remain in their households for extended periods of time, providing labor and experiencing forms of reciprocity that complicate the issue of family-based violence. In exploring this issue, the chapter reveals what Peter Geschiere refers to as the "riddle" of how family bonds can endure despite terrible suspicions.[5] Geschiere was one of the first to recognize that violence can come as much from inside the family as from outside it. He also convincingly posits that violence by intimate relations does not necessarily destroy or sever relations because of the conditions of what lies beyond the domestic sphere. It is thus in the space of the state and the reach of its power (or lack thereof) where the behaviors of family members take their shape.

The public/private divide as conceived by modern liberalism has direct implications for how African women negotiate claims for protection and redress against forms of family violence. Seyla Benhabib's analysis of various meanings of the "private sphere" in modern political thought forwards that "privacy has been understood as the sphere of moral and religious conscience" and that even in modern liberal societies, government has regarded the household, or the "intimate sphere," as a space formally and informally "outside" the "political sphere," where the values of equality and consent reign (1998, 86). Legal scholar and immigration law practitioner Karen Musalo claims there is "a historical resistance to recognizing women's rights as human rights" (2014, 46), but when examining violence against women more broadly, one encounters even more resistance to recognizing violations by family members as constituting serious violations worthy of recognition in the form of compensation, remedy, or refugee protection.[6]

In explaining domestic spaces as sites of insecurity and violence to American judges overseeing cases involving West Africans, experts and advocates must weave together both macroscale analyses of the forms of violence experienced and microinvestigations that examine the individual in their social setting. Testimonies that deploy family-based violence to justify various kinds of claims (the right to compensation or the right to immigrate) reveal both deep bonds and painful conflicts within African communities that must be carefully positioned within what geographer Jennifer Fluri describes as a "broad spectrum of violence" (2011, 280). In this chapter, the "broad spectrum" is the socioeconomic context in which family violence in Cameroon takes place and how, specifically, severe poverty created by state policy gives rise to social relationships in which exploitation and various forms of violence are routine features.

Within this volume, this chapter illuminates the late capitalist context in which a particular African state (Cameroon) determines economic realities for its citizens and how this reality ultimately annihilates many rights-based projects and protections. Specifically, Cameroon also does not fully comply with the Convention on the Elimination of All Forms of Discrimination Against Women (CEDAW). Even though the Cameroon government has ratified the convention, public awareness of the protections that CEDAW offers women is not widespread, and violence and discrimination against women are still enshrined in Cameroon's national laws and affirmed in its customary practices (OMCT International Secretariat 2004; Nkwidja 2006; United Nations 2008; Muma 2014). This volume as a whole investigates how human rights arguments are embedded in African statecraft and in forms of African political agency, but this chapter proposes that human rights arguments positioned in law are undercut by economic realities that are oftentimes beyond the capabilities of African governments to implement. Thus, in their current form, international human rights and the national laws they inspire are rendered purely utopian ideals within neoliberal globalization. Moreover, as humanitarianism has emerged as the most salient, visible, and practiced form of human rights in Africa, and the private sphere is often beyond the reach of humanitarian initiative (focused as it is on crisis and rupture rather than what exists as a steady state), family/domestic spaces continue to be ones in which human rights struggle to be defined, let alone implemented.

### How the State Shapes the "Private" Sphere: Legislation and Adjudication

Family violence has occupied an uncertain and uncomfortable space in American law as in legal systems of countries around the world. In 1824 an American court judged in the case of *Calvin Bradley v. The State* (of

Mississippi) that "family broils and dissensions" are often best left as private matters so as "to screen from public reproach those who may be thus unhappily situated" and prevent "mutual discredit and shame" of the family members involved.[7] In 1978 there were only nine US states that had legislation addressing the issue of domestic violence (Schelong 1994, 95). In a similar vein, there are no laws against spousal abuse, marital rape, or other forms of family violence such as forced marriage in the West African countries of Cameroon, Côte d'Ivoire, and Burkina Faso, and other countries either have no specific penalties for family violence or encourage the settlement of family violence through private (nongovernmental) mediation (Zellner 2003; International Rescue Committee 2012; Amnesty International 2015; Immigration and Refugee Board of Canada 2016b). The US government formally recognized family violence as a federal crime only recently with the passage of the 1994 Violence Against Women Act (VAWA), reauthorizing and expanding it in 2000 and again in 2005. As the report to the UN Special Rapporteur on Violence Against Women states, "The passage of VAWA was unquestionably a bellwether moment in the fight against domestic violence in the United States" (Bettinger-Lopez et al. 2011). However, on its own, VAWA does not and cannot fulfill the United States' obligation to prevent, investigate, and punish violations of violence by family members inside the domestic space or within family networks.

In keeping with American traditions of construing family violence as "private" and beyond the reach of the law, on June 11, 2018, US attorney general Jefferson Sessions overturned a precedential asylum decision known as *Matter of A-R-C-G-*, 26 I&N Dec. 388 (BIA 2014), which dramatically altered the security prospects of tens of thousands of foreign women seeking refuge in the United States as a result of fleeing domestic violence in their home countries. The June 11 decision, *Matter of A-B-*, Respondent 27 I&N Dec. 316 (AG 2018), effectively ruled that victims of domestic violence rarely meet the definition of a refugee from persecution.[8] Sessions's reasoning addressed a number of factors limiting victims of domestic violence from qualifying for asylum, including rejecting victims' characterizations of themselves as members of a "particular social group" and arguing that most domestic violence victims suffer from "private violence," which is not equivalent to "persecution."[9] In short, Attorney General Sessions issued a decision declaring that family violence was "violent conduct of a private actor . . . someone unaffiliated with government."[10]

Although the decision of US District Court judge Emmet G. Sullivan in *Grace v. Whitaker* blocked US Citizenship and Immigration Services (USCIS) from applying the standards set forth in a policy memo to its asylum officers implementing the decision of former attorney general Sessions in *Matter of*

*A-B-*, it remains unclear whether the legal theories recognizing victims of domestic violence as refugees based on their particular social group that were stipulated to and memorialized in *Matter of A-R-C-G-* are entirely vacated or if they must be reformulated.[11] In the current moment, debates continue in immigration courtrooms across the United States as to whether violence by family members constitutes "persecution."

The early twenty-first century witnessed considerable dispute and inconsistency on the central issue of whether women fleeing domestic violence were entitled to asylum protection. As a result of Sessions's overturning of *Matter of A-R-C-G-* and Sullivan's subsequent decision in *Grace v. Whitaker*, which is binding on USCIS asylum officers but not necessarily on immigration judges, the legal standard once again is very unclear (Musalo 2014, 45). But claims for protection arising from gender-motivated rights violations have never been considered straightforward in the American immigration law system, and the definitions of "persecution" have never been precise—nor consistently applied—in American immigration rulings.[12] Likewise, as I witnessed in a civil case, there are significant barriers to proving that loyal family relations contain within them the possibility of severe violence. The difficulties of demonstrating how labor relations in a family context (labor by family members in a domestic space) can meet the definition of exploitation (i.e., unfair to the advantage of another) or enslavement (i.e., subjugation under the control of another) in a court of law, *especially* when assumptions about "traditional culture" come into play, confirm that African citizens must struggle all the more to define and claim their human rights.

What is necessary for fully and honestly assessing whether family violence constitutes persecution is an examination of structural factors such as poverty, youth unemployment, corruption, gender discrimination, educational underinvestment, and ineffective judicial systems and their devastating effects in the domestic sphere, including (1) the strengthening of the family network as the only "trust network" in the lives of citizens (Tilly 2010) and (2) the politics of inequality that support the rise of family, clan, and/or community leaders who assume responsibility while disempowering lower-ranked members.

Drawing on the work of feminist political geography (Oberhauser et al. 2018) and building on Fluri's (2015) work revealing the critical dimensions of seemingly apolitical sites and situations to better conceive of civilian security, this chapter examines family welfare as part of rather than separate from human security and the realization of human rights. African family life, rather than operating in an apolitical space, is deeply reflective of the political and economic insecurity of West African states. Therefore, Sessions's reasoning that domestic violence is "the violent conduct of a private actor ... someone unaffiliated with government" is operating under a fantasy of a "private sphere" that is neutral and apolitical and in which its members' behaviors and choices are disconnected from the realities crafted by government. Extending what Fluri (2011, 280) and other feminist political geographers have argued, which forwards that corporeal sites (i.e., human bodies) can no longer be considered apolitical, this chapter demonstrates that "private" social formations that attack or coerce bodies must also be considered in a political frame, as the precarity produced in intimate spaces is truly a function of statist and geopolitical dictates.

### Trafficking in Human Relations in Cameroon: Poverty, Family, and Interdependency

In Cameroon, young female family members are typically targeted for various forms of trafficking. In the case referred to at the start of this chapter, Christine, a young woman from Douala, traveled to the United States and worked in childcare and household labor for her relatives with the understanding that she would eventually be paid for her work (although she was not paid for many years). Christine's low social standing—defined by her poverty and low level of education relative to her family members who trafficked her—made it possible to convince Christine to travel to a foreign country and to maintain assumptions about promises of payment her relative/trafficker had made for years. But while Christine's loyalty was enforced through dependency, it was also shaped by social practices of reciprocity and mutuality that also contain elements of deception, unequal exchange, and advantage taking that have become commonplace in the past half century in Cameroon.

The United States Department of State (2013) has stated definitively that "Cameroon is a source, transit, and destination country for children subjected to forced labor and sex trafficking and a country of origin for women subjected to forced labor and forced prostitution." It has also stated, "The Government of Cameroon does not fully comply with the minimum standards for the elimination of trafficking." The nonprofit group Trauma Centre for Victims of Human Trafficking in Cameroon has been working to bring relief to women who have returned from situations where they were trafficked abroad. The center's vice president, Beatrice Titanji, has "called on the government to investigate and prosecute the agents, create jobs and mount guard at airports to discourage Cameroonians from [being trafficked]" (Chimtom 2015). However, little action has been taken by the government.

In the interviews that I conducted with Christine, she repeated that after two years of working without being paid (her relative/trafficker told her that she was putting Christine's salary into a bank account but did not allow her to access this bank account or indicate where it was), she eventually realized that her relative/trafficker was being "purely dishonest." However, even after becoming conscious of her manipulation, she continued to rely on her relatives and maintained the belief that they would eventually fulfill their pledges to compensate her. In other words, Christine was invested in her family cell and believed that with repeated requests, pleas, and reminders of their obligations, her relatives would eventually rectify the situation, making her unpaid work only a "temporary" state. Christine believed that pay for her work was possibly or even likely to be forthcoming in her future, despite comprehending that she had not been paid for many years. She reasoned that since she was completely dependent on her relatives for her livelihood, her relatives would have to acknowledge their duty to her and meet the terms of their arrangement, not because of a threat that she would go to the police or force their compliance but because the obligations of kin were so long-standing that mistreatment or exploitation was likely to be impermanent. This was a passing phase in the long cycles of a family relationship. In sum, Christine considered her exploitation to be an unpleasant cost of being part of a secure network that provided opportunities and that it was preferable to the prospects of seeking alliances with nonkin (police, social workers, etc.), which would rupture any kin dependencies and understandings of mutuality and could only result in a more permanent exploitation or ostracism.

A member of the Cameroonian family that had trafficked Christine testified in the family's defense, attesting, "Christine was with us everywhere we used to go. . . . She took care of the children and the chores like any member of the family." When discussing the work Christine had been brought to the United States to do, the family member stated: "It was more like doing a favor to a family member, extended family member." Lastly, the family member described Christine (a middle-aged woman with two children) as being "like one of the big kids who helps out with the little kids."[13] These statements speak to the understanding by the defendants that as a "member of the family" and "a big kid," or very nearly an older sibling, Christine assisted the family with requisite chores rather than performing a "job" that occupied sixteen hours of the day (as Christine testified). By not receiving any compensation, vacation time, days off, or sick leave, Christine was perceived as simply a family member "helping" rather than an employee performing labor.

International human rights organizations have unveiled that enslavement and forced labor have increased significantly in recent years in Cameroon (Kazé 2009; United States Department of State 2015). My own fieldwork in Cameroon and in the United States among Cameroonian asylum seekers has revealed to me that uncles, aunts, cousins, and extended kin—who are often referred to as "other mothers" and "brothers" to note their personal closeness with the individuals being interviewed—take over responsibilities for the care and well-being of younger or more vulnerable family members and, as a result, often obtain considerable power over them.[14] My interviews have revealed how transgressions and violations are enacted in the family sphere and how they result in situations of unbearable exploitation, including trafficking, forced marriage, and systematic sexual abuse. Nicolas Argenti's work in the Cameroon Grassfields has examined what he terms "the paradox of kinship systems: a tension at the heart of the affective life of the family," in which he perceives the family as a problematic and unreliable ally (2007, 2011). Argenti writes, "Over the past four centuries and right up to the 1930s . . . children were abducted into slavery, sometimes with the tacit consent or even the connivance of their parents, and still today many mothers send one or more of their children into foster care from a young age. In many cases, contemporary fosterage arrangements consign children to harsh conditions that they endure for protracted periods of time before returning home" (2011, 269). Argenti argues that socioeconomic strains from the early twentieth century through the present day have eroded the previously sacrosanct protective capacities of mothers and fathers and transferred the oversight and management of children to the most powerful elders and elites within the family network, who frequently exploit them.

Likewise, Geschiere (2003) emphasizes that one must not romanticize kinship and recognize that the increased scale of social relations by African societies has in fact made kinship both durable and potentially harmful. Put simply, as Africans engage with a broader and more diverse set of people, they come into contact with threats and vulnerabilities that make them aware of the precariousness of living out in the wider world—in urban centers and as migrants and expatriates. This makes African citizens adhere to their family networks as critical economic providers and social ties. This "holding together" of family members does not necessarily reinforce mutual affection or devotion; rather, it can cause strain. Geschiere focuses on higher status or wealthier kin who can "feel entrapped by the obligations of kinship" but who also command commitments and obligations from those they assist or protect.

Studies also point to the Cameroonian government's general lack of attention to this issue and refusal to address labor exploitation and trafficking in a strategic or serious way. Press reports repeatedly echo the troubling trend of trafficking Cameroonian girls abroad to work as maids or in service positions (Gwanfogbe 2015). Their traffickers often lure their own extended family members with promises to find them jobs, connect them with employers, locate housing for them, and assist them with the immigration process and paperwork. However, in reality, these women and children face dire circumstances in their working and living conditions (Chimtom 2015; Gwanfogbe 2015). The general lack of care for women and children in Cameroon and the lack of police protection form the link between increasingly high rates of exploitation and trafficking.

Since the economic crisis hit Cameroon in the 1980s, leading to multiple salary slashes, unemployment, daily price hikes, and general economic hardship, many Cameroonians began losing their ability to maintain their dignity by demanding just wages and working conditions (Fonchingong and Gemandze 2009). Trafficking in women became one of many symptoms of general economic malaise. Trafficking female family members has become a way for families to generate more income and use their assets to the greatest economic advantage. This reality is unfortunately extremely common in Cameroon, where women—particularly young women or women with children—are wards of their extended families, and they can be transferred, exchanged, given in marriage, or given as labor to any person or persons by the family (Roeland and Boerma 2004; Walker 2010). The High Commission of Canada in Cameroon (2015) has stated: "Many women in Cameroon are handed over to the custody of those claiming to provide free education or paid work." Being a poor woman in Cameroon very much implies a lack of the right to self-determination, as lower-status women are not only wards but also required to perform duties to those who assume care or authority over them (Domowitz 1981; Nsagha et al. 2012).

## The Political Economy of Cameroonian Family Networks and Its Significance in Cases of Sexual Violence within the Family

In asylum seeker testimonies and interviews with locals in Cameroon, individuals commonly attest to being victimized through forced marriage, which includes child marriage, arranged marriage, and widowhood rites such as levirate or sororate, as well as rape, incest, and sexual assault within the family. In nearly all the testimonies I have read, observed, or organized, the victim understood after the fact that the abuse was considered an obligation owed to the perpetrator or enacted to extract compensation in exchange for security (Ngoutsop 2017, 178).

In 1992 a group of African pediatricians published an article on the increase in cases of child rape in Cameroon, stating, "Child victims of sexual abuse and the severe physical trauma they endure . . . is a medicosocial reality which is new in Cameroon and needs attention" (World Health Organization 2010, 45–48). Many public health workers have likewise reported that in the case of Cameroon, rape and incest are taking up "more and more public space" (Ngoutsop 2017, 179). There are daily reports of rapes in the media and in community news forums, and one study demonstrated that in 2007, 4.69 percent of all medical reports filled in Cameroon's hospitals were for sexual assaults on minors (Bang 2007, 37). The nongovernmental organization EIP Cameroon, which is backed by the Canadian government and local child protection organizations, estimates that 40 percent of children are sexually abused in Cameroon (Voice of America 2011). Moreover, according to the German development agency GTZ (Gesellschaft für Internationale Zusammenarbeit), "Nearly one-fifth of the some 432,000 people raped in Cameroon were raped by a family member (based on interviews with 37,719 people across the country)." Flavien Ndonko, anthropologist and head of GTZ's HIV/AIDS program, has reported that rape in Cameroon has increased sharply over the years: "In the 1970s cases of rape were extremely rare—0.1 percent of women and girls. But since the 1980s we are seeing an explosion of sexual attacks, targeting adolescents in particular" (Ndonko et al. 2009, 14–15).[15]

A growing body of research points to the increasing levels of family-based child sexual assault and incest in Cameroon, which speaks to the authority and power held within family networks, the weak position of the police and the law vis-à-vis the family domain, and the increasing desperation of the country's citizens, who turn on their most vulnerable and easily exploitable individuals in their kin networks to instrumentalize their influence and authority over them for personal gain. In 2011 Catherine Moto Zeh, the secretary-general of the international NGO School as an Instrument of Peace, stated: "The sexual abuse of children in Cameroon is far more rampant than previously thought" (Voice of America 2011). The World Health Organization (WHO) notes that about 13 percent of school-going children in sub-Saharan Africa are sexually abused. In Cameroon, watchdog organizations say the figure in 2009 was closer to 40 percent, and of those, almost every fifth attack was carried out by a family member (Lazareva 2017). Officials in the Ministry of Social Affairs say the numbers are exaggerated, but they have no statistics. Even the Ministry of Women's Empowerment and the Family admits they rely nearly entirely on civil society organizations to address the issue of child sexual abuse, rape, and incest in Cameroon (Lazareva 2017). Cameroon has ratified several treaties protecting children, but they are not strictly enforced. The Cameroon Society for the Prevention of Child Abuse and Neglect says the few abusers who are eventually taken to court are either acquitted for lack of enough evidence or are given lenient sanctions. Sometimes perpetrators offer money to relatives of victims to avoid prosecution or threaten the victims so they will keep quiet. The widespread phenomenon in Cameroon of "breast ironing," or using a hot roller to pound and massage a pubescent girl's breast buds with the intent of protecting a child from the attention of the opposite sex and avoiding rape and early pregnancy, confirms the widespread nature of sexual violations against women and girls in the country (Chishugi and Franke 2016).

One way to comprehend this disturbing phenomenon is to uncover the uncommon strength of dependencies in family networks in Cameroon. These networks reflect the security or insecurity of their various members and are often negotiated through marriages, sexual exchanges, and/or presumed sexual permissions. One example of dependencies creating insecurities is described by Cameroonian anthropologist Péguy Ndonkou. In this instance a woman sent her eldest daughter to live with the woman's brother after her husband's death, knowing that the daughter's uncle had more capacity to provide for her. The girl's uncle then proceeded to rape her for the next nine years. According to Ndonkou's (2015) interviews, the uncle determined that sexual access was an obligatory indemnity for providing living and schooling expenses and mitigated the burden of taking in vulnerable family members. Several Cameroonians with whom I have worked have echoed such accounts of rape and sexual assault by members of their family either as children who were violated by caretakers or substitute parents during situations of parental incapacity or as adults who were violated by those from whom they received temporary or long-term financial assistance.[16]

Ndonkou's (2015) analysis reveals that in a great number of the interviewed victims who were raped, the perpetrators depended on the pressures to maintain family solidarity to shield them from criticism, censure, or punishment for their assaults, while the victims experienced the pressure to maintain family solidarity at all costs. Knowing that very few victims will risk unsettling family solidarities or straining the bonds and alliances within the family unit, family members who commit acts of sexual (or other forms of) violence against individual kin typically do so without facing consequences. Moreover, the consequences would be potentially most devastating for the family of the victim, who would have to decide punitive measures or manage the separation of the perpetrator from the family cell, thereby removing a (likely) valuable member of a vulnerable unit that depends on his or her membership to survive. Cohesion is institutionalized in family units not through long-standing traditions of unity—as many anthropologists presumed in previous decades—but rather through severe political and economic insecurity, which necessitates a structure of dependency (Ndonko et al. 2009, 12–14).

Charnelle Lumière, a Cameroonian rape and incest survivor who is a member of RENATA, known as "the national aunties network," which assists victims of sexual abuse, incest, violence, and early pregnancy, recounted that when she sought shelter with a neighbor after being raped by her uncle at the age of thirteen, she was allowed to stay only one night. The neighbor confided to Lumière, "What happens in the family, should stay in the family, one should never interfere," and sent the young girl back home (Lazareva 2017). As Lumière's case demonstrates, not only do *members* of families maintain cohesion, but *outsiders* also enforce societal attitudes and behaviors, promoting family unity as essential to security provision, even in the face of demonstrable evidence that it is causing profound *violations* of individual security, welfare, and human rights.

Ndonkou (2015) argues that the resurgence of rape and incest in Cameroonian society is in large part a result of a "rise in sectarian practices" and "the total social and economic insecurity in which Cameroonian families flounder." This analysis dovetails with that of John Chishugi, who argues that Cameroonian societies "maintain strong communal cultural roots where the 'good of society' is often paramount" (Chishugi and Franke 2016, 625–26). Highly localized loyalties and alliances stand in when state or regional welfarism collapses, tightening the bonds of kinship, even in the face of brutality or violence committed by members of the kin group. Even if trust is broken between individual members of the kin group, the belief in the stability and security of the collective and its redistributive powers and surety provision withstands interpersonal conflicts or abuses. West African sociologist Moïse Tamekem Ngoutsop (2017, 178) argues that the family is a "micro-context" in which violence against women can be witnessed and interpreted. Interpersonal relations in the family and the clan are *affected* by intrafamilial sexuality, but they are not *determined* by them (178). In other words, violations against women, junior men, or less powerful members can be tolerated in order to maintain the integrity of the only organizational structure that can counter scarcity and extreme deprivation.

### Feminist Political Geography and the Translation of Political-Economic Inequality to Family Inequality

Feminist political geographers have confirmed that both poverty *and* inequality, or wealth gaps, are forms of structural violence (Roberts 2008; Fluri 2015). Numerous West African countries exhibit this fundamental kind of human insecurity, which domestic spaces both mirror and attempt to mitigate in a variety of ways. The United Nations describes many countries in

West Africa as experiencing "intensive" deprivations in education, health, and living conditions and term this state "severe multidimensional poverty" (United Nations Development Programme 2016). The UN Development Programme describes Cameroon as exhibiting a high number of households living in severe multidimensional poverty and ranks it as a "low human development category," positioning it at 153 out of 188 countries and territories in terms of development. Cameroon suffers from what economists have summarized as "limited inclusiveness of economic growth and low growth" and "present disparities in the redistribution of economic growth" (Tabi Atemnkeng and Mbu Tambi 2018, 56). Poverty reductions in urban areas have been matched by poverty increases in rural areas (57).

While UNDP surveys carefully include gender comparisons for each country and investigate beyond mere income poverty to include assessments of other serious forms of deprivation and dispossession, including political oppression, there are few comprehensive studies on how material and political privation is linked to violence in the family domain. Localized studies from throughout the Global South have linked economic crisis to the commodification of marriageable girls and women; authoritarianism has been linked to the revival of local customs that encourage misogynistic practices and demand generational and gender conformity; and sectarian politics can influence the entrenchment of forms of behavioral control, leading to the disciplining of heterodoxy or individuality, which is often carried out by kin or elders (Ngou 2007; Jean-Baptiste 2008; Burrill, Roberts, and Thornberry 2010; Glass 2014; Puttick and Minority Rights Group International 2015).

Emily Burrill and Richard Roberts (2010) have explored how the colonial transition and the violence it wrought contributed to domestic and family violence in French Soudan. Burrill and Roberts examined domestic violence in a context where shifts or disruptions "threaten the obligations and expectations that b[ind] people together in hierarchical relationships" (33). Their work brings greater nuance to the feminist political geography discourse on seemingly apolitical sites as spaces of political violence by demonstrating that societies under pressure and in transition demonstrate an impetus to form new family units and new social networks, which are often achieved through exchanges and marriages and, more explicitly, the caregiving, servitude, and/or sexual labor (imposed, coerced, or uncompensated) of women or children. Burrill and Roberts examined the "moral economy of the household"—or systems of exchange and materiality embedded in the mores and values governing marriage and the family (34). The moral economy of the household is affected by the political economy of the state when the state imposes threats (or fails to control threats) that disrupt interpersonal mutuality and fair, equitable interdependence among family groups. Therefore, one of the ways the family is "made political" and thus central to different kinds of rights-based claims is in the ways structural violence, political disenfranchisement, and economic marginalization play out at the level of the family.

While trust networks in Cameroon are almost entirely based on ethnicity and language and have historically been strong, contemporary realities of severe poverty, a contracting economy, an entrenched dictatorship, and limited job opportunities have created an atmosphere that is ripe for exploiting one's trust network for personal gain (Africa Desk 2008; Pemunta 2011; Doumara 2012; Caballero 2014; Mouendé 2014). In some societies and regions in Cameroon, one's extended family members are considered emotionally closer and beholden to greater obligations to assist one than one's own biological parents (Todd 1982, 85; Essomba Fouda 2010, 34–35). Reciprocally, young family members often are entrusted with greater obligations to serve and minister to powerful relatives and elders than to their own parents (Argenti 2011).

Data gathered as part of my work representing victims of family-based violence indicate that despite the incidence of abuse and exploitation of family members by their more powerful kin, low-status individuals, those with little access to education, salaried positions, or regular incomes, are often eager to trust those blood relations who make promises or offers of assistance in matrimony, employment, schooling, political favors, or finances. Distressingly, as extended family members have considerable authority over their relations, depending on other kinds of power they possess in terms of their income, inherited cultural position, social class, or political connections, they frequently are in a position to abuse their relations, whether through sexual abuse, exploitation, trafficking, arranged marriage, forced labor, or other forms of indenture or servitude (Koki Ndombo et al. 1992; Voice of America 2011; United States Department of Labor 2015; United States Department of State 2015).

In American courts of law, both judges and many lawyers working on cases of family violence involving African claimants operate with the beliefs that kinship is resilient because it constitutes a safety net, a safe harbor, and a benevolent and sympathetic bonded group. To better understand social patterns and recent traditions, an expert witness is charged with untangling the paradox of kinship ties that remain durable despite the fact that they can be injurious to certain members of the kin group and advantageous to others. Geschiere writes that despite the tensions of mutual obligations, the family bond endures and lineage or kin networks cohere because of the increasingly perilous prospects of seeking cooperation or advantageous connections outside of the family sphere. Many of the African asylum seekers with whom I have worked are typically seeking refuge from persecution committed by their family members but often jeopardize their own claims by demonstrating that they were reluctant to sever their kinship ties, as their actions indicate a marked distinction from testimonies and claims of those suffering persecution by government agents.

The labor and sexual exploitation of women and children by their family members is important for understanding power dynamics and the mutation of the concept of "wealth in people" that has been occurring in late twentieth-century and early twenty-first-century Cameroon. Family networks throughout the world, but especially in Cameroon, are rife with uneven levels of socioeconomic status, cultural and political prestige, and rural and urban divisions, creating conditions that are ripe for both competition and exploitation.

According to Gus Correa, group supervisor for the US government's Homeland Security Investigation's local Anti-Trafficking Coordination Team, "All traffickers do the same thing. . . . They prey on people who are vulnerable. . . . They strip away their identity" (Bankston and Martinez 2014). However, in the case of Christine, who was trafficked by her extended family, while she was vulnerable, her relatives did not strip away her identity as much as they imposed (and enforced) her identity as *kin*, that is, as a constituent member of the private sphere performing household chores essential for achieving solidarity and cohesiveness of that sphere. By simultaneously emphasizing Christine's vulnerability and her security only within the kinship domain, her traffickers were able to ensure her loyalty and obligation for many years.

### Conclusion: Possibilities for Recognition, Remedy, and Redress

Christine was lucky to extricate herself from a trafficking situation and receive compensation for her unpaid work through litigation in an American court of law. In Cameroon, however, there are few means of redress for those who are abused, exploited, or trafficked by their family members. Without specifying the region or the outcome, the US Department of State country report on human rights practices for 2011 indicated that the courts in Cameroon heard *one* case of forced labor in 2010 (United States Department of State 2012), and the 2013 report claimed that the Cameroon courts secured *one* conviction for child trafficking in that year. Overall, in 2013 Cameroon only initiated five trafficking prosecutions, even though "sources indicated that 120 cases of trafficking and related offenses, including kidnapping of minors, kidnapping with fraud and violence, forced marriage, and slavery, were reported to law enforcement and NGOs in the Littoral, South West, and South regions in Cameroon in that year" (United States Department of State 2013).

Despite the fact that trafficking and family violence are widespread and a problem affecting hundreds or even thousands of women and young people across the country, the government of Cameroon does not effectively police or prosecute (let alone convict) those who have committed crimes of this nature. This means that others in Cameroon like Christine have very little hope that the government or judiciary will lend support for the cause of assisting those in abusive family or domestic arrangements. Therefore, asylum and refugee status in the United States are critical outlets for many individuals fleeing family violence and forms of domestic and family exploitation in Cameroon and other parts of Africa. In many ways, crime and exploitation can be understood as a diagnostic of intimacy rather than an indication of wrongful acts between unfamiliar bodies that are purely motivated by the self. Rather than operating within the dynamics of society or unrelated groups, family violence and exploitation are microcontexts in which the stressors and conflicts of the "broad spectrum" exact their toll on individuals.

As many studies show, not only is poverty increasing in Cameroon, but income inequality is also rising, which further diminishes the economic prospects of everyday people (Johannes, Etoh-Anzah, and Tafah 2009). As public expenditure on health care, education, and other economic investments decreases, Cameroon's citizens are increasingly turning to their kin networks for assistance (Nyamnjoh and Rowlands 1998; Pelican, Tatah, and Ndjio 2008). Geschiere terms this phenomenon "the stretching of kinship relations," or "people's talent for 'discovering' relatives who can serve as footholds." This, he argues, puts kinship under heavy strain: "New elites dread the pressure of their 'brothers' in the village who want them to redistribute from their new wealth—all the more so, since there seems to be no limit to those who claim to be 'brother'" (Geschiere 2003, 44). In some cases in which I was called as a witness, wealthy family members who were expected to bear heavy financial burdens for many kin believed the appropriate measure of compensation was the labor of or sexual access to those they had assisted. In both northern and southern Cameroon, family members receiving assistance are often asked to perform unpaid labor, sexual labor, or difficult labor or to engage in other kinds of indenture and servitude in a "payment in kind" arrangement (Argenti 2011; Sinderud 2013). When Cameroonians who live on the economic margins of society are asked to perform such kinds of labor, they rarely feel that they can refuse.

These facts are critical to understanding the realities of family violence in Cameroon. In my experience interviewing women fleeing family violence or trafficking in Cameroon (or from Cameroon), the person most likely to have "sold," forcibly married, exploited, or sexually abused these individuals was a family member (the most common family member was the paternal uncle, but grandfathers, stepparents, older siblings, and cousins were also frequently abusers and/or traffickers).[17] In some cases, a family member's spouse has also been a trafficker and exploiter of children and young women in Cameroon (Walker-Said 2015, 2016).

While trafficking women and children between families (to be used as household help, caregivers, or spouses) is technically criminalized, it is a phenomenon that is largely ignored by police (Kazé 2009; Nsom 2009; Bishops of Cameroon and Atanga 2013). Given the remarkable authority and control family leaders have over other family members (depending on their position in the generational hierarchy, their cultural status, their social class, or their political connections), the police do not interfere in what they deem "family affairs," even though the results of family decisions might be illegal, unjust, dehumanizing, cruel, or exploitive (Koki Ndombo et al. 1992; Burrill, Roberts, and Thornberry 2010; Mabuse 2011; CamerounWeb 2015; Immigration and Refugee Board of Canada 2016a).

The research on trafficking, forced labor, the exploitation of women and children, and child abuse in Cameroon exposes the political and economic frameworks that enforce the heavy influence and involvement of immediate and extended family in Cameroonian citizens' lives. This means that exploitation, violence, and dehumanization—in a word, persecution—are in fact *more* difficult to extricate oneself from than violence by state or governmental agents. They are also potentially more lethal, as victims face dual adversaries in their family members and the government, which constructs the family as a "private sphere" free from government "interference."[18]

## Notes

1. I served as an expert witness in these cases for the plaintiffs in civil court.

2. For the purposes of this chapter, I will use this name to refer to this woman involved in the trafficking and exploitation case in order to guard her anonymity. The T nonimmigrant status (T or T1 visa) was created for those who had been victims of human trafficking. It allows victims to remain in the United States to assist in an investigation or prosecution of human trafficking. This stipulation is important: in order to qualify for the T visa, an applicant must comply with law enforcement to assist in the investigation or prosecution of their case, with very limited exceptions. Once a T nonimmigrant visa is granted, a victim can apply for permanent residence after three years. The US Justice Department estimates that between 14,500 and 17,500 people are trafficked into the country every year, but other sources estimate that the number could be as high as 50,000 annually. See United States Citizenship and Immigration Services n.d.

3. In October 2000 Congress created the T nonimmigrant status by passing the Victims of Trafficking and Violence Protection Act (VTVPA). Motivated by the alarming rise in human trafficking into the United States, this legislation strengthened the ability of law enforcement agencies to investigate and prosecute human trafficking and also offered protection to victims (Armaline, Glasberg, and Purkayastha 2011, 212–19).

4. One can trace the emergence of a distinctly "private" realm in various legal doctrines that sought to stake out a sphere or domain free from the encroaching power of the state (see Horwitz 1982; Macpherson 2011).

5. Geschiere quotes Eric de Rosny's (1981) recounting of the Duala saying "One has to learn how to live with one's witch."

6. Musalo argues that this is all the more legally inconsistent in that being a member of a family or kin group is an "immutable trait," which is recognized as a criterion for refugee protection. According to US Citizenship and Immigration Services, the key board decision on the meaning of "a particular social group" requires that members of the group share a "common, immutable" trait. See Matter of Acosta, 19 I&N Dec. 211 at 233 (BIA 1985). In *Matter of Acosta*, the Board of Immigration Appeals codified at 208.15(C)(1) that "a particular social group is composed of members who share a common, immutable characteristic, such as sex, color, kinship ties, or past experience, that a member either cannot change or that is so fundamental to the identity or conscience of the member that he or she should not be required to change it."

7. Bradley v. State, 2 Miss. (1 Walker) 156 (1824) (Schelong 1994).

8. This decision vacated a Board of Immigration Appeals (BIA) decision of December 6, 2016, in *Matter of A-B*, as well as overruled the decision in the *Matter of A-R-C-G-*, upon which the BIA had relied to decide *A-B-*.

9. Matter of A-B-, Respondent Decision by U.S. Attorney General Jeff Sessions, 27 I&N Dec. 316 (AG 2018).

10. The category of inquiry known as "family-based violence" is coming increasingly into play as examinations of violence in the private sphere reveal that "domestic violence," which heretofore has been used principally to refer to spousal abuse, must uncover violations and conflicts between all members of a nuclear family or extended household, including interpersonal struggles between generations, genders, kin, spouses, in-laws, and others (Fluri 2011; Shively 2011; Leask 2017; see also Puttick and Minority Rights Group International 2015).

11. Matter of A-B-, Respondent, Decided by Attorney General June 11, 2018, 27 I&N Dec. 316 (AG 2018). (Matter of A-R-C-G-, 26 I&N Dec. 338 [BIA 2014] is overruled.) For the best analysis of the conclusions and implications of Sessions's ruling in *Matter of A-B-*, see Jeffrey S. Chase, "How Far Reaching Is the Impact of Grace v. Whitaker?," *Opinions/Analysis of Immigration Law* (blog), December 24, 2018, https://www.jeffreyschase.com/blog/2018/12/24/how-far-reaching-is-the-impact-of-grace-v-whitaker.

12. Inconsistency has been a hallmark of American immigration courts for over a decade (see Wheeler 2009; Trac Immigration 2016).

13. Transcript of videotaped deposition of [name redacted], July 21, 2016, Chicago, Illinois, 86, 88.
14. Interview, John the Baptist Zamcho Anyeh, SJ, May 25, 2014, Maison Jesuite, Mvolyé, Cameroon; interview, Fr. Philippe Azeufack, SJ, May 30, 2014, Résidence St. François Xavier, Yaoundé, Cameroon; phone interview, Cameroonian asylum seeker #3, November 2, 2018; interview, Walters Nkwi, March 19, 2019, Douala, Cameroon.
15. In Cameroon rape is a crime punishable by up to life in prison, but only about one in twenty rapists is convicted (Kazé 2009).
16. Field interview notes, asylum cases, January 13, 2016, February 9, 2017, March 6, 2018.
17. Interview, Adèle Nimboh, July 6, 2007, Kribi, Cameroon; Charlotte Walker-Said, interview records, May 12–13, 2014, Yaoundé, Cameroon; interview, "Christine," February 11, 2017, New York.
18. It is perhaps worthwhile noting that before Article 16 of the Universal Declaration of Human Rights, which states, "The family is the natural and fundamental group unit of society and is entitled to protection by society and the state," comes Article 12, which affirms that families be protected from "arbitrary interference." This can be interpreted in many ways, including a conservative reading that might suggest that a human rights priority for the family is "noninterference." UN General Assembly, Universal Declaration of Human Rights, December 10, 1948, 217 A (III), https://www.refworld.org/docid/3ae6b3712c.html.

## References

Africa Desk. 2008. "Anti-Government Rioting Spreads in Cameroon." *New York Times*, December 7, 2008.
Amnesty International. 2015. "Burkina Faso: Les droits des femmes toujours autant ignorés." Amnesty International Belgique Francophone, July 15. https://www.amnesty.be/infos/actualites/article/burkina-faso-les-droits-des-femmes.
Argenti, Nicolas. 2007. *The Intestines of the State: Youth, Violence, and Belated Histories in the Cameroon Grassfields*. Chicago: University of Chicago Press.
———. 2011. "Things of the Ground: Children's Medicine, Motherhood and Memory in the Cameroon Grassfields." *Africa: Journal of the International African Institute* 81 (2): 269–94.
Armaline, William T., Davita Silfen Glasberg, and Bandana Purkayastha. 2011. *Human Rights in Our Own Backyard: Injustice and Resistance in the United States*. Pennsylvania Studies in Human Rights. Philadelphia: University of Pennsylvania Press.
Bang, G. A. 2007. "Contribution à l'étude des abus sexuels intra-familiaux envers les mineurs à Yaoundé (Cameroun)." PhD diss., Université de Yaoundé I, Cameroon.
Bankston, Amanda, and Aaron Martinez. 2014. "Merchants of Modern Slavery: Sex Traffickers Use Deception, Manipulation to Control Victims." *El Paso Times*, May 4, 2014.

Benhabib, Seyla. 1998. "Models of Public Space: Hannah Arendt, the Liberal Tradition, and Jürgen Habermas." In *Feminism, the Public and the Private*, edited by Joan B. Landes, 73–98. Oxford: Oxford University Press.

Bettinger-Lopez, Caroline, Rachel Natelson, Christina Brandt-Young, and Sandra Park. 2011. "Domestic Violence in the United States: A Preliminary Report Prepared for Rashida Manjoo, U.N. Special Rapporteur on Violence against Women." Version 04-04-11 UM HRC edits/forwarded to UVA Clinic.

Bishops of Cameroon, and Mgr. Joseph Atanga. 2013. *Declaration of the Bishops of Cameroon on Abortion, Homosexuality, Incest, and Sexual Abuse of Minors.* Bertoua, Cameroon: National Episcopal Conference of Cameroon.

Burrill, Emily S., and Richard L. Roberts. 2010. "Domestic Violence, Colonial Courts, and the End of Slavery in French Soudan, 1905–12." In *Domestic Violence and the Law in Colonial and Postcolonial Africa*, edited by Emily S. Burrill, Richard L. Roberts, and Elizabeth Thornberry, 33–53. Athens: Ohio University Press.

Burrill, Emily S., Richard L. Roberts, and Elizabeth Thornberry, eds. 2010. *Domestic Violence and the Law in Colonial and Postcolonial Africa*. Athens: Ohio University Press.

Caballero, Andres. 2014. "Pentecostal Churches Accused of Exploiting Cameroon's Poor." NPR.org, April 12. http://www.npr.org/2014/04/12/302166602/revivalist-churches-accused-of-exploiting-cameroons-poor.

CamerounWeb. 2015. "20% of Women in Cameroon Are Victims of Sexual Abuse." December 16. http://www.cameroonweb.com/CameroonHomePage/NewsArchive/20-of-women-in-Cameroon-are-victims-of-sexual-abuse-348829.

Chimtom, Ngala Killian. 2015. "In Search of Jobs, Cameroonian Women May End Up as Slaves in Middle East." *Inter Press Service*, July 15. http://www.ipsnews.net/2015/07/in-search-of-jobs-cameroonian-women-may-end-up-as-slaves-in-middle-east/.

Chishugi, Dr. John, and Dr. Trixy Franke. 2016. "Sexual Abuse in Cameroon: A Four-Year-Old Girl Victim of Rape in Buea Case Study." *Journal of Child Sexual Abuse* 25 (6): 619–26.

Domowitz, Susan. 1981. "The Orphan in Cameroon Folklore and Fiction." *Research in African Literatures* 12 (3): 350–58.

Doumara, Aissa Ngatansou. 2012. "Hunger and Patriarchy in Cameroon." OpenDemocracy, October 2. http://www.opendemocracy.net/5050/a%C3%AEssa-ngatansou-doumara/hunger-and-patriarchy-in-cameroon.

Essomba Fouda, Antoine. 2010. *Le mariage chrétien au Cameroun: Une réalité anthropologique, civile et sacramentelle*. Paris: L'Harmattan.

Fluri, Jennifer L. 2011. "Bodies, Bombs and Barricades: Geographies of Conflict and Civilian (In)Security in Afghanistan." *Transactions of the Institute of British Geographers* 36 (2): 280–96.

———. 2015. "Feminist Political Geography." In *The Wiley-Blackwell Companion to Political Geography*, edited by J. Agnew, V. Mamadouh, A. Secor, and J. Sharp, 235–47. London: Wiley-Blackwell.

Fonchingong, Tangie Nsoh, and John Bobuin Gemandze. 2009. *Cameroon: The Stakes and Challenges of Governance and Development*. Johannesburg: African Books Collective, 2009.

Geschiere, Peter. 2003. "Witchcraft as the Dark Side of Kinship: Dilemmas of Social Security in New Contexts." *Etnofoor* 16 (1): 43–61.

Glass, Michael. 2014. "Forced Circumcision of Men (Abridged)." *Journal of Medical Ethics* 40 (8): 567–71.

Gluckman, Max. 1953. "Bridewealth and the Stability of Marriage." *Man* 53:141–43.

Gwanfogbe, Helen. 2015. "International Trafficking in Cameroonian Slaves Is Real." *Cameroon Tribune* (Yaoundé), July 22. http://allafrica.com/stories/201507220901.html.

High Commission of Canada in Cameroon. 2015. "Dinard Declaration on the Partnership for a Comprehensive and Sustainable Strategy to Combat Illegal Trafficking in the Sahel Region." https://www.international.gc.ca/world-monde/international_relations-relations_internationales/g7/documents/2019-04-06-sahel.aspx?lang=eng.

Horwitz, Morton J. 1982. "The History of the Public/Private Distinction." *University of Pennsylvania Law Review* 130:1423–28.

Immigration and Refugee Board of Canada. 2016a. *Benin: Domestic Violence, Including Availability of State Protection and Support Services (2009–2015)*. Report BEN105406.FE. February 9. http://www.refworld.org/docid/56d7f6b44.html.

Immigration and Refugee Board of Canada. 2016b. *Cameroon: Domestic Violence, Including Legislation; Protection Provided by the State and Support Services Available to Victims (2014–2016)*. April 21. Report CMR105382.FE. https://www.refworld.org/docid/5729a55e4.html.

International Rescue Committee. 2012. "Let Me Not Die before My Time: Domestic Violence in West Africa." International Rescue Committee. https://www.rescue-uk.org/sites/default/files/document/990/newircreportdomviowafricauk.pdf.

Jean-Baptiste, Rachel. 2008. "'These Laws Should Be Made by Us': Customary Marriage Law, Codification and Political Authority in Twentieth-Century Colonial Gabon." *Journal of African History* 49 (2): 217–40.

Johannes, Tabi Atemnkeng, Peter Angyie Etoh-Anzah, and Akwi Tafah. 2009. "Who Benefits from Combined Tax and Public Expenditure Policies in Cameroon." *Journal of Developing Areas* 43 (1): 1–23.

Kazé, Reinnier. 2009. "CAMEROON: Bringing Rape out of the Shadows." *New Humanitarian* (*IRIN News*), June 2. http://www.irinnews.org/report/84670/cameroon-bringing-rape-out-of-the-shadows.

Koki Ndombo, P. O., I. F. Biyong, N. Eteki Tamba, G. Grüselle, D. Lantum, and M. Makang-Ma-Mbog. 1992. "Child Victims of Sexual Abuse in Cameroon." *Annales de Pédiatrie* 39 (2): 111–14.

Lagon, Mark P. 2011. "The Global Abolition of Human Trafficking: The Indispensable Role of the United States." *Georgetown Journal of International Affairs* 12 (1): 89–98.

Lazareva, Inna. 2017. "Cameroon's 'Auntie Army' of Rape Survivors Battles Sex Abuse of Girls." *Reuters*, May 16. https://www.reuters.com/article/us-cameroon-women-rape/cameroons-auntie-army-of-rape-survivors-battles-sex-abuse-of-girls-idUSKCN18CoBU.

Leask, Anna. 2017. "Family Violence: New Holistic Approach Announced." *New Zealand Herald*, June 6.

Mabuse, Nkepile. 2011. "Breast Ironing Tradition Targeted in Cameroon." *CNN*, July 27. http://www.cnn.com/2011/WORLD/africa/07/27/cameroon.breast.ironing/index.html.

Macpherson, C. B. 2011. *The Political Theory of Possessive Individualism: Hobbes to Locke*. Oxford: Oxford University Press.

Mouendé, Matthias. 2014. "'Witch-Hunt' Riot Rocks Cameroon Town." *France 24*, January 1. http://observers.france24.com/content/20140113-witch-hunting-turns-violent-cameroon.

Muma, Roland. 2014. "Cameroon's Female Judges Discuss Gender-Based Violence." *Face2Face Africa*, April 7. https://face2faceafrica.com/article/violence-against-women-cameroon.

Musalo, Karen. 2014. "Personal Violence, Public Matter: Evolving Standards in Gender-Based Asylum Law." *Harvard International Review* 36 (2): 45–48.

Ndonko, Flavien, Olivia Bikoe, Gerd Eppel, and Kouo Ngamby. 2009. *Viol et inceste au Cameroun: Rapport Final*. Yaoundé, Cameroon: Colorix-GTZ.

Ndonkou, Péguy. 2015. "Le viol et l'inceste au Cameroun: Une pratique sournoise et occulte." Yaoundé, Cameroon: Association Soutien aux Victimes d'Agressions Sexuelles Rechercher. http://savas-asso.org/index.php/veille/veille-2014/42-19-05-2014-le-viol-et-l-inceste-au-cameroun-une-pratique-sournoise-et-occulte.

Ngou, Honorine. 2007. *Mariage et violence dans la société traditionnelle Fang au Gabon*. Paris: L'Harmattan.

Ngoutsop, Moïse Tamekem. 2017. "La question de l'appui institutionnel aux jeunes filles victimes de viols et d'incestes au Cameroun: Quelle gouvernance dans la gestion de ce 'problème genré' de santé publique." *Africa Development / Afrique et Développement* 42 (1): 177–97.

Nkwidja, Aggée. 2006. "Violence contre les femmes: La bastonnade comme preuve d'amour." *Le Messager*, December 8, Cameroon-Info.net edition. http://www.cameroon-info.net/article/violence-contre-les-femmes-la-bastonnade-comme-preuve-damour-99384.html.

Nsagha, Dickson S., Anne-Cecile Z. K. Bissek, Sarah M. Nsagha, Jules-Clement N. Assob, Henri-Lucien F. Kamga, Dora M. Njamnshi, Anna L. Njunda, Marie-Therese O. Obama, and Alfred K. Njamnshi. 2012. "The Burden of Orphans and Vulnerable Children Due to HIV/AIDS in Cameroon." *Open AIDS Journal* 6 (October): 245–58.

Nsom, Kini. 2009. "Girls Testify Being Raped by Own Fathers." *Cameroon Post*, June 5. http://www.cameroonpostline.com/girls-testify-being-raped-by-own-fathers/.

Nyamnjoh, Francis, and Michael Rowlands. 1998. "Elite Associations and the Politics of Belonging in Cameroon." *Africa: Journal of the International African Institute* 68 (3): 320–37.
Oberhauser, Ann M., Jennifer L. Fluri, Risa Whiston, and Sharlene Mollett. 2018. *Feminist Spaces: Gender and Geography in a Global Context.* New York: Routledge.
OMCT International Secretariat. 2004. *Violence against Women in Cameroon: A Report to the Committee against Torture.* Organisation Mondiale contre la Torture (OMCT) / World Organization against Torture. https://www.omct.org/files/2004/07/2409/eng_2003_03_cameroon.pdf.
Parreñas, Rhacel Salazar, Maria Cecilia Hwang, and Heather Ruth Lee. 2012. "What Is Human Trafficking? A Review Essay." *Signs* 37 (4): 1015–29.
Pelican, Michaela, Peter Tatah, and Basile Ndjio. 2008. "Local Perspectives on Transnational Relations of Cameroonian Migrants." *African Sociological Review / Revue Africaine de Sociologie* 12 (2): 117–27.
Pemunta, Ngambouk Vitalis. 2011. "Challenging Patriarchy: Trade, Outward Migration and the Internationalization of Commercial Sex among Bayang and Ejagham Women in Southwest Cameroon." *Health, Culture and Society* 1 (1): 166–92. https://doi.org/10.5195/hcs.2011.58.
Podgers, James. 2013. "Taking on Trafficking: House of Delegates OKs Key Measure for Adoption by the States." *American Bar Association Journal* 99 (10): 62.
Puttick, Miriam, and Minority Rights Group International. 2015. *The Lost Women of Iraq: Family-Based Violence during Armed Conflict.* Report of the Ceasefire Project. London: Ceasefire Centre for Civilian Rights and Minority Rights Group International. http://minorityrights.org/wp-content/uploads/2015/11/MRG-report-A4_OCTOBER-2015_WEB.pdf.
Roberts, David. 2008. *Human Insecurity: Global Structures of Violence.* New York: Zed Books.
Roeland, Monasch, and J. Ties Boerma. 2004. "Orphanhood and Childcare Patterns in Sub-Saharan Africa: An Analysis of National Surveys from 40 Countries." *AIDS* 18 (2): 555–65.
Rosny, Eric de. 1981. *Les yeux de ma chèvre: Sur les pas des maîtres de la nuit en pays douala.* Paris: Plon.
Schelong, Katherine M. 1994. "Domestic Violence and the State: Responses to and Rationales for Spousal Battering, Marital Rape, and Stalking." *Marquette Law Review* 78 (1): 79–120.
Shively, Kim. 2011. "When Domestic Violence Is Not 'Intimate Partner Violence': Cases from Turkey and Elsewhere." *Practicing Anthropology* 33 (3): 13–16.
Sinderud, Marte Bogen. 2013. "Royal Concubinage in Ngaoundere, Northern Cameroon, ca. 1900–1960." *International Journal of African Historical Studies* 46 (1): 1–25.
Tabi Atemnkeng, Johannes, and Daniel Mbu Tambi. 2018. "Growth-Equity and Sectoral Decompositions of Aggregate Poverty Changes in Cameroon: The Role of the Labour Market." *African Journal of Economic and Management Studies* 9 (1): 56–71.

Tilly, Charles. 2010. "Cities, States, and Trust Networks: Chapter 1 of Cities and States in World History." *Theory and Society* 39 (3): 265–80.
Todd, Loreto. 1982. *Cameroon*. New York: John Benjamins.
Trac Immigration. 2016. "Asylum Outcome Increasingly Depends on Judge Assigned." December 2. http://trac.syr.edu/immigration/reports/447/.
United Nations. 2008. Committee on the Elimination of Discrimination Against Women (CEDAW). *Responses to the List of Issues and Questions with Regard to the Consideration of the Combined Second and Third Periodic Reports: Cameroon*. CEDAW/C/CMR/Q/3/Add.1.
United Nations Development Programme. 2016. *Human Development Report 2016: Human Development for Everyone*. Briefing notes for countries on the 2016 Human Development Report: Cameroon. http://hdr.undp.org/sites/all/themes/hdr_theme/country-notes/es/CMR.pdf.
United States Citizenship and Immigration Services. *Victims of Human Trafficking: T Nonimmigrant Status*. n.d. Accessed September 28, 2017. https://www.uscis.gov/humanitarian/victims-human-trafficking-other-crimes/victims-human-trafficking-t-nonimmigrant-status.
United States Department of Labor. 2015. *Cameroon: Child Labor and Forced Labor Reports*. Report by the Bureau of International Labor Affairs, https://www.dol.gov/agencies/ilab/resources/reports/child-labor/cameroon.
United States Department of State. 2012. *2011 Country Reports on Human Rights Practices: Cameroon*. Washington, DC. https://2009-2017.state.gov/j/drl/rls/hrrpt//index.htm.
———. 2013. *Trafficking in Persons Report 2013*. https://www.state.gov/j/tip/rls/tiprpt/2013/index.htm.
———. 2014. *2013 Country Reports on Human Rights Practices: The Gambia*. Washington, DC. https://www.refworld.org/docid/53284a6014.html.
———. 2015. *Cameroon: 2015 Trafficking in Persons Report*. Report by the Office to Monitor and Combat Trafficking in Persons. http://www.state.gov/j/tip/rls/tiprpt/countries/2015/243410.htm.
Voice of America. 2011. "Child Sexual Abuse Growing in Cameroon, Study Says." *Voice of America News*, August 17. https://www.voanews.com/a/child-sexual-abuse-growing-in-cameroon-study-says-128016228/161660.html.
Walker, Charlotte. 2010. "The Trafficking and Slavery of Women and Girls: The Criminalization of Marriage, Tradition, and Gender Norms in French Colonial Cameroon, 1914–1945." In *Sex Trafficking, Human Rights, and Social Justice*, edited by Tiantian Zheng, 150–69. New York: Routledge.
Walker-Said, Charlotte. 2015. "Sexual Minorities among African Asylum Claimants: Human Rights Regimes, Bureaucratic Knowledge, and the Era of Sexual Rights Diplomacy." In *African Asylum at a Crossroads: Activism, Expert Testimony, and Refugee Rights*, edited by Benjamin Lawrance, Iris Berger, Trish Redeker-Hepner, Jo Tague, and Meredith Terretta, 203–24. Athens: Ohio University Press.

———. 2016. "Fleeing Patriarchy, Contesting Heteronormativity: Expert Testimony, Asylum, and Forced Marriage in Sub-Saharan Africa." In *Marriage by Force? Contestation over Consent and Coercion in Africa*, edited by Benjamin Lawrance, Annie Bunting, and Richard Roberts, 199–224. Athens: Ohio University Press.

Wheeler, Russell. 2009. *Seeking Fair and Effective Administration of Immigration Laws*. Washington, DC: Brookings Institution. https://www.brookings.edu/research/seeking-fair-and-effective-administration-of-immigration-laws/.

World Health Organization. 2010. *Violence and Health in the WHO African Region*. Brazzaville, Congo: WHO Regional Office for Africa. http://www.afro.who.int/sites/default/files/2017-06/mvi-violence-health-15-04-11.pdf.

Zellner, Sara L. 2003. "Condom Use and the Accuracy of AIDS Knowledge in Côte d'Ivoire." *International Family Planning Perspectives* 29 (1): 41–47.

# 7

## Colonial Legacies, Electoral Politics, and the Production of (Anti) homosexuality in Senegal

CHEIKH IBRAHIMA NIANG,
ELLEN E. FOLEY, AND NDACK DIOP

For the past decade, the status of Senegal's legal statute criminalizing homosexuality has been a central theme in national politics. In the wake of highly publicized violence against suspected homosexuals in 2008 and 2009, global human rights groups urged Senegal to decriminalize homosexuality and to protect the rights of sexual minorities. In spite of this vocal pressure, the Senegalese government has given no indication that it is reconsidering the current legal framework outlawing homosexual acts. On the contrary, during US president Barack Obama's visit in 2013, Senegalese president Macky Sall asserted that he would not overturn Senegal's laws criminalizing homosexuality during his presidential term, a promise he repeated throughout his first term in office. Media coverage of Sall's refusal is illustrative of the political stakes of legislating sexuality in Senegal. A *New York Times* article titled "Senegal Cheers Its President for Standing Up to Obama on Same-Sex Marriage" relays several enthusiastic Senegalese newspaper headlines following President Obama's visit: "No, We Can't" (*Libération*); "Macky Says No to Obama" (*Walfadjri*); "Obama Makes a Plea for the Homos, Macky Says No!" (*Le Populaire*); "President Sall Has Closed the Debate on Homosexuality" (*L'Observateur*) (Nossiter 2013).

A rising tide of violence against homosexuals and efforts to criminalize same-sex sexuality have been noted elsewhere on the African continent in recent years (Tamale 2007; Boyd 2013; Kretz 2013). Yet incidences of violence against suspected homosexuals in Senegal seem to stand in stark contrast to past norms. Gender-nonconforming individuals have a long and visible history in Senegal; the Wolof word for these individuals, *goorjigeen*, merges the word for man (*goor*) with the word for woman (*jigeen*) into a compound term that demarcates gender fluidity (Niang 2010; Broqua 2017).[1] The historical acceptance of non-binary-gender expression in Senegal makes the recent public rejection of sexual minorities by political leaders all the more surprising.

In this chapter, we draw upon anthropologist Gilbert Herdt (2009) to consider the ways that Senegal's backlash against homosexuality in 2008 and 2009 operated as a sexual panic. Herdt builds on the 1972 work of British sociologist Stanley Cohen and offers a further elaboration of Cohen's conceptualization of moral panics: large-scale events in which a perceived threat by alleged evildoers provokes strong reactions. Herdt identifies sexual panics as a form of moral panic. Similar to the folk devil in a moral panic, a key element of a sexual panic is the identification of a sexual scapegoat. During a sexual panic the perceived threat of the sexual other is out of proportion, and "the cultural imagination becomes obsessed with anxieties about what this evil sexuality will do to warp society and future generations" (Herdt 2009, 5). Herdt argues that in the most extreme panics "the rights of these persons are qualified and revoked, undermining citizenship" (2).

Senegal's sexual panic was characterized by the figure of the homosexual as a devil whose very person was a threat to the nation. In the midst of the panic, religious reformers and other commentators called upon the state, elected officials, and politicians to protect the nation by denouncing homosexuality and imprisoning (or exterminating) suspected homosexuals. In multiple acts of mob violence and vigilante justice, citizenship rights, due process, and bodily autonomy were revoked from suspected gay men whose very persons (and in a few cases corpses) threatened the social body. This sexual panic rests on a form of heteronationalism that represents the Senegalese nation as always-already patriarchal and heterosexual (Imam, Amina and Sow 1997; Jaunait, Le Renard, and Marteu 2013; M'Baye 2013).[2] Assertions of a heteronormative nation are not unique to Senegal. Yet this depiction erases a historical record and cultural reality in which non-binary-gender expression was once relatively ordinary. In what follows, we examine the conditions that produced this wave of sexual panic in Senegal and consider the longer-term implications for human rights protections for sexual minorities and legislating sexuality more broadly. Ironically, the move away from single-party rule and the broadening of Senegal's political field likely enabled the emergence of conservative religious reformers with antihomosexual platforms. The Senegalese case illuminates why postcolonial African states may engage in repression of LGBTQ individuals to defend those states' moral legitimacy in moments of political and economic uncertainty.

### Gender Expression and *Goorjigeen*: Past and Present

In the midst of the 2008 sexual panic in Senegal, pundits and religious leaders asserted that homosexuality had never been an African practice and was instead a perverse colonial import and a sign of ongoing neocolonial influence (M'Baye 2013). As Babacar M'Baye (2013) and others note, this claim of externality appears frequently in homophobic discourses throughout Africa (Epprecht 2004; Ahlberg and Kulane 2011; Tamale 2011). Here we present evidence from the colonial and postcolonial periods of queer spaces of sociality, non-binary-gender expression, and same-sex sexual practices in Senegal. We rely upon published material, as well as ethnographic research conducted in Senegal by Niang and his university students from 2000 to 2012. Our analysis makes use of oral histories, interviews, and cultural practices conveyed through expressions, proverbs, and songs.

This body of evidence serves as a counterpoint to the depiction of a heteronormative nation that was under threat during Senegal's sexual panic. Instead, we present a social and cultural context in which gender fluidity was visible and somewhat ordinary and in which *goorjigeen* occupied recognized and valued social positions in the complex social hierarchy of feminine networks of leisure, recreation, and ceremonial economic exchange. Yet, following historian and sociologist Jeffrey Weeks's (1996) work on the invention of homosexuality, while gender fluidity and same-sex sexual practices have always existed in Senegal, "homosexuals" as such did not. The outbreak of sexual panic in Senegal rested on the transformation of a benign person exhibiting gender fluidity (*goorjigeen*) into an alleged sexual devil whose deviant sexual practices threatened the moral fiber of society. The term *goorjigeen* has now become synonymous with homosexual, in essence collapsing previously socially acceptable gender fluidity with same-sex sexual practices (Niang 2010; Mills 2011; Broqua 2016). This evolution of the meaning of *goorjigeen*, in particular, its synonymy with homosexual acts, contributed in part to Senegal's homophobic backlash.

There is long-standing evidence of gender fluidity and homosexuality in precolonial and colonial Senegal. M'Baye (2013) and Christophe Broqua (2017) summarize key works of European colonial officers and social scientists who described gender fluidity and same-sex relationships in Senegal. Each highlights the work of Armand Corre (1894, 118), who described "effeminate men" and the Wolof designation (likely *goor-jigeen*) for them, and that of Geoffrey Gorer (1935, cited in M'Baye 2013, 121), who describes homosexuals and transgender women who were integrated into Senegalese society.

One of the most cited depictions of *goorjigeen* prior to Senegal's independence in 1960 comes from the work of historian Michael Crowder, who toured West Africa just prior to decolonization: "Today one can even see Jollof men dressed in women's clothes. I once met one in a small bar outside Dakar. He was obviously pathetically feminine. The Jollof must be used to this since they even have a word for them—Gor Digen. The elders and faithful Muslims condemn men like this, but it is typical of African tolerance that they are left very much alone by the rest of the people" (1959, 68). Crowder's description of a "pathetically feminine man" reflects his Eurocentric conception of gender. Nonetheless, he confirms the visibility of *goorjigeen* in the public sphere, as well as social and religious tolerance of their presence. English journalist Michael Davidson ([1970] 1998) echoes Crowder: he refers to Dakar in 1949 as a "gay" city and describes transgender sex workers who frequented Dakar's bar scene without incident in 1958.

Although archival sources are relatively silent on the topic of *goorjigeen* in the colonial period, much richer documentation about *goorjigeen* and their embeddedness in the social lives and social networks of *drianke* (grandes dames, or middle-aged women with financial means and high social status who were known to have sex with other women) is available through oral history and ethnographic fieldwork. In Saint Louis, Niang and his students conducted more than twenty oral history interviews and several focus groups with elderly women and men, some of whom were *goorjigeen*. These research participants shared recollections of social life in colonial Saint Louis. Saint Louis historically had the reputation of being a cosmopolitan locale where women and *goorjigeen* played significant roles in elite society; thus, the city serves as a rich site for oral histories.[3] Interviews solicited research participants' memories about the existence and social life of *goorjigeen* in Saint Louis, as well as the powerful *drianke* who often served as their protectors. Many research participants could identify specific European residents of the city known to have same-sex relationships. (Some interlocutors used the word "pederast" to designate these individuals, a term that conflates same-sex relationships with pedophilia.)

In contrast, no one associated the label *goorjigeen* with Europeans (Niang 2013). *Goorjigeen* is a status, an identity, and a cultural category with a set of roles and relationships that excludes Europeans; it is a Wolof concept.

Interviews and oral histories reveal that in Wolof cultural settings, *goorjigeen* were integrated into the female social world and played social roles typically reserved for adult women. While *goorjigeen* may combine elements of masculine and feminine gender expression, their social position is decidedly female. *Goorjigeen* belong to the social world of women.[4] They are known masters of the female arts of cooking, dance, fashion, clothing design, and makeup. The linguistic specificity of the term *goorjigeen*, documentation of their visible social roles in pre- and postcolonial Senegal, and anthropological evidence point to a local gender category.

*Goorjigeen* may have worn women's clothing exclusively or much of the time, particularly during activities such as dance parties, when frequenting cruising spots, and when cooking or serving meals for festive ceremonies. While dressing in women's clothing is a distinctive marker, the practice of cross-dressing in Senegalese society is not limited to *goorjigeen*. One of the most commonplace examples of gender play in Senegal occurs during Tajabone. On this holiday, children dress up as the opposite sex and go door-to-door asking for holiday treats (similar to Halloween in the United States). Male participants in *ndep* ceremonies (healing ceremonies for mental illness) also wear women's clothing (Ndoye 2010). These practices suggest familiarity with and acceptance of gender play and non-binary-gender expression that go beyond the existence of *goorjigeen*.

As *goorjigeen* occupied female roles in the Wolof social order, they participated in female spaces of sociality from which men and children were generally excluded. *Goorjigeen* attended and participated in gatherings where women transmitted cultural and bodily knowledge about sex, eroticism, and sexuality, often through crude or obscene oral poetry and dance (McNee 2000). *Goorjigeen* were also integrated into women's organizations called *mbotaay* (collectives of women belonging to a similar demographic group based on age or ethnicity). *Mbotaay* meet regularly and may operate as rotating credit associations, as social support groups, and as social groupings that organize festive activities.[5] Contrary to the inclusion of *goorjigeen* in these female spaces, men are not admitted except in the case of *gewel* (musicians and genealogists), who often serve as the musical accompaniment to women's song and dance.

Prior to independence and through the 1960s and 1970s, *goorjigeen* were known to organize dances and ceremonies called *tànnëbéer*. These events, particularly those organized in cities and towns in the North, were attended by the whole community. Etymologically, the word *tànnëbéer* is composed of the verb *tàn*, which can be translated as "making a personal choice," and *béer*, which is a plant species, conveying the idea of making a choice of sexual partner. These events offered an opportunity to meet potential partners for heterosexual sex and same-sex encounters. Similarly, in the 1970s, *drianke* organized *tànnëbéer* sessions with drumming and dancing for other women of their status, with the participation of *goorjigeen*. These events took place in public and were part of the ceremonial life of urban public space. They were not viewed as a violation of local moral conventions.

Oral histories indicate that *goorjigeen* sometimes married, and they also celebrated rites of passage (losing their virginity) typically reserved for young women. *Goorjigeen* were sometimes married to men who were not *goorjigeen*. Male partners of *goorjigeen* are similar to the "shirted" *yan daudu* in Hausa society described by Rudolf Pell Gaudio (2009) who publicly conform to gender norms but have sexual relationships with men. In Wolof these male partners were called *gorgi* (the man) or *jekker* (husband).[6] These marriages did not always involve cohabitation, but they could, particularly in cases where the person designated as the husband could afford to live relatively isolated from the local community. Marriages also existed between younger and older *goorjigeen*, with the elder taking on the role of the provider. The wedding receptions for such unions were more social event (e.g., an occasion to reinforce ties within and between social networks) than a consecration of the couple and their establishment of a new household, as in a heterosexual marriage. Nonetheless, much like other weddings of the urban elite, the weddings of *goorjigeen* were occasions for extravagant spending and conspicuous consumption. The organization of *goorjigeen* weddings follows the model of women's ceremonies, with ritual sequences of gift exchanges and large communal meals. One well-known anecdote describes a convoy of hundreds of cars accompanying a *goorjigeen* bride to her wedding in Dakar in the 1960s.

In contrast to widespread familiarity with the term *goorjigeen*, there are no known words to designate transgender men or lesbians. While sex between *goor* and *goorjigeen* is conceptualized as sex between individuals of different genders (similar to sex between men and women), sex between women is viewed as homosexual sex (sex between individuals of the same gender) (Niang 2013). Nonetheless, there is language to denote sex between women in Wolof (*këppënté* and *dëppënté*). Sexual relationships between women often take place within a community sharing the same experience of same-sex sexuality. The phrase "wa koñ bi" (the members of the local neighborhood) is used as coded language to designate a community of shared values and a web of networks in which women meet and come to know and trust each other.

While these networks are deeply hidden, ethnographic research reveals the long-standing existence of communities of gender nonbinary and same-sex-desiring individuals in urban Senegal. Nonetheless, historically the social category *goorjigeen* emphasized gender expression rather than sexual practices. Unless one was a member of their social networks, there were no visible indicators of the sexual practices of *goorjigeen*. As Broqua argues, "Their sexuality was not questioned. . . . Their sexual orientation was not an issue. *Goorjigeen* was a gender category and not a sexual orientation. The majority of Senegalese were unaware of their sexual practices since they were not spoken of" (2016, 171). While the term *goorjigeen* is part of the everyday lexicon in Senegal, there is no word in Wolof that designates homosexuality; hence, those who would decry the presence of homosexuality in Senegal have historically relied on French terms such as *pédé*, *PD*, *pederast*, and *les homos*.

Beginning in the 1980s, the term *goorjigeen* increasingly became synonymous with "homosexual" and acquired the status of an offensive epithet (Niang 2010). By the late 1990s hearing the word *goorjigeen* evoked fear on the part of gay men: "The term [*goorjigeen*] is like a siren sound that we expect to be followed by insults, blows, or stones thrown at us by out-of-control mobs" (Niang et al. 2003, 505). The increasing visibility of same-sex practices in Senegal over the past three decades (due in part to the proliferation of tabloid publications, ongoing moral campaigns against homosexuality, the inclusion of men who have sex with men [MSM] in national AIDS programming, and the emergence of networks of MSM who established linkages with global gay rights movements) has enabled this slippage in meaning (Foley 2014; Broqua 2017).[7] This visibility also diminished acceptance of transgender individuals, who are now assumed to be gay. In the following section we describe this transition to an increasingly hostile social setting that was prime for a sexual panic.

### Politics and Moral Legitimacy

The criminalization of homosexual acts in Senegal dates to the mid-twentieth century, when the French Penal Code, including its provisions penalizing homosexual acts (acts against nature), was applied in Senegal by the decree of November 19, 1947 (Camara 2009). The provision stands today in Articles 318 and 319, which outlaw "anyone committing an indecent or unnatural act with an individual of the same sex." Offenders can be fined or punished with imprisonment of up to five years (Camara 2009). Despite this provision, moral campaigns against homosexuality did not enter the public sphere until the 1980s. Here we argue that the rise in antihomosexual political discourse in

Senegal coincides with the broader process of democratization. We highlight two of the most significant consequences of Senegal's shift from one-party rule to contested elections. First, political parties and political candidates had to establish their moral legitimacy to earn the trust of the electorate. Second, religious leaders were newly empowered to issue critiques of the secular state and immoral political platforms and to advocate for political parties and candidates that they believed to be the best protectors of the Muslim nation. These shifts in Senegal's political sphere produced a favorable environment for antihomosexuality (which is portrayed as being synonymous with Islamic values) to become a litmus test for moral legitimacy and hence electability.

In the 1980s, Muslim religious reformers began to criticize the secular state and organize themselves to combat a variety of "social evils," from poverty to addiction and AIDS (Broqua 2016). As feminist and gender scholar Codou Bop (2008) recounts, the early efforts of these would-be Islamist reformers targeted Senegal's Family Code in the 1990s. A coalition calling itself the Islamic Committee for Reforming the Family Code argued against the legal and civil provisions accorded to women in the Family Code and for the creation of an alternative Code of Conduct inspired by Sharia law and adjudicated by an Islamic court (Bop 2008). These efforts were stalled indefinitely when President Abdoulaye Wade stated unequivocally that there would be no changes to the Family Code during his presidency. Yet as political scientist Leonardo Villalón (2010, 2015) argues, more significant than the failure of the campaign is the reformers' success in generating public political debate about issues that were seemingly settled in Senegal: *laïcité* (secularism), the Family Code, and women's access to a judicial system that would protect their rights in marriage and divorce.

Scholars assessing the process of "democratization" in predominantly Muslim West African countries since the 1990s have noted a marked increase in the religiosity of intellectuals and politicians, the proliferation of Islamic candidates and explicitly Islamic political platforms, and the power of religious leaders and reformers to win concessions from elected officials in spite of their limited ability to attain elected office (Gellar 2005; Soares 2009; Villalón 2010, 2015; Diouf 2013; Kang 2015; Babou 2016). Here again, the power of religious leaders and their public discourses may be less in their ability to win seats or official representation in seats of power than in their ability to sway public opinion and to hold politicians accountable to moral and religious concerns.

The backdrop of economic precarity provided fertile ground for these Islamic critiques of state failure and political corruption. Herdt (2009, 32) argues that panics emerge in times of social, economic, and political change and moments of conflict between state mechanisms of control and free expression of sexuality. This description corresponds with Senegal's social, economic, and political turbulence in the 1990s and 2000s. Many Senegalese have experienced economic distress since the advent of structural adjustment programs in the 1980s and the devaluation of the Central African franc in 1994, leading to significant frustration with the status quo.

Senegal's first democratic regime change (Alternance) occurred in 2000, when longtime opposition leader Abdoulaye Wade and his Parti Démocratique Sénégalais (PDS, Senegalese Democratic Party) finally beat the ruling Parti Socialiste (PS, Socialist Party), which had successfully held the presidency since independence in 1960. While scholars of Senegal describe the first decade of the twenty-first century as a period of reinvigoration of democratic activity and political organizing, most Senegalese did not experience significant improvements in their quality of life despite the political transition (Diouf and Leichtman 2009; Mills 2011; Villalón 2015). High unmet expectations for a responsive and transparent state fostered civic unrest and despair (Melly 2017).

In the years immediately prior to the surge in homophobic violence, Senegal experienced a decline in its main growth indicators. While the country registered an average growth of 4.4 percent between 1996 and 2006, with 5.3 percent in 2005, the growth rate of the GDP fell to 2.1 percent in 2006 and 2.8 percent in 2007. There were significant disruptions and in some cases complete bankruptcies among some of the country's largest businesses (Agence Nationale de la Statistique et de la Démographie 2008). The informal sector experienced sluggish growth, and workers rioted against regulatory measures. Youth unemployment in particular remains widespread in working-class neighborhoods, inland towns, and the suburbs of Dakar. Citizens suffered through a crisis in the energy sector with untimely load shedding, breaks in the supply of butane gas, and rising prices for fuel, electricity, and gas. From 2006 to 2007, the inflation rate went from 1.9 percent to more than 5 percent in the context of state reduction of subsidies for essential goods. The state's failure to provide for citizens' basic needs left it vulnerable to attacks on many fronts, including from religious authorities who questioned the state's moral legitimacy.

As in other Muslim nations in West Africa, social issues concerning gender, family life, marriage, and sexuality feature prominently in the political campaigns of conservative or reformist political parties and religious leaders who are pursuing greater alignment between religion and state policy (Villalón 2010). The Islamic organization Jamra, whose affiliate NGO would later become active in HIV prevention as a faith-based organization, was an early entrant in this emerging field of explicitly Islamic NGOs that lobbied for the application of religious values to state policy and priorities. Broqua (2016) offers a detailed historical overview of Jamra's development and its strident efforts to combat homosexuality. The organization was created in 1982 by Latif Guèye, who founded it as an Islamic organization that also published a monthly magazine. The mandate of the organization and the magazine was to combat social ills, particularly those affecting Senegalese youth. From its earliest inception the publication condemned homosexuality as one of the social evils threatening Senegalese society. Guèye became known for his work on drug addiction and AIDS, and in 1989 Jamra was selected by the National AIDS Control Programme to carry out HIV/AIDS awareness campaigns (Broqua 2016). Guèye became a leader in Senegal's robust civil society arena working on HIV/AIDS, and in 1993 he created a parallel nongovernmental organization, also called Jamra.

In Broqua's (2016) telling, Jamra occupied a pivotal dual role that allowed it to blur the boundaries between moral commentary and public health interventions. On the one hand, the religious organization deployed religious rhetoric to wage highly mediatized social and moral campaigns against homosexuality and other social ills. At the same time, the inclusion of the NGO in Senegal's national AIDS program meant that its leaders were keenly aware of Senegal's increasing focus on outreach to vulnerable populations, including MSM. While Jamra was officially charged with carrying out HIV education and awareness that would be sensitive to religious sensibilities, it also operated as an Islamic watchdog that publicly denounced alleged violations of Muslim values and homosexuality (Broqua 2016). It proved successful at swaying public opinion, and its public reach was illustrated when it closed down a nightclub in 1999 after the media reported that a parade of transvestites had taken place there.

Jamra's activities are situated within a much broader process of contestation and debate about the political, economic, and moral legitimacy of the Senegalese state. The opening up of the political field to opposition parties, including fundamentalists who have created their own political parties or run on religious platforms, has meant that public officials are continuously subjected to aggressive questioning about the compatibility of their actions, programs, and policies with religious values. As Villalón describes it, "The liberalization of political life has opened the door to religious critiques of the political order, and hence to a more assertive role for religion in public life" (2010, 380). Given Senegal's deep religiosity, individuals appealing to a higher moral ground may gain rapid traction and an immediate constituency for their policy positions. Jamra's campaign against homosexuality succeeded in creating a heightened sense of threat and producing an atmosphere of hypervigilance. Senegal's past tolerance of gender fluidity has been replaced by a "transphobic" public domain, one characterized by expressions of fear or anger about the public transgression of gender norms (Epprecht 2004, 16).

## "Outing" Homosexuals: Tabloid Coverage and Sexual Panic

As Herdt (2009) argues, moral panics and sexual panics are the culmination of many social forces, but they are often sparked by a triggering event. Most commentators suggest that the publication of photos of an alleged marriage between two men in the tabloid magazine *Icone* in February 2008 was the cataclysmic event that unleashed the panic (IGLHRC 2010; Mills 2011; M'Baye 2013).[8] In addition to the salacious photos, the text accompanying the article claimed that the publisher and author were alerting the authorities about the dangerous rise of homosexuality among Senegalese youth. The magazine sold out, and the article made headlines in a number of local press outlets, accompanied by hostile commentary. In Herdt's framework this event was a moral shock, "a socially significant incident or threat that galvanizes public outrage and is commonly associated with the idiom of disgust" (2009, 4).

Within days of the magazine's publication, the Senegalese police arrested ten people and placed them in custody for four days before releasing them without explanation (Bop 2008). This was the first in a series of events in which police and ordinary citizens targeted suspected homosexuals for arrest, detention, physical assault, and public shaming. In December 2008, nine young men were arrested in Sicap Mbao, a peri-urban neighborhood at the outskirts of Dakar, while they were conducting an HIV/AIDS prevention activity. The Senegalese Nine, as they were known in the global press, were accused of homosexuality and sentenced to eight years in prison and a fine of 500,000 West African francs for "indecent and unnatural acts and criminal association." The nine eventually won their appeal, and their sentences were overturned. In another incident in 2009, the body of a suspected homosexual man was exhumed from a Muslim cemetery in the city of Thiès. After his family reburied him, his corpse was disinterred a second time and dumped outside his family's house. His family ended up burying him within their family compound (IGLHRC 2010; Mills 2011).[9]

This wave of events was punctuated by repeated vocal condemnations of homosexuality by religious leaders, particularly those affiliated with anti-Sufi or fundamentalist organizations.[10] Islamists seized the opportunity to denounce homosexuality, to proclaim themselves the moral protectors of the nation, and to accuse the Senegalese state of being weak at best and complicit with moral decline at worst (Bop 2008).[11] The Collectif des Associations Islamique du Sénégal (CAIS, Collective of Islamic Associations of Senegal) circulated a press release that called on the state to "fight against homosexuality before it is too late." Seizing the opportunity presented by the heightened media coverage, the CAIS used multiple platforms to circulate antihomosexual rhetoric and to position itself as the moral protector of Senegal's Muslim population. Among other tactics, CAIS called on all imams of Senegal to decry the degeneration of morality and the rise of homosexuality in their Friday sermons. The group attempted to organize a protest march against "the depravity of morality and against the release of the jailed homosexuals" on a Friday afternoon after the main prayer session. State authorities eventually banned the protest for fear of further violence (Broqua 2016). Though the march was cancelled, the organizers benefited from extensive media coverage, during which they announced that they would put forward candidates in the upcoming local elections (Bop 2008).

Throughout 2008 and 2009 private radio and television stations provided a platform for representatives of Islamist associations, imams, and politicians who denounced homosexuality as a non-Senegalese and un-African phenomenon. After the release of the nine suspected homosexuals, leaders of twenty Islamic associations formed the Islamic Front to Defend Ethical Values, which was dedicated to oppose the threat of homosexuality. They referred to the release of the nine individuals as "an attack against Islam"; the president of Jamra read a public statement from the front asserting that "a shadow lobby has hatched a dangerous conspiracy against religious values in order to legalize homosexuality" (Agence France Press 2009). Another Muslim leader issued a public statement to journalists calling for the death of homosexuals if they did not comply with being banned from society (Agence France Press 2009). Private media broadcast repeated calls for the murder of homosexuals. Lists of names of suspected homosexuals circulated via social media and created a volatile climate exacerbated by a rumor that the police would be looking for those named on these lists. In fear for their lives, some men sought refuge in the Gambia, while others traveled to Mali, Guinea-Bissau, and the United States (Bop 2008). The sexual panic was in full swing.

Members of the fundamentalist movement employed incendiary rhetoric to invoke notions of a Muslim community under threat. They invoked a firm boundary between the Muslim community and homosexual others, thereby reinforcing a perception that defending the civil rights of sexual minorities was incompatible with Islam. In spite of their limited representation in government, they issued warnings to elected officials that the cost of defending homosexuals would be the erosion of voter support. Global and national human rights advocates spoke out against the reigning atmosphere of persecution, recalling that Senegal is a signatory to the African Human Rights Charter and the International Covenant on Civil and Political Rights, both of which protect the right to privacy and to equal treatment under the law (Bop 2008). Nonetheless, the sensationalist Islamist rhetoric was effective at silencing most of civil society. An ad hoc crisis committee of medical providers and NGOs that had worked the most closely with MSM organizations and leaders in Senegal's AIDS response found themselves operating in crisis mode as they tried to maintain a minimal level of activities while protecting their staff and clients (Foley 2014).

The heightened sense of crisis slowly subsided, but the backlash of 2008 and 2009 disrupted the grassroots activities of gay men and MSM who had been engaged in HIV education and other advocacy efforts (Poteat et al. 2011; Foley 2014). These networks operated not as a political movement to advance the civil or human rights of LGBTQ individuals but as vehicles for information sharing, peer education, leadership training, and social support.[12] Much of this organizing has ceased or has been driven entirely underground. Lingering effects of the sexual panic continue to shape what is politically and pragmatically possible in HIV/AIDS work. In 2010 the ad hoc crisis committee of AIDS NGOs successfully blocked the release of two human rights reports on Senegal's homophobic crisis, fearing that global media attention and calls for decriminalization would reignite homophobic violence (Foley 2014). Some members of this committee worked on an advocacy document with policy recommendations for countering homophobia, protecting the civil rights of MSM, and promoting tolerance of sexual minorities.[13] The document, which was always intended to be an internal document for the NGO community, was never officially released, because the Conseil National de Lutte Contre le SIDA (CNLS, National Committee to Combat AIDS), bowing in part to Jamra's opposition, did not want to contradict official state policy criminalizing homosexuality (Broqua 2016). These events indicate that antihomosexuality has not only come to dominate the public sphere but also greatly reduced the ability of nonstate actors to pursue advocacy work.

In the wake of the sexual panic, accusations of homosexual sympathies remain a powerful tool to discredit political opponents. These accusations were rife during the 2012 presidential campaign: the son of President Abdoulaye Wade was accused of being gay, and a Jamra leader accused another political group of being "infiltrated by homosexuals" (Broqua 2016). Macky Sall himself was castigated as being "the candidate for homosexuals" after he made an ambiguous statement about homosexuality that some commentators interpreted as support for decriminalization (Broqua 2016). Similar accusations swirled during the rest of the presidential campaign. They resurfaced in 2013, prompting President Macky Sall to make a definitive statement that there were no plans to decriminalize homosexuality.[14] Sall reiterated this stance during US president Barack Obama's visit in June 2013. It seems that Senegalese politicians are now faced with making assertive declarations of their support for continued criminalization, or they risk facing considerable public pressure and hostile accusations. Displaying a willingness to defend Senegal's legislation criminalizing homosexuality has become a litmus test for electability.[15]

## Legislating Sexuality: What Future for Sexual Minorities in Senegal?

We argue here that the homophobic incidents of 2008–9 in Senegal follow the pattern of a sexual panic (Herdt 2009). The conditions for this panic were rooted in widespread disillusion with the state, the increasingly visible and assertive role of religion in public life, and widespread resentment among Senegal's citizens due to prolonged economic precarity (conditions that are shared by citizens in other poor African countries). While the tabloid story of the gay wedding operated as a triggering moral shock, the sexual panic escalated in the context of cultural anger over decades of failed development and renewed mistrust of the nation's elites. As Herdt explains, cultural anger "marshals intense emotion across diffuse domains and arenas of action to unite disparate individuals and groups in political pursuit of a common enemy or sexual scapegoat" (2009, 5). In neighboring Gambia, it was former president Yahya Jammeh himself who served as the catalyst for widespread sexual panic: his introduction of antihomosexuality legislation and vicious antigay rhetoric represented an attempt to distract public debate away from his own illegitimacy and weakening grip on power.

Sensationalist media coverage about homosexuality and suspected homosexuals offered religious entrepreneurs and would-be social reformers a convenient and vulnerable target. In a trend that one commentator referred to as "the radicalization of homophobia in Senegal," a continuous drumbeat of homophobic warnings from religious commentators rose to a fever pitch (Bangré 2009). Fundamentalist discourses incited general panic about moral threats to the nation and destabilized confidence in the state's ability to counter these threats. The fundamentalist movement has attracted adherents in poor, densely populated neighborhoods on the outskirts of Dakar, including Mbao, Guinaw Rail, and Yeumbeul, and these sites were also the locations of homophobic violence that were reported in local media. As Lydia Boyd (this volume) argues for Uganda, political unease and economic distress are reframed as moral threats stemming from a destabilized social order.

At the time of the panic, the leader of the Islamic NGO Jamra referred to the fight against homosexuality as not only a moral campaign but also a civic and patriotic duty (Bangré 2009). The assertion that President Macky Sall's defiant public rejection of homosexuality is at once an expression of piety and a patriotic gesture reveals a significant shift in sociocultural norms in Senegal. Virulent expressions of intolerance stand in sharp contrast to historical evidence of non-binary-gender expression and same-sex sexual practices in Wolof society (Crowder 1959; Schenkel 1971; Teunis 1996; Davidson [1970] 1998; Boulaga and Akana 2007). In both the distant and more recent past, gender fluidity in which genderqueer individuals inhabited the social category *goorjigeen* and occupied feminine spaces in the social order provoked little social concern. Over the past forty years, forms of gender expression that previously needed no defense became indefensible.

Human rights advocates and individuals working in Senegal's AIDS response have lamented this erosion of cultural flexibility regarding gender expression. While Senegal's history of varied gender expression would seem to offer a basis for human rights protections and tolerance of sexual minorities, this past tolerance rested in part on both unwitting and willful ignorance about the sexual practices of gender-fluid individuals. Genderqueer or gender-fluid individuals were part of a legible social order, and their rights were assured by their integration in the wider social fabric. As religious and political discourses about homosexuality came to dominate Senegalese headlines and the word *goorjigeen* became synonymous with the word "homosexual," the cultural flexibility that accepted fluid gender expression has eroded. Religious leaders have successfully mobilized Islamic discourses to depict homosexuals as being outside the bounds of the social body and an affront to the *umma* (the faithful community of Muslims). The press release following the creation of the Islamic Front asserted that the Prophet encouraged the faithful to kill individuals who are guilty of immoral acts (like homosexuality): "These words from Allah and the Prophet's hadith require us to respond to all attacks against Islam" (Agence France Press 2009). By depicting homosexuality as an attack on Islamic values and the Muslim community, these religious leaders assert that homosexuals have no right to exist; they are undeserving of civil or human rights. Those who advocate for the civil rights of LGBTQ individuals in Senegal find little traction using a universal human rights framework. As in the Ugandan case (Boyd, this volume), rights are only successfully asserted as stemming from interdependence and social relatedness, and religious rhetoric has cast LGBTQ individuals as being outside the social order.[16] Any steps toward decriminalizing homosexuality in Senegal run the risk of being cast as an assault on Islam. Demands for protecting the human rights of sexual minorities in Senegal by global LGBTQ activists, as well as French president Nicolas Sarkozy's paternalistic comments about the imprisonment of alleged homosexuals in Senegal, may well have reinforced the convergence of antihomosexual and anti-imperialist rhetoric, as it has elsewhere on the continent (Boyd 2013; Broqua 2016).

The growing literature on transphobia or homophobia offers compelling evidence that non-gender-conforming individuals are highly vulnerable during moments of acute political frustration and social unease (Murray 2009). Gaudio (2009) evokes the shrinking sphere of tolerance and growing police harassment of sexual minorities in northern Nigeria in the midst of economic crisis and the establishment of Sharia law, while Marc Epprecht (2004) offers analysis of homophobic backlash in the midst of fear of AIDS and threatened masculinities in Zimbabwe. In the Senegalese case, latent anger and frustration with the state and uncertainty about the country's economic and social future are a volatile mix. In these moments of transition and uncertainty, particularly during electoral campaigns, accusations of supporting the decriminalization of homosexuality are believable, believed, and thoroughly delegitimizing. These accusations reinforce the structural vulnerability of LGBTQ individuals as politicians and other public figures condemn homosexuality in an effort to assure their electability.

Senegal's sexual panic offered a sensationalized distraction from longstanding and pervasive social, economic, and political challenges. But a sexual panic is also a social event during which particular actors (in this case, both politicians and religious leaders) attempt to consolidate power and discredit their opponents. As many African states face uncertain economic futures, political volatility, and a crisis in confidence of their citizens, the conditions are favorable for the eruption of panics. In the absence of human rights protections for LGBTQ individuals or a social climate favorable to establishing them, sexual minorities may continue to serve as sexual scapegoats for a variety of seemingly intractable problems in the years to come.

## Notes

1. The notion of genderqueer in queer theory may offer the closest approximation to *goorjigeen*. As described below, the term *goorjigeen* has taken on new meanings over time. In current usage it operates as a violent slur. It is no longer a term that queer, gay, transgender, or gender nonbinary individuals would use to describe themselves.

2. We stress, following Currier (2014) and Coly (2013), that these antigay discourses are not a reflection of "timeless African homophobia" but the product of a particular confluence of social and political events.

3. See Jones 2013 for an overview of the changing political and economic role of African and *métis* women in elite Saint Louis society.

4. See Niang 2010 for a more detailed explanation of the female kinship terms used in reference to age and generational hierarchies among *goorjigeen*.

5. These collectives of women have a deep history; Boilat 1984 describes these associations in Saint Louis in the nineteenth century.

6. More recent research reveals similar linguistic distinctions used by same-sex-desiring men who distinguish between effeminate receptive partners (*ibbi*) and masculine penetrative partners (*yoos*) (Teunis 2001; Niang et al. 2003).

7. Thomann's (2016) research in Côte d'Ivoire illustrates how the ubiquitous use of MSM in global AIDS programs simultaneously renders same-sex practices more visible, provides individuals who engage in same-sex practices with a new vocabulary for defining their identities, and obscures the tremendous diversity among LGBTQ people in terms of gender performance, sexual orientation, race, ethnicity, education, and class.

8. A similar wave of politicized homophobia occurred in Malawi in 2009 after the public wedding engagement ceremony of a transgender woman and a cisgender man (see Currier 2014).

9. For a comprehensive review of the series of events following the February 2008 publication, see IGLHRC 2010.

10. The past twenty years have seen the rise of Sunni Islam and other versions of Islamic fundamentalism (Augis 2005).

11. Bop's analysis of the Islamist movement highlights the parallels between the antihomosexual campaign of 2008 and a similar campaign in the 1990s that attempted to roll back legal protections for women mandated by Senegal's Code de la Famille. Using similar tactics, the campaign led by the Comité Islamique pour la Réforme du Code de la Famille au Sénégal argued that Senegalese feminists were "Westernized" and intent on destroying the foundations of the family (Bop 2008).

12. We are mindful of Stella Nyanzi's (2015) arguments that the absence of loud and boisterous proclamations of rights on the part of African LGBT individuals must not be assumed to stem from shame or oppression. She makes a forceful case that silence, particularly in the context of state-sponsored violence against homosexuals and same-sex-loving individuals in the Gambia, is a mode of self-protection and can be an expression of defiance.

13. Similar to Boyd's (this volume) allusion to making rights claims within culturally relevant relational obligations, this document alluded to Senegalese cultural values such as tolerance, discretion, and nonconfrontation as possible means of protecting LGBTQ individuals from persecution.

14. This pattern repeated itself again in 2016 when President Sall proposed a referendum to modify Senegal's constitution. The largest coalition of opposition parties accused the ruling party of seeking to decriminalize homosexuality.

15. Similar rhetoric and at least one murder of a suspected gay man took place during the 2019 presidential election cycle (Peyton 2019).

16. Similar to the case of Samson Mukisa, cases of assault and murder of suspected gay men in Senegal do not elicit sympathy, as LGBTQ persons are seen as being outside the bounds of kinship and social relationships of interdependence. Like Mukisa, their victimhood is illegible (Boyd, this volume).

## References

Agence France Press. 2009. "Création d'un Front islamique pour la defense des valeurs éthiques." *Jeune Afrique*, April 29. http://www.jeuneafrique.com/160403/societe/cr-ation-d-un-front-islamique-pour-la-d-fense-des-valeurs-thiques/.

Agence Nationale de la Statistique et de la Démographie. 2009. République du Sénégal, Ministère de l'Économie et des Finances, *Rapport d'activités 2008*. http://www.ansd.sn/index.php?option=com_docman&task=cat_view&gid=63&Itemid=277.

———. 2017. Enquête nationale sur l'emploi au Sénégal, deuxième trimestre 2017. http://www.ansd.sn/index.php?option=com_ansd&view=titrepublication&id=33.

Ahlberg, Beth Maina, and Asli Kulane. 2011. "Sexual and Reproductive Health and Rights." In *African Sexualities: A Reader*, edited by Sylvia Tamale, 313–39. Oxford: Pambazuka Press.

Augis, Erin. 2005. "Dakar's Sunnite Women: The Politics of Person." In *L'Islam politique au sud du Sahara: Identités, discours et enjeux*, edited by Muriel Gomez-Perez, 309–26. Paris: Karthala.

Babou, Cheikh Anta. 2016. "Negotiating the Boundaries of Power: Abdoulaye Wade, the Muridiyya, and State Politics in Senegal, 2000–2012." *Journal of West African History* 2 (1): 165–88.

Bangré, Habibou. 2009. "Comment les neuf homosexuels ont été libérés." *Jeune Afrique*, April 23. https://www.jeuneafrique.com/187335/politique/comment-les-neuf-homosexuels-ont-t-lib-r-s/.

Boilat, David. 1984. *Esquisses sénégalaises*. Paris: Karthala.

Bop, Codou. 2008. "Sénégal: Homophobie et manipulation politique de l'Islam." March 25. http://www.wluml.org/fr/node/4514.

Boulaga, Fabien Eboussi, and Parfait D. Akana. 2007. *L'homosexualité est bonne à penser*. Yaoundé: Academia Africana.

Boyd, Lydia. 2013. "The Problem with Freedom: Homosexuality and Human Rights in Uganda." *Anthropological Quarterly* 86 (3): 697–724.

Broqua, Christophe. 2016. "Islamic Movements against Homosexuality in Senegal: The Fight against AIDS as Catalyst." In *Public Religion and the Fight against Homosexuality in Africa*, edited by Adriaan van Klinken and Ezra Chitando, 163–79. London: Routledge.

———. 2017. "Góor-jigéen: La resignification négative d'une catégorie entre genre et sexualité (Sénégal)." *Socio* 9:163–83.

Camara, Fatou Kiné. 2009. "VIH et l'homosexualité." Roundtable presentation, Université Cheikh Anta Diop, Dakar, Senegal.

Coly, Ayo. 2013. "Introduction." *African Studies Review* 56 (2): 21–30.

Corre, Armand. 1894. *L'ethnographie criminelle d'après les observations et les statistiques judiciaires recueillies dans les colonies*. Paris: C. Reinwald.

Crowder, Michael. 1959. *Pagans and Politicians*. London: Hutchinson.

Currier, Ashley. 2014. "Arrested Solidarity: Obstacles to Intermovement Support for LGBT Rights in Malawi." *WSQ: Women's Studies Quarterly* 42 (3–4): 146–63.

Davidson, Michael. (1970) 1998. "A 1958 Visit to a Dakar Boy Brothel." In *Boy Wives and Female Husbands: Studies in African Homosexualities*, edited by Stephen O. Murray and Will Roscoe, 111–13. New York: St. Martin's.

Diouf, Mamadou. 2013. "Préface: Abdoulaye Wade et le régime liberal à l'examen; Réalisation, mirages, et abus d'une alternance démocratique." In *Le Sénégal sous Abdoulaye Wade: Le Sopi à l'épreuve du pouvoir*, edited by Momar-Coumba Diop, 13–20. Paris: Karthala.

Diouf, Mamadou, and Mara Leichtman, eds. 2009. *New Perspectives on Islam in Senegal: Conversion, Migration, Wealth, and Femininity*. New York: Palgrave Macmillan.

Epprecht, Marc. 2004. *Hungochani: The History of a Dissident Sexuality in Southern Africa*. Montreal: McGill-Queen's University Press.

Fal, Arame, et al. 1990. *Dictionnaire Wolof-Français suivi d'un index Français-Wolof*. Paris: Karthala.

Foley, Ellen. 2014. "Sites of Contention: The Politics of AIDS in Senegal." In *Medical Anthropology in Global Africa*, edited by Katherine Rhine and John Janzen, 89–96. Lawrence: University Press of Kansas.

Gaudio, Rudolf Pell. *Allah Made Us: Sexual Outlaws in an Islamic African City*. Malden, MA: Wiley-Blackwell, 2009.

Gellar, Sheldon. 2005. *Democracy in Senegal: Tocquevillian Analytics in Africa*. New York: Palgrave Macmillan.

Gorer, Geoffrey. 1935. *Africa Dances: A Book about West African Negroes*. New York: A. A. Knopf.

Herdt, Gilbert. 1997. *Same Sex, Different Cultures: Gays and Lesbians across Cultures*. Oxford: Westview Press.

———, ed. 2009. *Moral Panics, Sex Panics: Fear and the Fight over Sexual Rights*. New York: NYU Press.

IGLHRC (International Gay and Lesbian Human Rights Commission). 2010. *Words of Hate, Climate of Fear: Human Rights Violations and Challenges to the LGBT Movement in Senegal*. New York: IGLHRC

Imam, Ayesha, Amina Mama, and Fatou Sow, eds. 1997. *Engendering the Social Sciences in Africa*. Dakar: CODESRIA.

Jaunait, Alexandre, Amélie Le Renard, and Élisabeth Marteu. 2013. "Nationalismes sexuels? Reconfigurations contemporaines des sexualités et des nationalisms." *Raisons politiques* 49 (1): 5–23.

Jones, Hilary. 2013. *The Métis of Sénégal: Urban Life and Politics in French West Africa*. Bloomington: Indiana University Press.

Kang, Alice. 2015. *Bargaining for Women's Rights: Activism in an Aspiring Muslim Democracy*. Minneapolis: University of Minnesota Press.

Kretz, Adam J. 2013. "From 'Kill the Gays' to 'Kill the Gay Rights Movement': The Future of Homosexuality Legislation in Africa." *Northwestern Journal of International Human Rights* 11 (2): 207–44.

Le Corre, Maelle. 2013. "Sénégal: Cinq femmes arrêtées pour 'actes contre-nature.'" November 13. http://yagg.com/2013/11/13/senegal-cinq-femmes-arretees-pour-actes-contre-nature/.

M'Baye, Babacar. 2013. "The Origins of Senegalese Homophobia: Discourses on Homosexuals and Transgender People in Colonial and Postcolonial Senegal." *African Studies Review* 56 (2): 109–28.
McNee, Lisa. 2000. *Selfish Gifts: Senegalese Women's Autobiographical Discourses.* Albany: SUNY Press.
Melly, Caroline. 2017. *Bottleneck: Moving, Building, and Belonging in an African City.* Chicago: University of Chicago Press.
Mills, Ivy. 2011. "Gendered Honor, Social Death, and the Politics of Exposure in Senegalese Literature and Population Culture." PhD diss., University of California, Berkeley.
Murray, David A. B., ed. 2009. *Homophobias: Lust and Loathing across Time and Space.* Durham, NC: Duke University Press.
Murray, Stephen O., and Will Roscoe. 1998. *Boy-Wives and Female Husbands: Studies of African Homosexualities.* New York: St. Martin's.
Ndiaye, Seynabou. 2001. "Femmes et politique au Sénégal: Contribution à la réflexion sur la participation des femmes sénégalaises à la vie politique du 1945 à 2001." Master's thesis, Université de Paris I–Panthéon–Sorbonne.
Ndoye, Omar. 2010. *Le N'doep: Transe therapeutique chez les lebous du Sénégal.* Paris: GRAPPAF-l'Harmattan.
Niang, Cheikh Ibrahima. 2010. "Understanding Sex between Men in Senegal: Beyond Current Linguistic and Discursive Categories." In *Routledge Handbook of Sexuality, Health and Rights,* edited by Richard Parker and Peter Aggleton, 116–224. London: Routledge.
———. 2013. "Anthropologie de la sexualité: Philosophie, culture et construction sociale du sexe au Sénégal." PhD diss., Université Cheikh Anta Diop, Dakar, Senegal.
Niang, Cheikh. I., Placide Tapsoba, Ellen Weiss, Moustapha Diagne, Youssoupha Niang, Amadou Moreau, Dominique Gomis, Abdoulaye Sidibé Wade, Karim Seck, and Chris Castle. 2003. "It's Raining Stones: Stigma, Violence and HIV Vulnerability among Men Who Have Sex with Men in Dakar, Senegal." *Culture, Health & Sexuality* 5 (6): 499–512.
Nossiter, Adam. 2013. "Senegal Cheers Its President for Standing Up to Obama on Same-Sex Marriage." *New York Times,* June 28, 2013.
Nyanzi, Stella. 2015. "When the State Produces Hate: Re-thinking the Global Queer Movement through Silence in the Gambia." *Thamyris/Intersecting* 30:179–94.
Ouzgane, Lahoucine, and Robert Morrell, eds. 2005. *African Masculinities: Men in Africa from the Late Nineteenth Century to the Present.* Scottsville, South Africa: University of KwaZulu-Natal Press.
Peyton, Nellie. 2019. "Fear in Senegal as Presidential Campaign Stirs Up Homophobia." Thomson Reuters Foundation. https://www.reuters.com/article/us-senegal-election-lgbt/fear-in-senegal-as-presidential-election-stirs-up-homophobia-idUSKCN1Q92CV.
Poteat, Tonia, Daouda Diouf, Fatou Maria Drame, Marieme Ndaw, Cheikh Traore, Mandeep Dhaliwal, Chris Beyrer, and Stefan Baral. 2011. "HIV Risk among MSM in Senegal: A Qualitative Rapid Assessment of the Impact of Enforcing Laws That

Criminalize Homosexuality." *PLoS ONE* 6 (12): e28760. https://doi.org/10.1371/journal.pone.0028760.

Seck, Abdourahmane. 2010. *La question musulmane au Sénégal: Essai d'anthropologie d'une nouvelle modernité.* Paris: Karthala.

Schenkel, Ralf. 1971. "Le vécu et la vie sexuelle chez les Africains acculturés du Sénégal." *Psychopathologie Africaine* 7:313–58.

Soares, Benjamin. 2009. "The Attempt to Reform Family Law in Mali." *Die Welt des Islams* 49:398–428.

Tamale, Sylvia. 2007. "Out of the Closet: Unveiling Sexuality Discourses in Uganda" In *Africa after Gender*, edited by Catherine Cole, Takyiwaa Manuh, and Stephen F. Miescher, 17–29. Bloomington: Indiana University Press.

———, ed. 2011. *African Sexualities: A Reader.* Nairobi: Pambazuka Press.

———. 2013. Confronting the Politics of Nonconforming Sexualities in Africa. *African Studies Review* 56 (2): 31–45. doi:10.1017/asr.2013.40.

Teunis, Niels. 1996. "Homosexuality in Dakar: Is the Bed the Heart of a Sexual Subculture?" *Journal of Gay, Lesbian, and Bisexual Identity* 1:153–69.

———. 2001. "Same-Sex Sexuality in Africa: A Case Study from Senegal." *AIDS and Behavior* 5 (2): 173–82.

Thomann, Matthew. 2016. "HIV Vulnerability and the Erasure of Sexual and Gender Diversity in Abidjan, Côte d'Ivoire." *Global Public Health* 11 (7–8): 994–1009.

Villalón, Leonardo. 2010. "From Argument to Negotiation: Constructing Democracy in African Muslim Contexts." *Comparative Politics* 42 (4): 375–93.

———. 2015. "Cautious Democrats: Religious Actors and Democratization Processes in Senegal." *Politics and Religion* 8 (2): 305–33.

Weeks, Jeffrey. 1996. "What Do We Mean When We Talk about the Body and Sexuality?" In *Modernity: An Introduction to Modern Societies*, edited by Stuart Hall, David Held, Don Hubert, and Kenneth Thompson, 363–94. Malden, MA: Blackwell.

# Making Rights Visible

## The Embodied Nature of Debates over Sexual and Gender-Based Rights in Uganda

LYDIA BOYD

In the early months of 2014, Uganda was seized with a moral panic linked to concerns about women's clothing. Uganda's parliament had begun debating the Anti-Pornography Bill, a piece of legislation with the stated purpose of protecting women and children from becoming the victims of sexual crimes by legally "defin[ing] and creat[ing] the offense of Pornography."[1] Women's clothing was not mentioned in the bill anywhere, but in media coverage and popular discussions the legislation became known as the "anti–mini skirt" bill, and its existence was interpreted by many as license to police and limit women's choice of dress. In the wake of these debates, women on the streets of Kampala were assaulted, their clothing ripped from their bodies, and politicians made statements asserting that women who chose to wear miniskirts were to blame for such assaults (Tumusiime and Kiguli 2015, 32). In a perverse twist, mobs of men sought to levy the punishment of nakedness for the perceived offense of, to use the language of the bill, the provocation of "sexual excitement."[2]

As Ugandan feminist activists and other critics rightly argued, the bill's problems stemmed from its overly broad definition of pornography and the implicit blame it placed on the actions of women, who could elicit the desire of men by dressing in ways perceived to be sexually suggestive. Women's bodies became viscerally central to debates over the bill: public, tangible evidence

171

of less tangible, less visible tensions in Ugandan society. In the months following the bill's introduction, women's public nakedness became a means of social censure wielded not only by angry mobs of young, disenfranchised men but also by the state. In at least two instances, state police sought to arrest female members of the political opposition, in the process stripping and groping the politicians as officers dragged the women's half-naked bodies into police cars that were surrounded by shouting crowds of onlookers and media.[3] At a moment when the increasingly authoritarian nature of the Museveni regime was drawing criticism from both within and outside the country, it was the bodies of women opposition politicians that became the screen for these tensions, their public nakedness making the bald power of the state newly visible.

Much of the scholarly response to the Anti-Pornography Bill has focused on the symbolic resonance of the miniskirt, the sartorial evidence of a "modern girl," whose visibility has long stoked tensions in the Ugandan public sphere, as it has elsewhere throughout Africa (Allman 2004; Hansen 2004; C. Decker 2010; A. Decker 2014). At the same time, Ugandan feminists have argued that the miniskirt obscures as much as it reveals, deflecting public attention away from the pressing political and economic realities under an autocratic regime (Tamale 2013; Awondo, Geschiere, and Reid 2014; Ayebazibwe 2014; Nyanzi and Karamagi 2015; Tumusiime and Kiguli 2015). As fruitful as discussions of the miniskirt have been, what I found most striking about the response to the Anti-Pornography Bill was the symbolic power not of clothing but of nakedness. It was women's bodies that were being—forcefully, cruelly—stripped bare, their nakedness drawing contempt, stoking outrage, and titillating an anxious public. It was women's bodies—not just their skirts—that emerged as terrain upon which a debate over propriety, culture, and rights was borne out.

This chapter is an attempt to frame and answer this question: Why has the naked body become a response to and a tool with which to engage and resist debates over gender and sexual rights in Uganda today? Debates over the Anti-Pornography Bill were not just over the legitimacy of "women's rights" but more generally about where rights should be *located* and made *visible*. These were debates over how and for whom rights should engender empowerment and political agency. My interest is in how the body itself—exposed and made vulnerable—reveals a key tension underlying debates over gender-based and sexual rights in Africa today. Ultimately, such debates in Uganda hinge on an underlying conflict between two competing constructs for rights-based claims, one rooted in a liberal political ideology that privileges the autonomous individual and another that views political agency and moral action as functions of interdependence and social relatedness. In the first model, the vulnerable, often anonymous body compels a compassionate response, and such vulnerability serves as evidence of the erosion of a liberal ideal of equality. In the second, a rights-based claim depends on social embeddedness, on the relationships forged between the person seeking redress and the community. Rights in one case are dispassionate, staked on a belief in the sameness of social equals. In the second model, rights depend on the difference between social actors and the ability to highlight the obligations and relations between people. These are different perspectives on what kinds of rights establish just relationships within society. I argue that the conflict between these models underlies many of the debates over sexual and gender-based rights in African societies today.

The body is an important locus for these tensions because the public's reactions to different kinds of bodily vulnerability—the varying responses of pity, contempt, admonishment, or compassion that nakedness generates—reveal how Ugandans make sense of who deserves rights and under what conditions rights may be extended. The meaning attributed to a naked body—the meaning made of its vulnerability and its exposure—is an important lens through which to understand how Ugandans themselves contextualize, justify, and sometimes dismiss different kinds of rights-based claims, especially those attributed to gender and sex. In this way I hope to move past analyses that posit "culture" as being in conflict with human rights to better understand the competing frameworks that animate human rights in different historical and social contexts. Drawing on a set of examples in recent years where bodies have been publicly thrust into the center of debates over the rights of women and sexual minorities in Uganda, I examine the controversial role that the body itself—exposed and publicly visible—plays in rights-based projects and the kinds of rights claims such vulnerability both enables and denies.

## Moral Bodies, Moral Claims: Competing Frameworks for Rights-Based Agency

My interest in nakedness as a window onto rights-based struggles stems from a recognition of the important role the body has played in the modern history of human rights. Scholars of human rights have for some time understood the unique power that women's bodies in particular—their physical presence but also their assumed vulnerability—have in rights-based political projects. Female bodies, Dorothy Hodgson writes in her introduction to *Gender and Culture at the Limit of Rights*, are "sites of contestation" that pit cultural against judicial and international frameworks for rights-based claims (2011, 3). But more than terrain for the cultural resistance to global rights frameworks, women's bodies have also proved to be critical touchstones in the Western history of human rights practice itself. As Pamela Scully (2011) has cogently argued, victimized women—especially the bodies of black women—were important symbols for nineteenth-century abolitionists, missionaries, and other early humanitarians who framed their work as a response to the unacceptable bodily violation of those considered the most vulnerable: women. The expansion of modern human rights work has depended on the visibility of suffering, especially on the evidence that women's embodied victimhood could provide.

This early concern with bodily vulnerability introduces an important tension that weaves through the twentieth- and twenty-first-century practice of human rights. As Peter Redfield and Erica Bornstein note in their own history of human rights and humanitarianism, "Human rights discourse defines its version [of human good] through past failure" (2010, 6). That is, in seeking to improve the human condition, Western human rights frameworks demand that we imagine the violation of persons denied rights. Women, and black women in particular, have long provided the vulnerable bodies at the center of such projects: symbolic and tangible evidence that provides both the moral justification and the limits of rights themselves. This symbolic work helps reveal a contradiction that underlies the Western claim of rights-based equality. Western human rights rhetoric depends not only on an argument about the sameness of all individuals but also on the recognition of humanity's inherent *inequality*: the persistent presence of a vulnerable victim.

If the vulnerable body plays a central role in shaping Western human rights practice, I suggest that the body exposes a different set of tensions concerning rights in the Ugandan context. In Uganda reactions to the naked body do not tend to focus on the perceived violation of or need to protect claims of equality, as we see in Western contexts. Rather, debates over rights are oriented around the moral value of relationships of interdependence and the apparent threat that the disruption of such relationships poses. The result is that nakedness does not evoke an unequivocal response of moral outrage or abstract compassion for an anonymous victim, as it often does in Western human rights contexts. In the examples I discuss below, bodily vulnerability stokes titillation and sometimes provokes rebuke. In one instance, nakedness is claimed as a powerful moral tool that works to chastise the looker. In all cases, the response to nakedness—titillating, chastising, shaming—is not generated by a threat to an unassailable moral value of equality. Rather, it depends on a shared understanding of the value of inequality, difference, and relationality. These responses to nakedness are driven by a fundamental concern with the status of a social and moral relationship. Rights-based claims, in this context, gain moral authority not by revealing a threat to equality but by highlighting the failure of social obligations and relationships that are often unequal. This distinction has consequences for how communities evaluate certain rights claims as valid and others as not.

In order to examine this issue, I turn to two recent cases where public nakedness generated discussion and debate about the moral and political terms of certain rights and responsibilities in Uganda. These cases each generated very different reactions to the naked, vulnerable body. But in both I found that the public's reaction was driven by a concern for the ways the body was related to others and the ways that nakedness could be used to emphasize, solidify, or even undermine the kinds of moral (and rights-based) claims made possible by such relationships. More than anonymous victims, these exposed bodies reveal how rights claims are situational, dependent not on the abstract equality of individuals but on the relationships of difference, dependence, and inequality that have long provided the terms of moral arguments about obligation, justice, and rights in Uganda.

### Gendered Protest: Nakedness and the Obligations of "Rights" in Uganda

In April 2017 the Ugandan feminist and academic Stella Nyanzi was imprisoned on charges of "cyber harassment" and "offensive communication" following a post she made describing Uganda's president, Yoweri Museveni, as a "pair of buttocks" and criticizing the qualifications of the First Lady, Janet Museveni, who had recently been appointed the minister of education.[4] Nyanzi's imprisonment drew widespread criticism from the international press and foreign governments, which viewed it as a blatant effort to silence a public critic of the Museveni regime. While this political act thrust her into the international spotlight, Nyanzi had for some time been known in Uganda for her wildly popular writing on social media. On Facebook, her preferred platform, her posts ranged from incisive political critique to fictional (and very popular) storylines that followed her alter ego's sexual escapades to posts about her own workplace struggles as a researcher at the Makerere Institute for Social Research.[5] Her following is such that she has emerged as a tabloid favorite in Uganda, the subject of media fascination in her own right well before her high-profile political arrest. Her popularity on social media is due in no small part to the frankness and forthrightness of her writing, especially on issues relating to sexuality and relationships, as well as the boldness of her political commentary. She has developed a singularly brazen online persona, exposing the hypocrisy of everything from the struggles faced by single mothers in Uganda to tales of government corruption.

Before her arrest, Nyanzi was best known for a widely publicized and prolonged conflict she had had with her supervisor at Makerere, the political scientist Mahmood Mamdani. At the culmination of this conflict, in April 2016, Nyanzi staged what would become an infamous public protest in front of her office, her access to which had become a focal point of her argument with Mamdani. Calling news media to her university office building, she sought to document what she characterized as a violation of her work contract.[6] She smeared red paint on the building walls and stripped naked in front of an apparently locked building gate, an effort, she stated in her own descriptions of the protest, to shame Mamdani into restoring her access to her office and her position of good standing in the institute. Yelling profanities and shaking her bare breasts, Nyanzi was greeted by coworkers and onlookers, who alternated between cheering her and staring in stunned silence. The protest was eagerly followed by the press and avidly consumed on social media. (Nyanzi posted her own videos and photos of the incident to Facebook, and other media organizations uploaded broadcast clips of her protest to YouTube.)

Her decision to remove most of her clothing (she kept her underwear on) was widely and feverishly debated. She was mocked as "crazy" and "vulgar" by mainstream media outlets and political pundits and caricatured by cartoonists in the opposition's newspaper, the *Daily Monitor*. NBS TV, an independent television station in Kampala, described the protest as a "regrettable incident," "like a movie of some sort," and onlookers as "shocked."[7] Professor Sylvia Tamale, a former dean at Makerere's School of Law and a friend of Nyanzi's, described her own sense of disbelief upon being called to the protest site and seeing Nyanzi in a state of undress: "I was shocked and horrified; embarrassed and ashamed. I thought my friend had completely lost it" (2016, 2). Madness was a common theme in coverage of the event; Nyanzi was dismissed as a woman who was out of control, even insane, behaving in a way inappropriate to her level of education and social standing. (She is the mother of three children, a fact often cited by critics of her actions.) But others celebrated and supported her protest, which Nyanzi repeatedly characterized as a last-ditch effort to secure her livelihood in the face of a university administration that she believed was unfairly set against her.

In a high-profile lecture given in the wake of the protest, Sylvia Tamale characterized the debate that followed as one generated by Nyanzi's resistance to the "dominant scripts," or discourses, that shape bodily norms for gendered behavior in Uganda. Defying a moral code that dictates that women's bodies are dangerous sexual objects whose power must be mitigated by women's dress and demure conduct, she argued that nakedness can be defiant and empowering, causing us to "rethink our association of nakedness with shame and debasement" (Tamale 2016, 31). My own analysis of the response to Nyanzi's actions extends from this reading to ask how nakedness challenges *particular* kinds of moral norms and moral claims to propriety, obligation, and justice. The empowerment posed by the act of being naked can come in a Foucauldian sense, as Tamale argues, because it undermines and directly challenges moral norms that work to oppress women, inscribing them into gendered discourses that are inherently unequal. But nakedness also works by drawing attention to the relationship between the naked body and the onlooker, who is shamed into recognizing the ways the protesting body has been abused. Nakedness in this sense gives voice to an aggrieved individual, forcing the looker to recognize the ways he or she is party to another's violation. From this perspective, the power of nakedness does not extend from a claim of equality (I resist the social norms that mark me as different from you in order to demand that I be treated the same); instead, it makes a claim based on the difference, interdependence, and mutual obligation between social actors (your actions are a violation of your obligations to me, and my nakedness shames you into recognizing your complicity).

This reading of nakedness draws from some of the most famous cases of women's political protest in twentieth-century Africa, cases where women's naked bodies worked to highlight the violation of women's particular standing in society and in so doing sought to shame men by revealing their abusive and extractive behavior toward women. The tradition of using the naked body as a tool of protest has a long history in many parts of Africa, where women's (especially older women's) exposed bodies shamed powerful constituencies into recognizing and responding to grievances (Lawrance 2003; Diduk 2004; Page 2005; Fallon and Moreau 2016; Grillo 2018). In recent memory, Nobel Peace Prize winner Wangari Maathai's 1992 protest against the disappearance and detainment of political prisoners in Moi's Kenya provides one such example. In this instance, Maathai led a peaceful sit-in of the mothers of political prisoners in Nairobi's Uhuru Park. When the police were called to disband the protest forcibly, beating the protesters with sticks, several women stripped naked and ran at the police, yelling in their faces and placing their bodies between the armed men and prone or injured protesters. In this chaotic and violent moment, the naked body became a tool that sought not to challenge gendered norms but to use such norms to shame men who were morally compromised not only by their association with an authoritarian state but also by their violent mistreatment of women and mothers. As one protester sought to characterize the encounter, "What kind of government is this that beats women? Kill us! Kill us now! We shall die with our children" (Worthington 2001, 168).

Here, naked protest facilitates moral claims made by women who use their bodies to highlight the violation of a relationship of mutual dependence with men. The moral violation posed by the police was not of women's "right" to protest or of their right to claim a public, political space ordinarily ascribed to men. Rather, women used their position as women to highlight men's (and the state's) injustice. In this case, the *difference* of women (especially the status of these women as mothers) was important. The mothers had a moral right to be there, to protect their children, and to speak for them peacefully. The older women's nakedness brought to public attention the violation of the moral obligation of the state toward its citizens or, in more palpable terms, between the (younger) policemen and the (elder) women protesting, whose status (as elders, mothers, and women) was violated by men who (unjustly) sought to shame, violate, and abuse them.

During the 1929 Women's War, staged by Igbo women in colonial Nigeria—another famous and much-studied example of African women's political protest—women drew on modes of political action well known in southeastern Nigeria at the time, a practice that the Igbo called "sitting on a man" (Van Allen 1972). Historian Judith Van Allen has described the practice of sitting on a man as a "collective response to the abrogation of rights," one levied at individual men, or men collectively, at times when men were deemed to have violated their social and moral obligations toward women (176). During the women's war, Igbo women directed these tactics toward colonial administrators in an effort to resist taxation and other colonial policies. Igbo women protested in large groups throughout the region, occupying administrative offices, yelling, making obscene gestures, and violating norms of behavior and comportment. Nakedness, as it was during the protests in 1990s Kenya, was an important tool used by women (Tamale 2016, 7). Nakedness signaled—visibly, viscerally—the violation of social norms, in this way revealing how women themselves suffered from the state's mistreatment, the body signaling the state's disrespect of women's status and their collective rights. As Misty Bastian (2002, 270) has argued in her analysis of women's protests during this period, these were moral arguments that sought to highlight the devaluation of women's contribution to society during the colonial era, the ways women's "usefulness" (to use the phrase of one Igbo woman) and men's dependence on women's productive and reproductive work had increasingly become invisible, ignored, and disregarded. Here, as in Wangari Maathai's case, women's status as women was essential to the claims they sought to make. Women drew on a long tradition that permitted them to use the public shaming of others—a shaming demonstrated by the public loss of women's control—to highlight men's violation of women's rights and status. This was, as Van Allen argues, a political tool, one levied with forethought and one that drew on a shared understanding of the way rights were actualized through a respect for relationships of mutual obligation.

Stella Nyanzi, almost certainly familiar with both of these historical examples of women's protest, was likely attempting to make a similar claim with her naked body. From her perspective, the demands made by her employer were a violation of an established set of mutual obligations between supervisor and employee. In her writing about the conflict, she makes clear that she felt manipulated and coerced by her supervisor, left with few options, and faced with a university bureaucracy that she felt was weighted against her. Nakedness here, as in the other examples, is meant to reveal and make public the violation of a relationship and the moral and social obligations that shape such a relationship. She stripped naked in front of her office door—from which she claimed to have been locked out—to highlight an apparent abuse of power and the unjustified (in her view) disregard of her work and her position. In the end, however, she was derided by many who felt her act was out of touch with the scope of her complaints. The moral claim she sought to mobilize fell flat for many in Uganda, possibly because her own position in Ugandan society is one of relative status and privilege. Perhaps even more problematically, her protest was staged not with her superiors as a primary audience but for the cameras of traditional and social media. This targeting of the media may complicate the efficacy and the moral legitimacy of her protest, as it circumvents the very relationship she wishes to morally criticize, expose, and (ideally) restore. Ultimately, her protest was directed not toward a relational bond but rather toward a media forum that was largely abstract, anonymous, and unbound by personal moral obligations.

This reading of the ways public protest works (and the limits of its success in this case) speaks more broadly to how rights-based discourse circulates and is debated in Kampala today. When Nyanzi was arrested on charges of cyber harassment and offensive communication in 2017, a year after she staged her university protest, she was again thrust into the headlines.[8] At the beginning of that year she had made a series of posts on Facebook criticizing President Museveni for failing to fulfill a campaign promise to provide sanitary napkins to schoolgirls. (Many girls throughout Uganda miss school during their menstrual periods because they don't have access to such products.) Sections 24 and 25 of Uganda's 2011 Computer Misuse Act, under which she was charged, disallow persons from using the internet to "disturb the peace" or violate another citizen's "right to privacy."[9] In an account of her first court appearance, the UK newspaper *The Guardian* reported her response to the charges: "Offensive communication? Who is offended? . . . He [Museveni] lied to the voters that he would provide pads and Ugandans are offended that he is such a dishonourable man. It is we who are offended, not him" (Slawson 2017).

Her case has hinged on the court's interpretation of the limits of Nyanzi's right to free speech. From the perspective of many Western human rights advocates, Museveni's right to privacy is curtailed by his status as a public figure. A democratic society's commitment to free speech usually gives the public a right to criticize its political leaders. But in a widely watched one-on-one interview with a reporter for *Al Jazeera* soon after Nyanzi's arrest, Museveni, when pressed on Nyanzi's case, responded by emphasizing the ways rights are always limited by one's "responsibilities" to others: "Well, if I am an activist and commit an offense . . . because rights, to enjoy rights you must also *restrain the rights of others* [emphasis added]. You can't trample on the rights of others and you say it is 'my right' to abuse other people, to assault other people. Rights go with responsibilities, if you know anything about democracy."[10] Rights, from Museveni's perspective, are meaningful only in the context of a larger set of relationships that structure social obligations between members of society. This argument about the limits of individual rights is to some extent universal: one's right to free speech is curtailed by libel laws that limit one's ability to spread false information about another person, and one cannot threaten public safety by yelling "fire" in a crowded theater. Yet in Uganda rights talk is deeply informed not only by a sense of competition between sets of rights but also by the notion that rights are exercised through the relationships one has with others.

As Mikael Karlström (1996, 486) has written in his study of democracy and political change in Buganda, the Ganda concept of "rights," the root of which in Luganda is the word for "peace" or "liberty" (*eddembe*), is one that emphasizes how rights should reinforce rather than threaten the moral obligations between disparate and unequal members of society. Rights should, in effect, strengthen (and never undermine) the "peaceful" relations and responsibilities between groups that constitute civil society and that, by the very nature of society, are often unequal. This is an interpretation of rights-based practice echoed in Holly Porter's (2017) recent study of the adjudication of rape cases in northern Uganda, where "justice" is defined narrowly not in terms of the punishment of the convicted but in relation to a broader effort to reestablish "social harmony" between accusers and the accused. The moral value at the center of this interpretation of what rights mean and do hinges on the social good of interdependence rather than individual autonomy. It is this framework that allows Museveni to make the claim that Nyanzi's public criticism of him is unjustified: What public good comes from her undermining his status as a leader? It should also be noted that the reverse argument is made by Nyanzi: Museveni's failure to fulfill his social duty as a leader (to provide promised resources to schoolgirls) opens him up to a morally justified critique by his constituent, a criticism that, not coincidentally, hinges on bodily metaphor, shaming him into a response—though not the one that was desired. ("When buttocks fart, are we surprised? That is what buttocks do. They shake, jiggle, shit and fart. Museveni is just another pair of buttocks.")[11]

My interest in Nyanzi's political activism—first protesting her employer, then criticizing her government—is in the ways her case reveals a more situated understanding of how rights discourse circulates in Uganda and in turn shapes forms of political agency. The value of the naked body in this context—while contested and debated among Ugandans in the wake of her Makerere protest—works somewhat differently from how it might in a US or European context. Nakedness becomes a means to make a moral claim, but not one that hinges on the violation of "equal" rights; rather, this is a moral claim that hinges on a shared understanding of how a sector of society has failed in its particular obligations and collective responsibilities. Womanhood in this instance matters, as do age and other kinds of social status (the special moral obligations a leader has to the people, for instance). The particular nature of the relationship between the body exposed and the person and institution against which she protests is important. Nakedness is situational: it evokes and depends upon a recognition of the (often unequal) relationship it is meant to reveal; it is a means to compel a response from those who are responsible for and responsive to those who protest.

## The Limits of Rights: The Sexualized Body Seen and Unseen

If Nyanzi's protests reveal how the body can be an (imperfect) means of revealing and emphasizing a rights-based claim derived from a sense of moral obligation between social actors, I now turn to an example where the body's violation fails to do such work. In this case, the suffering of an exposed body becomes almost invisible and is unable to mobilize the response that Nyanzi and the historical examples discussed above were able to do. This failure is important because it emphasizes again how the body is shaped by the relationships that produce it. In this case the body's vulnerability is decontextualized, taken out of the social relationships that give it meaning. Because of this, the body's violation becomes almost invisible, even as it is discussed and debated in the most public forum: a Ugandan courtroom.

In July 2011 I had traveled to Uganda to continue fieldwork with a community of Ugandan born-again Christians involved in AIDS prevention work.

This community had in recent years become more active in another kind of social advocacy, one that had placed them at the center of an expansive social and political debate in Uganda over the issue of sexual rights, specifically, the rights of Ugandans to pursue same-sex relationships. In 2009 the Ugandan legislature had introduced the Anti-Homosexuality Bill, which expanded criminal penalties for same-sex relationships and introduced new penalties for actions considered to "promote" homosexuality in the country. The bill was deeply controversial in the international realm, drawing rebuke from US and European political leaders. But in Uganda the bill's proponents, including some of the pastors with whom I had long done fieldwork, enjoyed support and had expanded their public profiles as champions of Ugandan "cultural" values and opponents of the idea of equal rights for queer Ugandans.[12]

The court case that I was following in 2011 was not directly linked to the Anti-Homosexuality Bill, but it involved some of the pastors who had become public advocates for the bill, and at the center of the case was an accusation of homosexual sex. The case being tried stemmed from charges of conspiracy to cause injury (to trade and to reputation) brought against four pastors and two others who were accused of making false accusations of pederasty against another prominent pastor, Robert Kayanja.[13] Among the six accused were prominent religious leaders who had taken public roles supporting the Anti-Homosexuality Bill, including the pastors Martin Ssempa and Solomon Male. In 2009 these pastors made several public statements accusing Kayanja of coercing young boys and men in his congregation to engage in sexual acts with him. In the accounts of the boys who shared their stories at the behest of the pastors, Kayanja would ply them with gifts of travel, hotel stays, and food in exchange for engaging in anal sex with him. These explosive charges were made in carefully scripted televised appearances during which the pastors introduced the alleged victims of the sexual assaults and helped them present their statements before the assembled media.

By December 2010 initial interest in pursuing charges against Kayanja had turned into a civil case against the accusing pastors themselves.[14] That month the pastors and their assistants were arrested and charged with conspiracy to injure Kayanja's reputation. In June 2011, while the case against them was under way at the Buganda Road Chief Magistrate Court, I attended two days of their trial.[15] Most of both of these days was taken up with the testimony of first a police officer and then a forensic medical expert who had interrogated and later physically examined one of the boys who had accused Kayanja of sexual misconduct.

In the testimony of the medical examiner, the vulnerable, exposed body—that of Kayanja's alleged victim—took center stage. The elderly doctor who took the stand had been asked by police investigators in February 2009 to complete a forensic medical exam on one of the alleged victims, Samson Mukisa. The details of the exam he described were intimate; for much of his exchange with defense attorneys, he lingered on a description of the physical evidence of anal penetration. This was testimony that was in many ways an act of exposure: laying bare, debating, and considering coerced sex through the lens of a victim's body.

The testimony was notable for the way intimate details about sex and the victim's body were paired with an almost absurd degree of spatial and temporal abstraction. Samson Mukisa had accused Kayanja of soliciting and compelling him to have sex in 2007. According to the medical examiner, the Ugandan police had requested a physical exam of Mukisa on February 17, 2009. The gap between when the alleged sexual act happened and when the exam occurred was nearly two years, but this gap seemed to be irrelevant to the doctor, and it only became apparent upon further questioning by a defense attorney. The victim's body in the testimony is exposed in specific, detailed ways, but in other ways the body seems unmoored from the here and now, difficult to place in time. The body's violation is also debated in ways that further mark the victim as incomprehensible. The effect of queer sex on the body became a focal point of the testimony, one that was never really resolved. Because of these debates (when did this happen? to what effect?), the nature of the violation—the physical and emotional cost of the alleged assault—receded into the background. A victim was exposed, but in ways that made the violation difficult to understand. I am interested in how and why this public exposure ultimately makes the victim less visible and even less comprehensible.

The medical examiner began by explaining what he was looking for during the exam.

> DOCTOR: There are some substances found on a person who has been the victim of an act of sodomy. In cases of sexual assault it is normal . . .
> DEFENSE ATTORNEY: If someone has been sexually assaulted?
> DOCTOR: Sodomized, if someone has been sodomized the body should reveal the presence of spermatozoa. . . . These are the reproductive animals of the male.
> DEFENSE ATTORNEY: After two years, would they still be there?
> DOCTOR: I wouldn't even request for the exam.
> DEFENSE ATTORNEY: Why did you [in this case]?
> DOCTOR: Because he said the act happened the day before.

As I noted above, the doctor's response befuddled the defense attorney, as the accusations made by Samson Mukisa placed the assault in 2007, nearly two years before this medical exam took place. This may have been due to a lack of preparation on the part of the witness or the general sloppiness of the investigation, but the result was a sense of disorientation in the courtroom from the beginning of the cross-examination. The who and when of the alleged act seemed to be lost in these conflicting details.

The questioning of the doctor continued by describing the nature of the physical exam and what such an exam reveals about a sexually active body. The doctor emphasized the invasiveness of his exam, which he played up so as to generate laughter from those in the courtroom: "The examination I requested is disgustful to most people. I tell [the patient] I am going to inspect your privates and report to the President [laughter from courtroom]. Even the kings! Even the kings would prefer to keep out [not have the exam]. But when you go to the doctor . . . [you must submit]." The testimony then turned to the ways the exam provides evidence of anal penetration. Here, as in the discussion of the timeline of the assault, the attorney and the doctor struggled to find common ground regarding the effect that anal penetration has on the body.

> DOCTOR: In consensual sodomy you find it [the anal sphincter] remains open even after you visit the john [toilet]. The anus should "pucker" [*his hands show a closed thumb and index finger*]. This puckering is absent in someone who is in the habit of having consensual sodomy. There is no contraction of the sphincter.
> DEFENSE ATTORNEY: So you are effectively saying that there is a gaping hole?
> DOCTOR: Yes. Oh, it is not outright gaping but it is not the normal appearance of the puckered anal sphincter.
> DEFENSE ATTORNEY: If someone, a doctor, came and said someone in the practice of having anal sex has a normal sphincter, he is wrong?
> DOCTOR: Yes, quite possible. Even in heterosexual sex if the male organ is bigger than the female you get tears.

During this back and forth between the attorney and the doctor, there was a sense of confusion rooted, at least in part, in a lack of shared understanding of what anal sex might actually involve and the effect it might have on the body. The discussion of the "anal sphincter" continued for several minutes, often generating giggles and laughs from spectators. But it also provoked a sense of disbelief among others, including the defense attorney interrogating the doctor. Was the doctor testifying that men who have anal sex with other men sustain permanent damage to their anuses? Damage that might be evident even years later?

The testimony is notable for the way it became a debate over sex itself. What does anal sex involve? How does it mark and transform the body? The testimony contributed to and was shaped by a broader public discourse about homosexuality in Uganda that characterized queer sex as abhorrent and physically irregular, a kind of sex that marks the body in ways that help expose these sexual acts as different socially and morally (as well as sexually) from reproductive sex.

In the wake of Uganda's 2009 Anti-Homosexuality Bill, homosexual sex had become a topic of fascination for Uganda's tabloid media, a focus stoked by newly emboldened social activists who supported the bill and sought to portray homosexuality as a social threat to normative social relationships. Queer sex was popularly described as dangerous because it was supposedly the product of unchecked, insatiable desires. In one infamous public statement made during this time, Pastor Martin Ssempa (one of the religious leaders on trial here) made public comments about queer sex while projecting images from a gay pornographic film, observing that the actors were going to "eat the poo poo," a comment that almost instantly went viral online and made Ssempa, for a time, a household name synonymous with Ugandan homophobia.

The efforts of Ssempa and others to reveal the "secrets" of gay sex worked to mark this sex as nonnormative, the result of dangerous and uncontrolled appetites (see Boyd 2013, 715). Popular Ugandan tabloids like *Red Pepper* sold papers at the height of public debate over the Anti-Homosexuality Bill by featuring the faces of men the editors accused of harboring same-sex desires, effectively "outing" these men and exposing them to public rebuke and physical violence. In response, some queer Ugandan activists held news conferences wearing masks in a desperate effort to protect their anonymity in the face of very real threats to their safety and well-being. While necessary, the masks played into a broader view in Uganda that homosexuality dissembles, feigning normativity while masking baser, foreign desires that are out of step with or even counter to social relationships that shape moral sexual behavior. In public discourse during these years, the queer body was problematized, characterized as untethered to normative social relationships.

The doctor's testimony aligned with these broader social concerns about exposing homosexuality in Uganda, an effort that made homosexuals themselves appear loosed from the social relationships that shape moral and social status in Ugandan society. The doctor dwelled on intimate bodily details—the anal sphincter, spermatozoa—but at the same time worked to obscure the victimization and vulnerability of the boy who claimed to have been assaulted. The victim became both present in a way that made many uncomfortable (the doctor claimed that no one would readily consent to the probing exam he gave the boy), but these details did little to place this assault in social context, an effect that had consequences for the victim. The alleged victim remained a disjointed figure, unmoored even from a clearly fixed timeline of events.

As I have written elsewhere (Boyd 2013), the discourse of sexual rights that circulated in the international realm in response to Uganda's Anti-Homosexuality Bill in 2009, a discourse that drew heavily on Western constructs of sexual equality and personal sexual autonomy, clashed with alternative constructs for sexual personhood in Uganda, ones that tied sexual desire to a broader set of kin and gendered relationships that undergirded and shaped a moral and political emphasis on interdependence. This helped explain why characterizations of gay sex as disordered and ambiguous, as an act that dissembles and blurs together with acts of eating and defecation (as Ssempa emphasized in his public statements), were readily adopted and helped shape popular perceptions of queer sexuality and its dangers. Such portrayals also placed queer sexuality outside the kind of kin and gendered relationships of interdependence that colored Ugandans' own notions of what constituted moral, "proper" sexual relationships. The effect of this is that the alleged victim in this instance is put into public discourse in ways that untethered him from the kinds of relationships that would make his own victimhood more readily legible and his claims for redress and justice more readily accepted.

Here the body's exposure fails to make the kind of moral claim that even Nyanzi's controversial use of nakedness was able to achieve. Those in the courtroom who were made to see this victim, who were witness to his exposure and the intimate details of his body during testimony, were unable to see his socially, morally contextualized self. As was seen with Nyanzi's act of public protest, the body is made meaningful only when it is placed in context, understood in terms of a set of mutual obligations shaped by broader social emphasis on interdependence between social groups and persons. Whether or not Mukisa's story of sexual abuse is true, his treatment in court testimony reveals something more generally about the ways queer sex itself was considered and understood by the Ugandan public during these years. It was this emphasis on the sexual body "out of place" that seemed to characterize the public perception of queer sex and complicate efforts to forward a claim of "equal rights" for queer Ugandans. Both this case and the earlier discussion of Nyanzi's protest reveal the ways that rights-based claims in Uganda are effective when they play upon a broader set of obligations between social actors but seem to be less effective when they depend only upon the visibility of a vulnerable victim.

## Conclusion: Situating Bodies, Situating Rights

If, as Sally Engle Merry has argued, human rights are a form of "cultural practice" (2006, 228), then it is important to understand more about how particular cultures and historical moments shape the meaning given to rights-based claims and the tools available to forward such claims. The two examples I have discussed in this chapter are an attempt to illuminate the ways human rights discourse circulates and is shaped by cultural and historical orientations to sexual and gendered personhood in Uganda. At the center of my analysis is the exposed, vulnerable body. My argument has been that exposure (specifically, nakedness) is an important feature of rights-based claims in diverse cultural contexts but that the effect of such nakedness is different in different times and places. In the West, Scully (2011) has argued, the vulnerable body provides the visible, visceral evidence of the violation of rights and in this way provides moral justification for the defense of rights-based equality. In the examples I have discussed here, the body's exposure is most powerful when it is used to make a situated claim about rights in the context of mutual obligations. The body's nakedness and vulnerability become meaningful when the violation of the body is directed back toward and used to implicate those with more power. In the Ugandan context, it is the relationship between social actors that shapes rights-based claims. These different orientations to nakedness and the body help us better understand different ways rights themselves are conceived and brought into being, as well as the ways certain arguments about rights-based equality may be contested.

Rights in Uganda are rarely engaged as abstract or universal concepts; they are most widely accepted when they work to highlight and reinforce the relationships between different categories of persons. This orientation to rights poses particularly pressing problems for certain groups of people in Uganda. Queer Ugandans, as I have noted, are in a position in which their efforts to forward an argument for equal treatment have often been dismissed. Largely, as I have shown here, these dismissals have stemmed from a broader public inability to "see" and morally legitimize these claims because they are not rooted in established social hierarchies and relationships.

One way to change the perception of how sexual and gender-based rights might work in Ugandan society is not to focus on a dynamic that poses culture as a "problem" that complicates the expansion of rights-based claims but to examine the possibilities for making new kinds of claims within a culturally accepted framework. This might mean using and pursuing new kinds of relational obligations as the basis for rights claims—claims not only between women and men within a patriarchal family context but also between older and younger Ugandans or between other groups affiliated through clientship, clanship, or work. Such possibilities open up new avenues for protest and for viewing the body as a mechanism for claims-making that is empowered rather than passive and, importantly, situated within rather than imposed from outside Uganda.

The women's movement in Uganda has used this approach in recent efforts to recognize women's unpaid domestic labor, highlighting how such labor contributes to social and material relationships both within the family and outside of it. The social media hashtag #sharecarework was initiated to promote the issue of women's unpaid domestic labor and to push for more recognition of women's contribution to the household and for more family support of women's work lives. Here the effort is not only to argue that unpaid labor is unjust but also to point out that women's work supports a broad set of social and familial relationships and that women's investment in others demands respect and compensation. As Rita Aciro-Lakor, the director of the Ugandan women's organization UWONET, explained to me, "Rights need to be placed in local context, but with an emphasis on social change. For instance, communities need to know about their past and the kinds of rights and empowerment women historically had."[16] While there is a commitment to the language of "rights" among Uganda's women's organizations, there is also a recognition that the kinds of rights claims that are most tenable are those that reinforce moral arguments about obligation, justice, and empowerment, often by celebrating values like interdependence and reciprocity. In Aciro-Lakor's view, culture becomes not a stumbling block to rights but a means for seeing rights through a new, changing lens, providing a vision for how society can do better for vulnerable populations. Here the vulnerability of the body makes sense not as an abstract victim of society's disregard but as a body whose work demands the attention and respect of others.

## Notes

1. The Anti-Pornography Bill was signed into law by President Museveni in June 2014, becoming the Anti-Pornography Act. Republic of Uganda, "The Anti-Pornography Act, 2014," Uganda Legal Information Institute, https://ulii.org/system/files/legislation/act/2014/1/Anti%20Pornography%20Act%20of%202014.pdf.

2. The 2014 Anti-Pornography Act broadly defines "pornography" as "any representation through publication, exhibition, cinematography, indecent show, information technology or by whatever means, of a person engaged in real or stimulated [sic] explicit sexual activities or any representation of the sexual parts of a person for primarily sexual excitement."

3. In these cases, women members of the opposition party, Forum for Democratic Change (FDC), were arrested using force and in the process groped and stripped by the police in front of news cameras. Videos of the arrests, the first of Ingrid Turinawe in 2012, the second of Fatuma Zainab in October 2015, were posted by the Ugandan news media on YouTube. "Police Arrests FDC Official Fatuma Zainab," YouTube,

October 12, 2015, https://www.youtube.com/watch?v=AFFD18dgH6w; "Police Assault Turinawe as A4C rebrands to 4GC," YouTube, April 20, 2012, https://www.youtube.com/watch?v=wZ6ALwfIxBY.

4. The charges against Nyanzi were linked to a January 2017 Facebook post criticizing President Museveni in which she wrote: "Museveni matako nyo. Ebyo byeyayogedde e Masindi yabadde ayogera lutako." This translates from Luganda as "Museveni is very much a pair of buttocks. When he spoke in Masindi he was speaking as buttocks do." She continued in English: "I mean seriously, when buttocks shake and jiggle, while the legs are walking, do you hear other body parts complaining? When buttocks produce shit, while the brain is thinking, is anyone shocked? When buttocks fart, are we surprised? That is what buttocks do. They shake, jiggle, shit and fart. Museveni is just another pair of buttocks. Rather than being shocked at what the *matako* said in Masindi, Ugandans should be shocked that we allowed these buttocks to continue leading our country" (Rukundo 2018, 252).

5. By training, Nyanzi is a medical anthropologist and has an active research profile in this field.

6. Nyanzi claimed she had been barred entry to her regular office for failing to fulfill her contested duty to teach a graduate seminar.

7. "Dr Stella Nyanzi Shocks Nation," NBS TV, April 18, 2016, https://www.facebook.com/watch/?v=1022061667884798.

8. At the time of this writing (December 2019), Nyanzi remains in Luzira prison in Uganda after being arrested for a second time, in November 2018, on charges of offensive communication, this time in connection with a separate Facebook post, made in September 2018, that was deemed offensive to the president. In August 2019 she was found guilty of "cyber harassment" (see note 9) and sentenced to eighteen months in prison. She is expected to be released nine months after this conviction, gaining credit for time already served.

9. Nyanzi was charged in April 2017 in violation of Sections 24 ("Cyber Harassment") and 25 ("Offensive Communication") of the Ugandan *Computer Misuse Act* (2011). Section 25 states: "Any person who willfully and repeatedly uses electronic communication to disturb or attempts to disturb the peace, quiet or right of privacy of any person with no purpose of legitimate communication whether or not a conversation ensues commits a misdemeanour and is liable on conviction to a fine not exceeding twenty-four currency points (480,000) or imprisonment not exceeding one year or both" (Government of Uganda 2011, 17).

10. "Yoweri Museveni: A Five Time-Elected Dictator?," *Al Jazeera*, April 30, 2017, https://www.youtube.com/watch?v=hGQ6W4td72E&t=606s. Musveni's discussion of Nyanzi comes at the 11:30 mark.

11. See note 4 for Nyanzi's entire January 2017 Facebook post.

12. I adopt the Western term "queer" to refer to a broad range of sexual identities in Uganda, from gay men and lesbians to transgender folks. I use this term because it is the most broadly inclusive term available, even as its use in Uganda is relatively recent.

13. The accused were the pastors Martin Ssempa, Michael Kyazze, Solomon Male, and Robert Kaira, along with Deborah Anita Kyomuhendo, a businesswoman, and David Mukalazi, a musician.

14. It was unclear to me what provoked this change in the direction of the police investigation. There are several complicating factors that shape this case and that might shed light on the direction the investigation took (beyond the facts of the case). The pastors were considered rivals of each other, competing for visibility in Kampala's crowded and competitive religious landscape, a fact that many highlighted in order to explain the motivations of the accused to make such scandalous accusations. In interviews with me, some of the accused intimated that Kayanja (arguably the most successful of this group) had bribed the police into redirecting their investigation. I have no evidence one way or the other as to whether any of this actually happened or if it affected the course of the investigation, but these rumors circulated widely. This is all to say that this case intersected with a host of other questions about justice, power, and political agency in Uganda that are outside the scope of this chapter.

15. All quotes from the trial included in this chapter were taken from my own transcriptions of the trial proceedings on July 1, 2011, Buganda Road Chief Magistrate Court, Kampala, Uganda.

16. Interview with author, Kampala, Uganda, June 4, 2018.

## References

Allman, Jean, ed. 2004. *Fashioning Africa: Power and the Politics of Dress*. Bloomington: Indiana University Press.

Awondo, Patrick, Peter Geschiere, and Graeme Reid. 2014. "Homophobic Africa? Toward a More Nuanced View." *African Studies Review* 55 (3): 145–68.

Ayebazibwe, Agatha. 2014. "Women Activists Demonstrate over the Pornography Law." *Daily Monitor*, February 26, 2014. http://www.monitor.co.ug/News/National/Women-activists-demonstrate-over-the-pornography-law/-/688334/2222788/-/ntmewkz/-/index.html.

Bastian, Misty. 2002. "'Vultures of the Marketplace': Southeastern Nigerian Women and Discourses of the *Ogu Umunwaanyi* (Women's War) of 1929." In *Women in Colonial African Histories*, edited by Jean Allman, Susan Geiger, and Nakanyike Musisi, 260–81. Bloomington: Indiana University Press.

Boyd, Lydia. 2013. "The Problem with Freedom: Homosexuality and Human Rights in Uganda." *Anthropological Quarterly* 86 (3): 697–724.

Decker, Alicia C. 2014. *In Idi Amin's Shadow: Women, Gender, and Militarism in Uganda*. Athens: Ohio University Press.

Decker, Corrie. 2010. "Fathers, Daughters, and Institutions: Coming of Age in Mombasa's Colonial Schools." In *Girlhood: A Global History*, edited by Jennifer Helgren and Colleen A. Vasconcellos, 268–88. New Brunswick, NJ: Rutgers University Press.

Diduk, Susan. 2004. "The Civility of Incivility: Grassroots Political Activism, Female Farmers, and the Cameroon State." *African Studies Review* 47 (2): 27–54.

Fallon, Kathleen M., and Julie Moreau. 2016. "Revisiting Repertoire Transition: Women's Nakedness as Potent Protests in Nigeria and Kenya." *Mobilization: An International Quarterly* 21 (3): 323–40.

Government of Uganda. 2011. *Computer Misuse Act*. Acts Supplement to the *Uganda Gazette* CIV, no. 10.

Grillo, Laura S. 2018. *An Intimate Rebuke: Female Genital Power in Ritual and Politics in West Africa*. Durham, NC: Duke University Press.

Hansen, Karen Tranberg. 2004. "Dressing Dangerously: Miniskirts, Gender Relations, and Sexuality in Zambia." In *Fashioning Africa: Power and Politics of Dress*, edited by Jean Allman, 166–85. Bloomington: Indiana University Press.

Hodgson, Dorothy. 2011. "Gender and Culture at the Limit of Rights." In *Gender and Culture at the Limit of Rights*, edited by Dorothy Hodgson, 1–14. Philadelphia: University of Pennsylvania Press.

Karlström, Mikael. 1996. "Imagining Democracy: Political Culture and Democratisation in Buganda." *Africa* 66 (4): 485–505.

Lawrance, Benjamin N. 2003. "La révolte des femmes: Economic Upheaval and the Gender of Political Authority in Lomé, Togo, 1931–33." *African Studies Review* 46 (1): 43–67.

Merry, Sally Engle. 2006. *Human Rights and Gender Violence: Translating International Law into Local Justice*. Chicago: University of Chicago Press.

Nyanzi, Stella, and Andrew Karamagi. 2015. "The Social-Political Dynamics of the Anti-Homosexuality Legislation in Uganda." *Agenda* 29 (1): 24–38.

Page, Ben. 2005. "Naked Power: Women and the Social Production of Water in Anglophone Cameroon." In *Gender, Water and Development*, edited by Anne Coles and Tina Wallace, 57–73. Oxford: Berg.

Porter, Holly. 2017. *After Rape: Violence, Justice and Social Harmony in Uganda*. Cambridge: Cambridge University Press.

Redfield, Peter, and Erica Bornstein. 2010. "An Introduction to the Anthropology of Humanitarianism." In *Forces of Compassion: Humanitarianism between Ethics and Politics*, edited by Erica Bornstein and Peter Redfield, 3–30. Santa Fe, NM: School for Advanced Research Press.

Rukundo, Solomon. 2018. "'My President Is a Pair of Buttocks': The Limits of Online Freedom of Expression in Uganda." *International Journal of Law and Information Technology* 26:252–71.

Scully, Pamela. 2011. "Gender, History, and Human Rights." In *Gender and Culture at the Limit of Rights*, edited by Dorothy Hodgson, 17–31. Philadelphia: University of Pennsylvania Press.

Slawson, Nicola. 2017. "Fury over Arrest of Academic Who Called Uganda's President a Pair of Buttocks." *The Guardian*, April 13.

Tamale, Sylvia. 2013. "Exploring the Contours of African Sexualities: Statutory, Customary and Religious Laws." Paper presented at the conference "Law and Religion in Africa: Comparative Practices, Experiences and Prospects," University of Ghana, Accra, January 14–15.

———. 2016. "Nudity, Protest and the Law in Uganda." Inaugural professorial lecture, Makerere University, Kampala, Uganda. https://searchworks.stanford.edu/view/122 75421.

Tumusiime, Amanda, and Juliet Kiguli. 2015. "Unshackling Women's Sexuality? Miniskirts, the Law, and the Media in Uganda." In *Contested Intimacies: Sexuality, Gender and the Law in Africa*, edited by Derrick Higginbotham and Victoria Collis-Buthelezi, 31–45. Cape Town: Siber Ink.

Van Allen, Judith. 1972. "Sitting on a Man: Colonialism and the Lost Political Institutions of Igbo Women." *Canadian Journal of African Studies* 6 (2): 165–81.

Worthington, Nancy. 2001. "A Division of Labor: Dividing Maternal Authority from Political Activism in the Kenyan Press." *Journal of Communication Inquiry* 25 (2): 167–83.

# Epilogue

## *Entanglements of Law, Gender, and Sexuality in Africa*

DOROTHY L. HODGSON

In postcolonial Africa, fierce debates have occurred (and reoccurred) over so-called family laws that seek to regulate gender and sexuality by codifying appropriate marriage forms, legitimate sexual practices and partners, and even the distinction between who is considered a "child" or an "adult." The chapters in this volume illuminate how such legal efforts serve as what the coeditors call "moralizing enterprises," both reflecting and seeking to produce proper political subjects or, more accurately, proper *gendered* citizens. People and institutions desiring to regulate or "improve" society have long turned to the creation of "laws" to name, codify, and implement their ideals and norms. Over time, the dominant scale of such laws has changed from *customary legal regimes* based on community social norms, to *national legal regimes* that privileged state-level legislation, to the current ascendancy of *transnational legal regimes* like human rights law.[1] The overlaps and contradictions of these contemporaneous legal regimes fuel debate and disagreement, compliance and resistance, among differently positioned actors.

Human rights regimes, with their claims to universality and the support of powerful global institutions like the United Nations, have only intensified the legal disputes over gender and sexuality as some activists invoke human rights laws to buttress their positions, while others seek to protect customary norms in the face of elite disparagement. "Democratization" has further exacerbated these tensions in countries like Senegal (Niang, Foley, and Diop) and

Mali (Burrill) with the introduction of multiple political parties and the rise of "civil" society organizations. Competing politicians, NGOs, religious groups, activists, and a spectrum of other actors avow certain gender ideologies to claim moral legitimacy through inexpensive media technologies like radios, televisions, cell phones, WhatsApp, and the internet.

The authors explore these postcolonial efforts to legislate sex and gender in a range of situations and sites across the continent. Whether the focus is marriage (Burrill; Masquelier), land rights (Nébié), education (Silver), sexuality (Musiime and Eryenyu; Niang, Foley, and Diop; Boyd), or domestic violence (Walker-Said), interested parties invoke, invent, or interpret laws to define the "appropriate" gendered and sexual relationships between and among men and women or between citizens and the state. Who can marry or have sex, and when? What rights and responsibilities does "being married" entail? What kinds of bodies can go to school? What is (or should be) women's access to and control over land? Who has the power to define and defend dominant norms: Individuals? Communities? States?

So what insights do these chapters provide into the entanglements of law, gender, and sex in postcolonial Africa? First, several authors emphasize the continued, even heightened salience of regulating, monitoring, and controlling marriage to projects of nation building and elite aspirations of modernity. Activist efforts to "reform" marriage by passing laws to raise the marriage age, prohibit polygamy, require registration, and prescribe certain property rights clash with alternative understandings of the purposes, forms, and functions of the institution. Marriage, as these debates make clear, is often about much more than recognizing and legitimating companionate relationships. Instead, marriage can be a pathway to establish interdependent social networks, legitimate children, organize labor relations, determine inheritance rights, claim adult status, and earn respect. Emily Burrill's fascinating analysis of the debates, delays, and compromises produced by struggles to reform the 1962 Marriage and Guardianship Code in Mali reveals the centrality of marriage to political, religious, and feminist aspirations. The male elites who took power when Mali became independent codified a conservative, patriarchal version of marriage in the 1962 code: husbands provided protection to their wives in return for their wives' obedience, and husbands had the right to restrict the movement, travel, and economic initiatives of their wives. Women achieved certain concessions, however. They organized to ensure that marriage was premised on consent, to abolish divorce through repudiation, and to secure the right to divorce their husbands under certain circumstances. The reality, of course, was that few couples sought such civil marriages, and thus there were limited efforts to change the code for decades. By the late 1990s and early

2000s, however, as Burrill documents, much had changed as a result of the expansion of "women's rights as human rights" efforts in the 1990s, the rise of NGOs and civil society organizations such as Women in Law and Development in Africa (WiLDAF), and local and global pressure for "democratization" and other political and economic "reforms." These changes reinvigorated efforts to revise the 1962 marriage code, pitting Malian feminist activists, politicians, and religious leaders against one another under the glare of the media.

A similar confluence of forces in Niger created campaigns to prohibit the "early" marriage of girls. Advocates framed the campaigns as a way to protect girls' health (by preventing fistulas) and to promote their right to education. But as Adeline Masquelier argues, the early marriage of girls may actually be a more reliable pathway to respect and economic security than education in these precarious times of deep gender inequities. Indeed, "the vision of girl's rights promoted by rights activists and development experts is based on a narrow definition of empowerment that is not easily reconciled with what it means to have status, enjoy respectability, and claim power over others when one is young and female in Niger" (Masquelier, this volume). Masquelier explicates the distinct and often clashing ideologies of "girls," understandings of "marriage," and visions of the future underlying both customary marriage practices and the international campaigns against early marriage in Niger. Moreover, she shows how, as elsewhere, state elites, religious leaders, and international activists (like colonial administrators in the past) buttress their moral positions by invoking specters of vulnerable women and girls that obscure the complex realities of their lives.

Second, other chapters examine how the control of marriage depends on the definition and regulation of appropriate sexual relations and, usually, constraints on the sexual activities of unmarried women. In Malawi (Silver) and Uganda (Musiime and Eryenyu), debates about youth sexuality and schooling focus on the sexual practices of girls rather than boys. Rachel Silver analyzes the contradictions in Malawi's official Readmission Policy, which is often celebrated for supporting girls' rights. The policy banishes pregnant girls from their schools and only allows them to be readmitted once they have given birth under strict conditions. The sexually active schoolboys who often fathered the children are rarely, if ever, dismissed. Moreover, according to Silver, the ostensibly "progressive" policy is constrained by a conservative approach to youth sexuality that forbids comprehensive sexual education in schools, promotes abstinence, and prohibits the provision of contraception—all of which would, of course, reduce schoolgirl pregnancies in the first place and suggest a continued stigmatization of youth sexuality.

Eunice Musiime and Leah Eryenyu examine similar debates about the sexuality of boys and girls in Uganda, where the parliament banned the provision of comprehensive sexuality education in 2016. The lawmakers argued instead for the creation of a "values-based" approach that would reflect "traditional" family values, in which sexual intercourse is confined (at least for women) to heterosexual marriage relations and linked to reproduction rather than pleasure. The resulting program, the National Sexuality Education Framework, was launched in 2018. The program set guidelines for teaching sexuality to different age groups premised on promoting abstinence, sexual purity, morality, virginity, and faithfulness. As in Malawi, the program ignored the realities of adolescent sexual lives and emphasized the sexuality of girls over boys.

As part of their efforts to confine sexuality to heterosexual marriage, conservative politicians and religious leaders across the continent have also demonized and even criminalized same-sex intimate relations as "foreign" and un-African, despite documented histories of gender fluidity and same-sex relations. In 2009, for example, the Ugandan legislature introduced its controversial Anti-Homosexuality Bill, which proposed new penalties for same-sex relationships and actions considered to "promote" homosexuality in the country. Lydia Boyd explores how these ideas of gay sex as not just "nonnormative" but dangerous (especially to ideals of heterosexual marriage) shaped medical testimonies, media fascination, and popular and political debates in the country. Cheikh Ibrahima Niang, Ellen Foley, and Ndack Diop examine similar debates in Senegal, which criminalized homosexuality and has witnessed a comparable rise in homophobic insults and actions.

Third, all the chapters affirm the importance of assessing the historical, political, and economic context of legislative efforts. As in the colonial period (e.g., Allman 1996), some of the fiercest struggles over women's bodies, loyalties, and rights occur during times of rampant economic precarity and political turmoil. In Uganda, according to Lydia Boyd, leaders used the language of moral crisis to lobby for the Anti-Pornography Bill as a way to deflect attention from their assertions of political authoritarianism. Although the bill was framed as a measure to protect women and children from becoming the victims of sexual crimes by implementing a broad definition of pornography, it soon resulted in physical attacks on some urban women accused of wearing provocative clothing, including female members of the political opposition. Boyd explores how and why women's naked bodies became the site of fierce battles over not just gendered and sexual rights in Uganda but also the broader assertions of and challenges to the intensified authoritarianism of President Museveni's political regime. Similarly, Niang, Foley, and Diop argue that one reason for the recent rise of "sexual panics" over homosexuals in Senegal was the efforts of competing political parties and conservative religious reformers to claim moral legitimacy in the broadened political terrain created by democratization.

Moreover, although most of the chapters discuss contemporary legislative debates, they demonstrate that history matters, especially colonial legacies of regulating gender and generational relationships, histories of Christian evangelism, and, for some, the more recent influence of more conservative Islamist ideologies. The importance of a historical understanding is perhaps most vivid in the rise of antihomosexual fervor in Senegal, explored by Niang, Foley, and Diop. As mentioned above, Senegalese politicians and conservative Muslim religious leaders have criminalized homosexuality and advocated for a virulent and sometimes violent homophobia. But their fierce efforts to assert a form of "heteronationalism" ignore a long history in which gender-fluid individuals, called *goorjigeen* in Wolof (a term that combines the words for man [*goor*] and woman [*jigeen*]), were visible and accepted. Although the term *goorjigeen* has now become synonymous with gay and homosexual and is frequently used as a disparaging epithet, the authors show how *goorjigeen* was a local gender category that referred historically to men who usually dressed as women and participated in female activities, organizations, and social worlds.

Finally, several authors argue that the focus on individual rights often deflects attention from the structural factors that shape and constrain people's possibilities and potential. In Niger (Masquelier), Malawi (Silver), and Uganda (Musiime and Eryenyu), gender inequities in access to reproductive health care undermine the ability of unmarried pregnant schoolgirls to pursue education and, as a result, burden their families with demands for childcare and financial support. In a different context, Charlotte Walker-Said analyzes how poverty, corruption, and conflict in Cameroon have strengthened the interdependence of family members, leading in some cases to the forced labor, trafficking, and enslavement of their female dependents in the United States. In 2018 US attorney general Jefferson Sessions overturned a case that allowed thousands of foreign women fleeing domestic violence to seek asylum in the United States. In his decision, Sessions drew on liberal ideas of the public-private divide to reason that most domestic violence victims suffer from "private violence," which is not equivalent to "persecution." Walker-Said challenges his claims, arguing instead that the "precarity produced in intimate spaces is truly a function of statist and geopolitical dictates." Drawing on her knowledge of Cameroon and the testimonies of asylum seekers, she demonstrates how poverty, youth unemployment, corruption, state underinvestment in education, and sporadic civil conflicts have contributed to the rise of rape, incest, and domestic violence.

Similarly, Elisabeth Kago Ilboudo Nébié analyzes the limits of the quota-based legal remedies favored by international donors to address gender inequities in access to and control over land in the face of class divides, rural-urban disparities, and increased impoverishment and resource stress produced by climate change. Drawing on evidence from Burkina Faso, she argues that "rights-based frameworks are insufficient to promote gender parity because they typically do not translate to local practice, especially in rural areas where customary laws and values regulate gender relations." State leaders invoked rights-based discourses to require that a certain number of women serve on local resource management committees to strengthen their rights to land and other natural resources. Unfortunately, Nébié shows, local men ignored such "top-down" edicts, the elected women did not necessarily represent the interests of all women, and the quotas sometimes increased rural women's workload rather than improving their conditions.

Together, these chapters provide nuanced, thoughtful analyses of the perils and possibilities of national and international efforts to legislate sex and gender. They document how such "moralizing enterprises" are inherently contested, the product of efforts to reconcile often contradictory political, policy, and moral goals. Although some chapters try to disentangle "local" from "global" actors, laws, and interventions, most acknowledge that these are deeply interwoven. The landscape of these actors includes the state, feminist activists, NGOs, and religious groups, each with their own perspectives, mandates, and moral ideals. But they do not engage as equals. State agents are often more powerful, given their oversight of NGOs, influence over (if not control of) the media, and ability to implement and enforce legislation. But the state is not all-powerful: laws passed by elites in the capital may have little impact on the practices of police, people, and courts in rural areas. Indeed, as coeditors and authors argue, the privileging of individual rights and autonomy often ignores the social differences, historical legacies, and structural contexts that distinguish those same individuals, including their gender and sexuality.

## Note

1. I explore and explain these distinct but overlapping legal regimes further in Hodgson 2017.

## References

Allman, Jean. 1996. "Rounding Up Spinsters: Gender Chaos and Unmarried Women in Colonial Asante." *Journal of African History* 37 (2): 195–214.

Hodgson, Dorothy L. 2017. *Gender, Justice and the Problem of Culture: From Customary Law to Human Rights in Tanzania*. Bloomington: Indiana University Press.

Contributors

Lydia Boyd is an associate professor of African, African American, and diaspora studies at the University of North Carolina, Chapel Hill. She is the author of *Preaching Prevention: Born-Again Christianity and the Moral Politics of AIDS in Uganda* (2015).

Emily Burrill is an associate professor of history and women's and gender studies and the director of the African Studies Center at the University of North Carolina, Chapel Hill. She is the author of *States of Marriage: Gender, Justice and Rights in Mali* (2015).

Ndack Diop is a researcher at the SAHARA Program, Université Cheikh Anta Diop (Senegal).

Leah Eryenyu is the research advocacy and movement-building manager at Akina Mama wa Afrika, a feminist Pan-African leadership development organization based in Kampala, Uganda. She received her bachelor's degree in political science from Williams College.

Ellen Foley is a professor in the department of International Development, Community, and Environment at Clark University. She is a medical anthropologist and the author of *Your Pocket Is What Cures You: The Politics of Health in Senegal* (2010).

Dorothy L. Hodgson is the dean of the School of Arts and Sciences and a professor of anthropology at Brandeis University. She is the author and editor of ten books, including *Gender, Justice and the Problem of Culture: From Customary Law to Human Rights in Tanzania* (2017), *Being Maasai, Becoming*

*Indigenous: Postcolonial Politics in a Neoliberal World* (2011), and *Gender and Culture at the Limit of Rights* (2011).

Adeline Masquelier is a professor of anthropology at Tulane University. She is the author and editor of several books, including *Prayer Has Spoiled Everything: Possession, Power, and Identity in an Islamic Town of Niger* (2001), *Women and Islamic Revival in a West African Town* (2009), and *Fada: Boredom and Belonging in Niger* (2019).

Eunice Musiime is the executive director of Akina Mama wa Afrika, a feminist Pan-African leadership development organization based in Kampala, Uganda. She holds a bachelor's degree in law from the University of Dar es Salaam (Tanzania) and an MBA, majoring in public policy analysis, from the University of Birmingham (United Kingdom).

Elisabeth Kago Ilboudo Nébié is a postdoctoral research fellow at the International Research Institute for Climate and Society at Columbia University.

Cheikh Ibrahima Niang is a medical and social anthropologist based at L'Institut des Sciences de l'Environnement (ISE) at Université Cheikh Anta Diop (Senegal).

Rachel Silver is an assistant professor of education at York University. She received her PhD in anthropology and educational policy studies from the University of Wisconsin–Madison in 2019.

Charlotte Walker-Said is an assistant professor in the Department of Africana Studies at John Jay College–CUNY. She is the author of *Faith, Power and Family: Christianity and Social Change in French Cameroon* (2018).

# Index

"abject African," figure of, 7–8
abortion, 97, 102n13; Malawi, 87, 95, 97; Niger, 60n18; Uganda, 106, 109, 113
abstinence, 97, 113; and birth spacing, 61n25; and CSE, 120; Malawi, 86, 93; Uganda, 108–9, 111, 113–14
accountability: on human rights, 116–17; for resource use, 75
accusations of homosexual sympathies, 162
ACHPR (African Court on Human and People's Rights), 37–38
Aciro-Lakor, Rita, 188
adoption, 31
adultery, prosecution of, 60n9
Adupa, Larry, 111–12
Africa, human rights histories, 7–10, 21n4
African Charter on Human and Peoples' Rights, 12, 161; Protocol on Rights of Women in Africa (see Maputo Protocol)
African Commission on Human and Peoples' Rights, NGO Forum, 33
African nationalist movements, 9
African Union, 30, 56; Campaign to End Child Marriage, 60n10; and Maputo Protocol, 12

"African woman," figure of, 59n7; as hyperfertile, 42; as suffering, 42–44
age groups, in Uganda's National Sexuality Education Framework, 112–13
alimony, 27
Amadou, Hama, 45
Amnesty International, 6, 29
anal sex, 182–86
An-Na'im, Abdullah Ahmed, 121
Ansar Dine (Mali), 36–37
anticolonialism, 6, 8
antihomosexuality: Gambia, 163; Nigeria, 165; Senegal, 150–65, 196–97; Uganda, 115, 181–86, 196; Zimbabwe, 165
"anti–mini skirt bill" (Uganda), 171–73
anti-Sufi organizations, 160–61
APDF (L'Association pour le Progrès et la Défense des Femmes), 31–33, 37–38
AQIM (Al Qaeda in the Islamic Maghreb), 36–37
Argenti, Nicolas, 132
asylum seekers, West African, 125–41
autochthonization, 69, 71, 74
autonomy: bodily, 110, 117, 151; individual, 4, 14, 17, 48, 172–73, 180, 198; sexual, 186
AVV (Aménagements des Vallées des Volta), resettlement program, 74
awareness-raising workshops, 33

201

Bajaj, Monisha, 90
Bamako, 35–36; University of, 32
Bastian, Misty, 178
Benhabib, Seyla, 126
birth control, 54–55
birth control access, 97; Malawi, 85–87; Niger, 61n23, 61n26
birth spacing, 54, 61n25
Bissa people, 74
Bompani, Barbara, 114–15
Bop, Codou, 157, 166n11
Bornstein, Erica, 174
breast ironing, 135
Breusers, Mark, 69, 80
Broqua, Christophe, 153, 156, 158–59
Brown, S. Terreni, 114–15
Buganda, 180
Buganda Road Chief Magistrate Court, 182–84
Bunch, Charlotte, 12
Burkina Faso, 128, 198; land resource management, 65–81
Burnet, Jennie, 71
Burrill, Emily, 137
Butler, Judith, 101n5

CAIS (Collectif des Associations Islamique du Sénégal), 160–61
Cameroon, 197; family violence, 125–41; Ministry of Social Affairs, 134; Ministry of Women's Empowerment and the Family, 134
Cameroon Society for the Prevention of Child Abuse and Neglect, 134–35
Canada, High Commission of, in Cameroon, 133
Catholic Church, opposition to CSE in Uganda, 116
CEDAW (Convention on the Elimination of All Forms of Discrimination against Women), 33, 35, 55, 127
CEHURD (Centre for Health Rights and Development), 108, 118

Cheng, Sealing, 110
chiefs, decreasing power of, 68
childbirth, 59n6
"child bride," figure of, 42–44, 47–48, 58. See also marriage, early
childcare options, and school readmission, 88, 92
child custody: Mali, 27; Niger, 51, 56
"child marriage," 9, 53, 60n20. See also marriage, early
child rights/adult rights, in human rights approach, 101n11
Chilisa, Bagele, 88
Chishugi, John, 136
Christian missions, and regulation of youth sexuality, 90
Christian values, in Uganda, 108–9
Church of Uganda (CoU), 112; opposition to CSE, 116
climate change: Burkina Faso, 65–81; Malawi, 88
CNLS (Conseil National de Lutte Contre le SIDA), 162
COGES (Comité de Gestion), 67–70, 74–80
Cohen, Stanley, 151
cohesion, in family units, 135
coitus interruptus, as form of infanticide, 54
Collectif des Associations Musulmanes (Mali), 35
colonialism, 7–9, 21n4, 55, 152; Burkina Faso, 80; Malawi, 90; Mali, 25–26, 28, 35, 137; Niger, 51, 56; Nigeria, 178; Senegal, 153–54
colonization, and regulation of youth sexuality, 90
Comité Islamique pour la Reeforme du Code de la Famille au Sénégal, 166n11
Commission for Population and Development, 107
Compaoré, Blaise, 68

complicity, accusations of, in women's rights activism, 110
concubinage, 126
condom use, 93, 97. *See also* birth control access
Congo, Democratic Republic of, Sexual Practices against Nature Bill (2010), 15
conservatism, cultural, in Uganda, 119
constitutions, 11; Malawi, 100; Namibia, 11; Senegal, 166n14; South Africa, 11; Uganda, 11, 118
contraceptive access. *See* birth control access
Cornwall, Andrea, 11–12
Corre, Armand, 153
Correa, Gus, 139
corruption, in Malawi, 101n12
corvée labor system, 8
Côte d'Ivoire, 128, 166n7
coup d'état, Mali, 29, 35–36
cowives, 54–55, 69
criminalization of homosexuality, 156, 163
cross-dressing, 154
Crowder, Michael, 153
CSE (comprehensive sexuality education), in Uganda, 106–21, 196
CSOs (civil society organizations), in Mali, 34
cultural change, in international human rights discourse, 42–44
cultural practices, 9, 89, 152, 186
cultural transformation, internal, 121
cultural values, Ugandan, 112–16, 119
culture, in transnational human rights framework, 5
culture, viewed as in conflict with human rights, 5–6, 10–11; in Niger, 44–46, 58–59; in Uganda, 173, 186–88; in US, 129
"culture of rights," 44
customary legal regimes, 193
CVD (Comité Villageois de Développement), 68–69

Da Jorio, Rosa, 25
Dakar, Senegal, 153, 155, 163; Sicap Mbao neighborhood, 160
Davidson, Michael, 153
decriminalization, of homosexuality, 162, 165
De Haas, Billie, 113–14
democratization, 193–94; Senegal, 156–59
DFID (British Department for International Development), 99
Diakité, Fatoumata Siré, 32–33, 38
Diawara, Bintou Coulibaly, 38
dictatorship, in Mali, 32
Diori, Hamani, 56
displacement, 36
divorce, 27, 194; Mali, 27, 31–32; Niger, 51, 56; Uganda, 118–19. *See also* repudiation
domestic duties, as impediment to girls' education, 50
domestic labor, unpaid, 71, 188
"donor," use of term, 100n3
*drianke*, 153, 155

economic crisis: Cameroon, 133; Senegal, 158
economic imperatives, and schoolgirl pregnancy, 89
economic progress, linked to fertility control, 47
education. *See* girls' education
EFA (Education for All), 89, 100
EIP Cameroon, 134
embodiment, 171–88
empowerment, concept of, 44, 46, 49, 51, 58
Englund, Harri, 11
enslavement, 9, 126, 131
entanglements, of law, gender, and sex, 193–98
Epprecht, Marc, 165
evangelical Christians, 86. *See also* Pentecostal Christians; Pentecostal churches

"exceptional women" status, 78
exploitation. *See* traffic in women
"extrastate," use of term, 21n3

Facebook, 175, 176, 179, 189n4, 189n8
family: as basic unit in society, 112; crisis of, 28–29; large, 54; loyalty to, 126. *See also* family networks; family planning; family violence; marriage
family laws, 16, 18, 55–57, 193–98; Mali, 28–31, 34–35, 38; Niger, 44, 47, 55–57, 61n28
Family Life Network, 115
family networks, in Cameroon, 130–41
family planning: Malawi, 93; Niger, 55. *See also* birth control access; birth spacing; contraceptive access
family violence: Burkina Faso, 128; Cameroon, 125–41; Côte d'Ivoire, 128; in US law, 127–29
FDC (Forum for Democratic Change), 188n3
female circumcision, 126
female sexuality: control of, 52, 90, 92–96; as focus of sex education, 114
feminist approach, to CSE, 110–12
"feminist dictator," concept of, 33
feminist political geography, 129–30, 136–39
fertility control, in Niger, 46–48, 54–55
fertility rates, in Niger, 47, 60n11
firewood collection, 66
fistula, obstetric, 43–45, 47–48, 59n1, 59n3
Fluri, Jennifer, 127, 129
focus groups, 76–79; Burkina Faso, 72, 76–77; Mali, 33; Senegal, 153
forced labor, 131
Fourth World Conference on Women (Beijing, 1995), 29
free speech, 180
French Army, and Mali, 36

French colonial legacy, Niger and, 51, 56, 60n20
French language, in Burkina Faso, 72
French Soudan, 137. *See also* Mali
Fulße herders (Fulße, Fulani, Peulh, Fula, Felatta, Haalpullar; Burkina Faso), 69–70, 76–81; Fulfuldé dialect of, 72
FWP (Forum of Women Parliamentarians), 70

GABLE (Girls Attainment in Basic Literacy and Education), 87
Gambia, the, 161, 163
Gaudio, Rudolf Pell, 155, 165
gender and sexuality legislation, 13–17. *See also under names of countries*
gender-based rights, debate over: Niger, 42–59; Uganda, 171–88
gender complementarity, in Niger, 59
gender diversity, in land resource management, 67
gender equality: Niger, 58–59; Uganda, 119
gender equity, and girls' education, 48–51
gender fluidity, in Senegal, 151–56, 164, 196
gender nonconformity, in Senegal, 151–56
gender parity policies, 65–67, 80
genderqueer, 164, 165n1
gender quotas, 65–67, 77–78, 197–98; Burkina Faso and, 67–71
"geography of blame," 45
Germany, foreign aid from, 32
Geschiere, Peter, 126, 132, 138, 140
girls' education, 195; and early marriage, 60n13; human capital approach to, 89; Malawi, 15, 84–100; Niger, 43–44, 46, 48–51
girls' rights advocacy, 42–44. *See also* marriage, early

Global Gag Rule, 98, 102n13
global human rights norms, and vernacularization, 109–12
*goorjigeen* (Wolof), 151–56, 164, 165n1, 197
Gorer, Geoffrey, 153
*gorgi* (Wolof), 155
government schools, and school readmission policy, 92
Grant, Monica, 89
Gray, Leslie, 69
Groupe Pivot Droit et Citoyenneté des Femmes (Mali), 34
GTV (Gestion des Terroirs Villageois), 68–69
GTZ (Gesellschaft für Internationale Zusammenarbeit), 134
Guèye, Latif, 159
Guttmacher Institute, 109

Hannig, Anita, 47
Health Policy Project, 85
health services, provided through schools, 101n10
Heller, Alison, 47
Herdt, Gilbert, 151, 157, 160, 163
heteronationalism, 151, 197
HIV/AIDS pandemic, 61n26, 86, 92–93, 107, 159–62, 164, 166n7
Hodgson, Dorothy, 173
homophobia, 196–97; Malawi, 166n8; Senegal, 150–65; Uganda, 115, 181–86
homosexual, *goorjigeen* as, 156
"homosexual as devil," figure of, 151–52
homosexuality, 122n4; claim of externality, 152; and family violence, 126; Senegal, 150–65. *See also* antihomosexuality; homophobia
honor crimes, 126
humanism, indigenous, 21n4
human rights. *See* rights; rights-based approach
human rights language, 48, 53, 58–59

human rights organizations, 29; and Mali marriage reform, 33–34. *See also names of organizations*
Hutter, Inge, 113

Ibhawoh, Bonny, 6–7
Igbo women, and Women's War (1929), 178–79
IHRDA (Institute of Human Rights Development in Africa), 37–38
"immoral behavior," and school expulsion, 92–94
imperialism, European, 7–8
incest, 126, 133–36
income inequality, in Cameroon, 140
incontinence, and obstetric fistula, 43, 48
indentured servitude, 126
infant feeding, as issue in school return, 88
infant mortality, in Niger, 54
infertility, 55
inflation rate, in Senegal, 158
inheritance rights: Burkina Faso, 69; Mali, 29, 31, 37, 39; Niger, 56
interdependency, 130–33, 172–73, 180–81. *See also* social relatedness
international aid, for Mali, 36
International Conference on Population and Development, 106; Programme of Action, 107
International Covenant on Civil and Political Rights, 161
International Livestock Research Institute, 72
Inter-Religious Council (Uganda), 112
interviews: Burkina Faso, 72, 76; Cameroon, 131–35; Malawi, 101n7, 153; Senegal, 152–54; Uganda, 180, 190n14
Islam: in Mali, 32–34; Sunni, 60n19, 166n10
Islamic Committee for Reforming the Family Code (Senegal), 157

Islamic Front to Defend Ethical Values (Senegal), 161, 164
Islamic fundamentalism, 166n10
Islamic High Council (Mali), 32–33
Islamic law and tradition: Burkina Faso, 69–70; Mali, 37; Niger, 43–46, 50–54, 56–57, 60n9; Senegal, 157. *See also* Muslim identity; Muslim organizations
Islamic NGOs, 158–59
Islamic values, and antihomosexuality, 157, 160–61, 164
Islamist movement, 166n11
Islamist reformers, in Senegal, 157, 160–61
Izala Muslim movement, 45, 60n8

Jammeh, Yahya, 163
Jamra (Islamic organization), 158–59, 161, 163
*jekker* (Wolof), 155

Kachala, Faith, 88
Kaïbo-Nord V2 (Burkina Faso), 74
Kaira, Robert, 190n13
Kampala, Uganda, 108, 113, 115, 171, 179, 190n14
Karlström, Mikael, 180
Kaunda, Zikani, 93
Kayanja, Robert, 182–86
Keita, Ibrahim Boubacar, 36
Keita, Modibo, 29
Kendall, Nancy, 93
Kerner, Brad, 88
Kevane, Michael, 69
kinship, and family violence, 131–33. *See also* family networks
Konaré, Alpha Oumar, 29, 34
Kountché, Seyni, 56
Kyazze, Michael, 190n13
Kyomuhendo, Deborah Anita, 190n13

labor: corvée system, 8; forced, 131; migration, 66, 80

*laïcité*, 157
landownership, in Burkina Faso, 69
land resource management, in Burkina Faso, 65–81
land rights, women's, in Burkina Faso, 69–71
Larok, Arthus, 119
legal aid, for women seeking divorce, 32
legal literacy sessions, 33
legal system, Niger, 51–54
literacy rates: Burkina Faso, 78; Niger, 48
livestock raising, in Sondré-Est (Burkina Faso), 74
Liwewe, Olivia, 87
local actors, role of, 10–13
local committees, for land management, 68–69
Local Governance and Adapting to Climate Change in Sub-Saharan Africa project, 72
local-local dynamics, 6–7, 26
Luganda language, 180
Lumière, Charnelle, 136

Maathai, Wangari, 177
Magufuli, John, 85, 100n2
majority, women's age of, in Niger, 52
Makerere Institute for Social Research, 175
Makerere University, 109, 175–76, 181
Malawi, 195; Cashgate Scandal, 101n12; and climate change, 88; constitution, 100; "Discipline Policy on Girls Education," 91; homophobia, 166n8; Life Skills curriculum, 93–95; malnutrition, 88; Ministries of Education and Gender, 87; Ministry of Education, Science, and Technology (MoEST), 85–87, 91–99; Ministry of Health (MoH), 87; Readmission Policy, 15, 84–100, 195; starvation, 88; state of emergency, 88

*Malawi Demographic and Health Survey*, 85
Male, Solomon, 182–86, 190n13
male dominance, in land resource management, 66–67
male fertility, 61n24; and women's worth, 90
male heads of household, 77
male mediation, 78–79
male virility, 61n24
Mali, 194; Marriage and Guardianship Code (1962), 26, 194–95; marriage legislation, 27–30; marriage reform, 25–39; massacre of 80 soldiers, 35; Ministry for the Promotion of Women, Children, and the Family, 34; Ministry of Justice, 34; "NGOization" of, 30; northern provinces, 35–36; peace accord (2015), 36–37; Personal Status and Family Code ("Marriage Code," 2009), 31–34
Maliki legal tradition, 51–52, 60n19. *See also* Islamic law and tradition
malnutrition, 88
Mamdani, Mahmood, 176
Manga (capital of Zoundwéogo Province, Burkina Faso), 72
Mann, Gregory, 10
Maputo Protocol, 12, 26, 30, 33, 35, 37–38, 56
marital authority, husband's, 27, 35, 194; Burkina Faso, 70; Mali, 35
marital consent, 194; Mali, 27–28, 31, 39; Niger, 52, 60n20. *See also* marriage, early
marital faithfulness, 113
marital obligation, 39
marital reconciliation, 32
marriage: arranged, 133–36; civil/secular, 27–31, 194; customary, 27–28; family, 53–54; forced, 9, 53, 126, 128, 133–36; *goorjigeen* and, 155; levirate/sororate, 133; multiple "scripts" for, 25–26;

religious, 27–28, 35; and school return policy, 92
marriage, early, 53, 89; Cameroon, 133–36; Niger, 42–59, 195
marriage, minimum age of, 39; Mali, 29, 35, 37; Niger, 45, 51–52, 55–58, 60n20. *See also* marriage, early
marriage certificate, 31
marriage choice, in Niger, 53–54
marriagecraft, 25–26, 37, 39n1
marriage equality, in Mali, 29
marriage legislation: Mali, 27–30; Morocco, 34; Senegal, 29; Uganda, 118–19. *See also* family laws
marriage reform, 194–95; Mali, 25–39
marriage registration, in Mali, 31
marriage rights talk, in Mali, 26
marriage witnessing, in Mali, 31
married students, 101n9
masculinity, 61n24
massacre, in Mali, 35
Mayzel, Maria, 88
Mazloum, Nahid, 87
M'Baye, Babacar, 152–53
McCollum, Betty, 43
MDGs/SDGs (Millennium and Sustainable Development Goals), 89
media: BBC, 33; *Icone* magazine, 160; and Mali marriage reform, 33–34; NBS TV, 176; Voice of America, 33. *See also* newspapers; social media
menstrual periods, girls and, 179–81
Merry, Sally Engle, 14, 44, 109–10, 186
military wives and mothers, in Mali, 35–36
miniskirt, 171–73
MNLA (National Movement for the Liberation of Azawad), 36
Molyneux, Maxine, 11–12
moral conservatism, and youth SRH, 84–86
"moral economy of the household," 137–38

moralizing enterprises, 3, 193
moral panics, 151, 160, 171. *See also* sexual panics
Morocco, and Moudawana family code (2004), 34
Mosse, David, 86, 99
Mossi farmers (Burkina Faso), 69, 74, 80; Mooré dialect of, 72
Mouvement Démocratique (Mali), 32
Moyn, Samuel, 5–6
MSM (men who have sex with men), 156. *See also* homosexuality
Muhammad, Prophet, 52
Muhanguzi, Florence, 114
Mukalazi, David, 190n13
Mukisa, Samson, 166n16, 183–86
Musalo, Karen, 126
Museveni, Janet, 111–12, 175
Museveni, Yoweri, 13, 107–8, 172, 175, 179–81, 188n1
Muslim identity: Burkina Faso, 72–74; Niger, 45–46
Muslim organizations, in Mali, 32–33
Muyan, 79, 81

nakedness, public, 171–88
Namibia, constitution (1990), 11
National Human Rights Commission (Mali), 34
nationalization of land, in Burkina Faso, 68
National Union of Muslim Women's Associations (Mali), 32–33
"native woman," figure of, 7–8
*ndep* ceremonies, 154
Ndonko, Flavien, 134
Ndonkou, Péguy, 135–36
neocolonialism, 152
neoliberalism, 4, 30, 38–39, 68, 127
newspapers: *26 Mars*, 32; *Al Jazeera*, 180; *Daily Monitor*, 116, 176; *The Guardian*, 179–80; *InfoMatin*, 33; *Les Échos*, 32; *Le Soir de Bamako*, 33;

*New York Times*, 150; *Wall Street Journal*, 42
"NGOization" in Mali, 30
NGOs: and CSE, 114, 118; foreign, as threat to traditional cultures, 108; Islamic, 158–59; rise of, 6; and school return, 96–99. *See also names of organizations*
Ngoutsop, Moïse Tamekem, 136
Niger, 197; Campaign to End Child Marriage (2014), 47; Code de la Famille, 56; and debate over gender-based rights, 42–59; and early marriage, 42–59, 195; family law reform, 55–57; as Islamic culture, 43–46, 50–54, 59n4; legal system, 51–54; Mandel Decree, 51, 53, 60n20; Statut Personnel du Niger, 56
Nigeria: antihomosexuality, 165; colonial, 178–79; Gender Equality Law (proposed), 3; Same-Sex Marriage Prohibition Act (2014), 15; Women's War (1929), 178–79
Nike Corporation, 90
Ninsiima, Anna, 114
non-binary-gender expression, history of, in Senegal, 151–56, 164
nonconsensual sex, 94. *See also* rape
Nyanzi, Stella, 166n12, 175–81, 189n4, 189n6, 189n8, 189n9

Obama, Barack, 15, 150, 162
Obote, Milton, 9–10
"old maids," 53
Oloka-Onyango, Joe, 5
"one-hundred-meter rule" (Malawi), 93
Ongeng, Rev. Can. William, 112, 115
open schools, 101n9
outing, of homosexuals, 160–63, 185

parental involvement, in sexuality education, 112
parental rights, in Mali, 27

PASMEP (Plate-Forme d'Actions à la Sécurisation des Ménages Pastoraux), 79
pastoralism, in Burkina-Faso, 72–79
PDS (Parti Démocratique Sénégalais), 158
peace accord, Mali (2015), 36–37
"pederast," use of term, 153
pederasty, 181–86
peer pressure, as factor in early marriage, 50
Pentecostal Christians, 114–16, 181–86
Pentecostal churches, 115
PEPFAR (US President's Emergency Plan for AIDS Relief), 86, 98
permissiveness, 117
"persecution," use of term, 128–29
Platform for Action (1995), 12
police, and traffic in women, 133, 140–41
policy language, 120
policy review process, for Malawi Readmission Policy, 94–96
political activism: Niger, 55–57; Uganda, 171–88
politics of partnership, and school return policy, 98
polygamy, 27
polygyny, 54. *See also* cowives
population growth, in Niger, 60n12
pornography, 171–73, 185, 188n2, 196
Porter, Holly, 180
postcolonialism, 6–7, 25–26, 28, 35, 38, 152, 193–98; Burkina Faso, 80; Malawi, 90
poverty: in Cameroon, 130–33, 140; and climate change, 66; and early marriage, 47; and family violence, 127; as form of structural violence, 136–37; multidimensional, 136–39; in Niger, 57; and school return policy, 100
power relations, in resource management, 76–79

precarity, 57, 100, 101n5, 130, 157, 163, 196–97
pregnancy: out-of-wedlock, 42, 50, 52–53, 60n22; and school expulsion, 84–100; and school readmission policies, 84–100; teenage, 106, 113; unintended, 109; unwanted, 106
pregnancy-related complications, as cause of death/disability of young Ugandan women, 113
"pregnant girl as vulnerable victim," figure of, 101n8
primary schools, 89; Malawi, 84, 88; Niger, 49, 60n14. *See also* girls' education; government schools; open schools
private landownership, in Burkina Faso, 68
private sphere, 126; and family violence, 130; state and, 127–30; as women's space, 80
procreation, as goal of marriage, 54
prosecution, for traffic in women, 139
prostitution, repression of, 60n9
provocation of "sexual excitement," 171
PS (Parti Socialiste [Senegal]), 158
public health approach, to youth sexuality, 96–99
public health campaigns, suspicions of, 61n26, 61n27. *See also* HIV/AIDS pandemic
public/private divide, and redress against family violence, 126. *See also* private sphere; public sphere
public protest, Stella Nyanzi and, 176
public sphere, women's exclusion from, 76–80
purity, issue of, 44

queer sex, 182–86
queer theory, 165n1
"queer," use of term, 189n12

RAF (Réorganisation agraire et foncière), 67–68
RAHU (Reach a Hand Uganda), 118
rape, 97, 126, 133–36, 143n15; child, 133–34; spousal, 52, 60n21, 128
redemption, school readmission policy as, 91
Redfield, Peter, 174
refugees, West African, 125–41
refugee status in US, for victims of family violence, 128–29
religious communities, Ugandan, and opposition to CSE, 108
religious culture, and reform, 121
RENATA ("the national aunties network"), 136
reproductive rights, vernacularization of, 116–20
repudiation, 56, 194
resilience, of family networks, 138–41
resistance, to school return policy, 91–92
resource sharing, 74
Rich, Adrienne, 110
rights: as alternative to values, 117–18; as externally imposed, 117; as individual freedoms, 10–11; as tools of donor nations, 117
rights-based agency, and women's bodies, 173–75
rights-based approach: as challenge to state power, 118; to CSE, 106–21; to education, 89–91, 99–100; and gender parity, 80; to land resource management, 65–67; and local context, 110; to school return, 96, 98–99
"rights of culture," 44
rites of passage, *goorjigeen* and, 155
Roberts, Richard, 137
Rosny, Eric de, 142n5
rural population, in Mali, 37
rural women, and gender quotas, 71
Ruranga, Mar. Rubaramira, 118
Rwanda, 70; Land Law (2004), 70

Saint Louis, Senegal, 153
Salam, Sheikh Abdou, 42, 45
Sall, Macky, 15, 150, 162–64
Samati, Madalo, 88
same-sex sexuality, in Senegal, 150–65
Sankara, Thomas, 68
Sarkozy, Nicolas, 164
school absenteeism, in Malawi, 88
School as an Instrument of Peace, 134
school dropouts, 85, 88
school readmission policy for young mothers, Malawi, 84–100, 195
schools, for parents, 85
Scully, Pamela, 11, 55, 174, 187
SDGs (Sustainable Development Goals), 100
secondary schools: Malawi, 84, 88; Niger, 48–51, 60n14. *See also* girls' education; government schools; open schools; primary schools
"secondary virgin," young mother as, 95
"second chances," and student sexuality, 91–94
"second shift," unpaid domestic work as, 71
Senegal, 15, 193, 196–97; and antihomosexuality, 150–65; constitution, 166n14; Family Code, 157, 166n11; French Penal Code, 156; marriage and family legislation, 29; National AIDS Control Programme, 159; Touré's exile in, 35
Senegalese Nine, 160–61
Sessions, Jefferson, 128–29
sex education, school-based, 86, 93–95. *See also* CSE
sexual abuse, early marriage as, 43
sexual and gender-based rights, Uganda, 171–88
"sexual excitement," provocation of, 171
sexual initiation, and girls' education, 89
sexual panics, 196; Gambia, 163; Senegal, 150–65

sexual personhood, 186–87
sexual violence: Malawi, 94; Mali, 37; Niger, 60n21; in schools, 50–51, 60n16
shaming, public, in women's protest, 175–81
silence, as mode of self-protection, 166n12
silencing, of women activists in Niger, 57
"sitting on a man," 178–79
slavery. *See* enslavement
social embeddedness, 172–73
social media, 175–76, 179, 188, 189n4, 189n8
social practice, rights work as, 14–17
social relatedness, 172–73; and rights-based claims, 187–88
Sondré-Est (center-south Burkina Faso), 65–81
sons, men's preference for, 54
South African constitution (1996), 11
Sowe, Gaye, 38
spiritual attack, 51, 55
Spivak, Gayatri Chakravorty, 7–8
spousal abuse, 128
SRH. *See* youth sexuality and reproductive health (SRH)
SRHR (Sexual and Reproductive Health Rights). *See* youth sexuality and reproductive health (SRH)
Ssempa, Martin, 182–86, 190n13
starvation, 88
state, role of, 10–13
state of emergency, in Malawi, 88
Stern, Steve, 91
Straus, Scott, 91
suffering, visibility of, 174
Sullivan, Emmet G., 128
Sunni Islam, 60n19, 166n10
Swidler, Ann, 99

Tajabone holiday, 154
Tamale, Sylvia, 5, 13, 120, 176–77
*tànnëbéer* (Wolof), 154–55
teacher predation, 94

teachers, role in CSE, 114
Terretta, Meredith, 8
Thiès, Senegal, 160
Titanji, Beatrice, 130
Tomusange, Peninah, 118
Touré, Amadou Toumani, 31–36
traffic in women: Cameroon, 125–41, 197; and early marriage, 46
transactional sex, 88, 97
transgender individuals, 153, 156
transhumance, 74
transnationalism, 4–6, 9–13, 30, 100n4, 193
transphobia, 159
Traoré, General Moussa, 29, 32
Trauma Centre for Victims of Human Trafficking in Cameroon, 130
triggering event, for moral/sexual panics, 160, 163
Trump, Donald, 98, 102n13
trust network, 131–32, 138
Tuareg people, 36
Turinawe, Ingrid, 188n3

UFN (Union des Femmes du Niger), 56
Uganda, 13, 195; AIDS Commission, 118; Anti-Homosexuality Bill (2009, 3, 15, 20, 21n1, 115, 181–86, 196; Anti-Pornography Bill (Anti-Pornography Act), 171–73, 188n1, 188n2, 196; Bureau of Statistics, 106; Common Man's Charter (1968), 9–10; Computer Misuse Act (2011), 179, 189n9; constitution (1995), 11, 118; CSE (Comprehensive Sexuality Education), 106–21, 196; Marriage and Divorce Bill, 118–19; Ministry of Education and Sports, 107–9; National Sexuality Education Framework (2018), 109, 111–16, 196; parliamentary ban on CSE (2016), 107, 112, 118, 121n1; Presidential Initiative on AIDS Strategy for Communication to

Uganda (*continued*)
Youth, 113; sexual and gender-based rights, 171–88
*uhuru* (Swahili word for "freedom"), 10
UNFPA (United Nations Population Fund), 60n10, 90, 98–99, 118; Operation Guidance for CSE, 107
UNICEF, 60n10, 99
United Nations, 8–9; Convention on Consent to Marriage (1964), 9, 28, 45; Convention on the Rights of the Child, 33, 46; Declaration on the Elimination of Violence against Women (1993), 12; International Technical Guidance on Sexuality Education, 107; Special Rapporteur on Violence Against Women, 128; Supplementary Convention on the Abolition of Slavery, the Slave Trade, and Institutions and Practices Similar to Slavery (1956), 9; Sustainable Goals, 46; Universal Declaration of Human Rights (1948), 8, 89, 143n18
United States: *Calvin Bradley v. The State*, 127–28; Department of State, 130; *Grace v. Whitaker*, 128–29; Homeland Security, Anti-Trafficking Coordination Team, 139; Justice Department, 141n2; *Matter of A-B-*, 128–29; *Matter of A-R-C-G-*, 128–29; T visa, 141n2, 142n3; USCIS (US Citizenship and Immigration Services), 128, 142n6; VAWA (Violence Against Women Act, 1994), 128; VIVPA (Victims of Trafficking and Violence Protection Ace), 142n3
Unterhalter, Elaine, 88
urban women, and gender quotas, 71
USAID, 86, 98–99
US-RDA (Union Soudanaise Rassemblement Démocratique Africain), 28–29
UWONET, 188

values-based approach to CSE (Uganda), 111, 196
Van Allen, Judith, 178
vernacularization, 14; of global human rights norms, 109–12; of reproductive rights in Uganda, 106–21; of women's rights, 110–12, 120
victimhood, and early marriage, 58
village groups, women and, 79–81
Villalón, Leonardo, 157, 159
violence: domestic, 126, 137, 142n10 (*see also* family violence); "family-based," 142n10; gender-based, in Malawi, 88 (*see also* antihomosexuality; sexual panics); against homosexuals, 150–65 (*see also* antihomosexuality; homophobia); in Mali, 35–37; private, 128, 197. *See also* family violence; sexual violence
virginity, 60n22
vulnerability, bodily, 171–88
vulnerability, of girls to male predators, 94

Wade, Abdoulaye, 157–58, 162
"wa koñ bi," 155
wards, women as, in Cameroon, 133
water fetching, 66
Watkins, Susan, 99
wealth gaps, as form of structural violence, 136–37
"wealth in people," 139
weddings, of *goorjigeen*, 155
Weeks, Jeffrey, 152
Wekesa, Violet, 88
WHO (World Health Organization), 134; and minimum-age-of-marriage laws, 47
widow inheritance, 126
WiLDAF (Women in Law and Development in Africa), 30, 195
witchcraft, 55
Wolof language, 151, 197

women: *goorjigeen* as, 154; sex between, 155
women's associations, 81; Burkina Faso, 79–81; Mali, 27–28, 34; *mbotaay*, 154, 166n5
women's bodies, and women's rights debate in Uganda, 171–88
women's clothing, 171–73, 196
women's land rights, in Burkina Faso, 69–71
women's movement, in Uganda, 119, 188
women's rights: Mali, 37–38; Senegal, 157; and vernacularization, 110–12, 120
women's status as women, and women's protest, 175–81
Women's War (Nigeria, 1929), 178–79
World Agroforestry Center, 72

Yadsé people (Burkina Faso), 74
young fathers: and school expulsion, 88; and school readmission policy, 91–92
young mothers: and school readmission policies, 84–100; and "secondary virginity," 95
youth morality: Malawi, 92–94; Mali, 28–29
youth sexual behavior, in Uganda, 113
youth sexuality, 195; control of, in Malawi, 92–96
youth sexuality and reproductive health (SRH): Malawi, 84–100; Uganda, 106–21
youth unemployment, in Senegal, 158

Zainab, Fatuma, 188n3
Zeh, Catherine Moto, 134
Zimbabwe, and antihomosexuality, 165

# Critical Human Rights

*Memory's Turn: Reckoning with Dictatorship in Brazil*
REBECCA J. ATENCIO

*Prisoner of Pinochet: My Year in a Chilean Concentration Camp*
SERGIO BITAR; translated by ERIN GOODMAN; foreword and notes by PETER WINN

*Legislating Gender and Sexuality in Africa: Human Rights, Society, and the State*
Edited by LYDIA BOYD and EMILY BURRILL

*Bread, Justice, and Liberty: Grassroots Activism and Human Rights in Pinochet's Chile*
ALISON J. BRUEY

*Archiving the Unspeakable: Silence, Memory, and the Photographic Record in Cambodia*
MICHELLE CASWELL

*Court of Remorse: Inside the International Criminal Tribunal for Rwanda*
THIERRY CRUVELLIER; translated by CHARI VOSS

*How Difficult It Is to Be God: Shining Path's Politics of War in Peru, 1980–1999*
CARLOS IVÁN DEGREGORI; edited and with an introduction by STEVE J. STERN

*Trauma, Taboo, and Truth-Telling: Listening to Silences in Postdictatorship Argentina*
NANCY J. GATES-MADSEN

*From War to Genocide: Criminal Politics in Rwanda, 1990–1994*
ANDRÉ GUICHAOUA; translated by DON E. WEBSTER

*Innocence and Victimhood: Gender, Nation, and Women's Activism in Postwar Bosnia-Herzegovina*
ELISSA HELMS

*Inside Rwanda's* Gacaca *Courts: Seeking Justice after Genocide*
BERT INGELAERE

*Amending the Past: Europe's Holocaust Commissions and the Right to History*
ALEXANDER KARN

*Civil Obedience: Complicity and Complacency in Chile since Pinochet*
MICHAEL J. LAZZARA

*Torture and Impunity*
ALFRED W. MCCOY

*Elusive Justice: Women, Land Rights, and Colombia's Transition to Peace*
DONNY MEERTENS

*Conflicted Memory: Military Cultural Interventions and the Human Rights Era in Peru*
CYNTHIA E. MILTON

*Historical Justice and Memory*
Edited by KLAUS NEUMANN and JANNA THOMPSON

*The Wars inside Chile's Barracks: Remembering Military Service under Pinochet*
LEITH PASSMORE

*Buried Histories: The Anti-Communist Massacres of 1965–1966 in Indonesia*
JOHN ROOSA

*The Human Rights Paradox: Universality and Its Discontents*
Edited by STEVE J. STERN and SCOTT STRAUS

*Human Rights and Transnational Solidarity in Cold War Latin America*
Edited by JESSICA STITES MOR

*Remaking Rwanda: State Building and Human Rights after Mass Violence*
Edited by SCOTT STRAUS and LARS WALDORF

*Beyond Displacement: Campesinos, Refugees, and Collective Action in the Salvadoran Civil War*
MOLLY TODD

*The Social Origins of Human Rights: Protesting Political Violence in Colombia's Oil Capital, 1919–2010*
LUIS VAN ISSCHOT

*The Soviet Union and the Gutting of the UN Genocide Convention*
ANTON WEISS-WENDT

*The Politics of Necessity: Community Organizing and Democracy in South Africa*
ELKE ZUERN

WITHDRAWN